W9-BKX-779

Tiger Lilies, Toadstools, and Thunderbolts

ENGAGING K–8 STUDENTS WITH POETRY

Iris McClellan Tiedt

Minnesota State University at Moorhead
Moorhead, Minnesota, USA

LIBRARY
FRANKLIN PIERCE COLLEGE
RINDGE, NH 03461

INTERNATIONAL
Reading Association
800 Barksdale Road, PO Box 8139
Newark, DE 19714-8139, USA
www.reading.org

IRA BOARD OF DIRECTORS

Donna M. Ogle, National-Louis University, Evanston, Illinois, *President* • Jerry L. Johns, Northern Illinois University, DeKalb, Illinois, *President-Elect* • Lesley Mandel Morrow, Rutgers University, New Brunswick, New Jersey, *Vice President* • Gregg M. Kurek, Bridgman Public Schools, Bridgman, Michigan • Jeanne R. Paratore, Boston University, Boston, Massachusetts • Lori L. Rog, Regina Public Schools, Regina, Saskatchewan • Carol Minnick Santa, Montana Academy, Kalispell, Montana • Rebecca L. Olness, Kent Public Schools, Kent, Washington • Doris Walker-Dalhouse, Minnesota State University Moorhead, Moorhead, Minnesota • Patricia L. Anders, University of Arizona, Tucson, Arizona • Timothy V. Rasinski, Kent State University, Kent, Ohio • Ann-Sofie Selin, Cygnaeus School, Åbo, Finland • Alan E. Farstrup, Executive Director

The International Reading Association attempts, through its publications, to provide a forum for a wide spectrum of opinions on reading. This policy permits divergent viewpoints without implying the endorsement of the Association.

Director of Publications   Joan M. Irwin
Editorial Director, Books and Special Projects   Matthew W. Baker
Senior Editor, Books and Special Projects   Tori Mello Bachman
Permissions Editor   Janet S. Parrack
Production Editor   Shannon Benner
Assistant Editor   Corinne M. Mooney
Editorial Assistant   Tyanna L. Collins
Publications Manager   Beth Doughty
Production Department Manager   Iona Sauscermen
Supervisor, Electronic Publishing   Anette Schütz
Senior Electronic Publishing Specialist   Cheryl J. Strum
Electronic Publishing Specialist   R. Lynn Harrison
Proofreader   Charlene M. Nichols

Project Editor   Shannon Benner

Cover   Design: Linda Steere
              Photographs (from left):   Image 100, Lloyd Wolf, Image 100

Copyright 2002 by the International Reading Association, Inc.
All rights reserved. No part of this publication may be reproduced or transmitted in any form or by any means, electronic or mechanical, including photocopy, or any information storage and retrieval system, without permission from the publisher.

Library of Congress Cataloging-in-Publication Data
Tiedt, Iris M.
    Tiger lilies, toadstools, and thunderbolts : engaging K–8 students with poetry / Iris McClellan Tiedt.
        p.   cm.
Includes bibliographical references (p.) and index.
    ISBN 0-87207-170-7
1. Poetry—Study and teaching (Elementary)   2. Poetry—Study and teaching (Middle school)
I. Title.
    LB1575 .T54 2002
    372.64—dc21

                                                                                    2001008045

— CONTENTS —

TO THE READER

v

CHAPTER 1
Tiger Lilies, Toadstools, and Thunderbolts:
Discovering the Magic of Poetry

1

CHAPTER 2
Be Like the Bird:
Teaching With Poetry

13

CHAPTER 3
"Fire! Fire!" Cried Mrs. McGuire:
Sharing Poetry Orally

37

CHAPTER 4
Like a Thunderbolt:
Infusing Poetry Into Your Reading Program

61

CHAPTER 5
Simple Simon:
Exploring Mother Goose Rhymes Across the Grades

91

CHAPTER 6

Swift Things Are Beautiful:
Writing Original Poetry
107

CHAPTER 7

I Hear America Singing:
Infusing Poetry Into the Total Curriculum
135

CHAPTER 8

I'm Nobody! Who Are You?
Celebrating Poetry
163

AFTERWORD
180

APPENDIX A

Thinking + Lesson Plans
181

APPENDIX B

Further Resources for the Teacher
204

REFERENCES
211

COPYRIGHT ACKNOWLEDGMENTS
219

INDEX
221

"Come with me," invites the poet. As teachers, we join poets in inviting students to listen to poetry, to recite poetry, to read poetry, and to compose original poems. Thus, we enhance our teaching as we stimulate students' thinking abilities.

Our students need poetry. They need the rhythm and music of poetry. They need the humor and whimsicality of poetry. And, they need the serious treatment of feelings and commentaries on life around us. We can open the door to poetry for students in a variety of ways that I will cover in detail throughout this book.

I wrote this book to help you engage students in K–8 classrooms with poetry in exciting ways. Eight chapters help you bring theory and practice together as you enhance your teaching. I have selected many fine poems for you, and I show you how to begin working with poetry right now and how to continue in the years ahead.

The emphasis throughout the lessons included in this book remains on sharing poetry with obvious enjoyment—dramatizing playful poems, recording voices, discovering poetry in unusual places, and making presentations that invite other students and parents to share poetry, too. This book shows you how the poet has something important to communicate to us all. Listen to the words of poet William Carlos Williams:

> It is difficult
> To get the news from poems;
> Yet men die miserably every day
> For lack
> Of what is found there.

Our job, then, is to facilitate communications between poets and our students, so that young people "get the news" that will nourish them throughout their lives. This book is designed to help you infuse poetry into the total curriculum that you share with your students. By opening doors to poetry at an early age, you will expand children's vision and creativity, build esteem and empathy, and enrich their worlds.

Let's celebrate poetry together!

Iris M. Tiedt

DECEMBER LEAVES

The fallen leaves are cornflakes
That fill the lawn's wide dish,—
And night and noon
The wind's a spoon
That stirs them with a swish.—

The sky's a silver sifter
A-sifting white and slow,
That gently shakes
On crisp brown flakes
The sugar known as snow.

— KAYE STARBIRD

CHAPTER 1

Tiger Lilies, Toadstools, and Thunderbolts: Discovering the Magic of Poetry

"Bright is the ring of words!" wrote poet Robert Louis Stevenson. Poetry expands our thinking; it stirs our creative spirits. The poet speaks to us, sharing joy, sorrow, sheer good humor, the mysteries of life. "Poetry is my kind of fooling," wrote genial Robert Frost, as he penned hundreds of charming poetry vignettes, commentaries on life—"Stopping by Woods," "The Hired Man," and many more. My favorite is the delightful poem "The Pasture," in which he invites us in simple language to walk with him through the meadow to check the spring and to see a newborn calf. Reading such poetry enriches our lives. Sharing this poetry in your classroom enriches the lives of children.

Poetry is a form of literature teachers usually enjoy. However, you may not know how to engage students with poetry effectively so that they, too, will learn to enjoy it. The purpose of this book is to bridge that gap by giving you a variety of learning activities that focus on creating a classroom climate that invites children to experience poetry as well as ideas for using specific poems for clear purposes. Here, you will find ways of approaching poetry that will cause students to smile as they listen to your reading of a favorite poem and to delight in creating original verses of their own.

In this introductory chapter, I begin to define the special attributes of poetry as compared to prose and to explore the variety of poems available for use in elementary and middle school classrooms. I also look at what poets communicate and how teachers can facilitate that communication.

What Is Poetry?

"Poetry is a mystery, but it is a mystery children can participate in and master," writes Kenneth Koch in *Wishes, Lies, and Dreams: Teaching Children to Write Poetry* (2000, p. 22).

Historically, poetry is one of the primary literary forms, for it can be traced to early oral traditions in all cultures. The minstrel singing the stories of Roland, the chants of the Indian medicine men, the calls of the shepherds in Grecian fields—all are poetry of the people.

Clearly, poetry was an important part of life in early civilizations. Today, it may be overlooked in our lives or it may be taught poorly in schools. As Pamela Tiedt notes in *Language Arts Activities in the Classroom* (Tiedt, Tiedt, & Tiedt, 2001),

> In an assessment-driven curriculum, poetry is not typically given a large place. The few poems that are taught...tend to be analyzed to death and torn apart looking for symbolism and the author's intent. Not surprisingly, many students come to believe that poetry is boring. Yet, poetry has a power to reach people, to communicate experience and emotion, and create a bridge between people in a different way than prose. Unlike narrative or expository prose, with its focus on clarity and organization, poetry can open up students' imaginations as they play with the twists and turns of language, and it can bring an unusual level of personal engagement to the classroom experience. (p. 259)

How, then, can you avoid killing students' interest in poetry before the poet has a chance to reach them? How do you engage their interest in reading and writing poetry? Let's begin by exploring various ways people, especially poets, perceive poetry. It is not easy to define poetry, for poetry is many things to different people. Poetry is special, and it is elusive. It also entails a personal response.

Poetry Is Special

"Poetry is special," says poet Karla Kuskin (1979), but

> poetry isn't special, to be reserved for deep thoughts and auspicious occasions. It can be as natural a form of expression as shouting or singing. Cultivate poetry and it will provide the shortest distance between an emotion and its articulation, the direct route from saying anything in any way to saying something special. (p. 3)

This is the attitude toward poetry we want to share with elementary and middle school children. Poetry is special, mysterious, and magical, yet it is real, dealing with ordinary people and common things. When poetry enters the classroom, there should come with it a feeling of excitement to which children can respond.

Poetry Is Elusive

Many noted scholars have defined poetry, but no definition fits as well as that expressed by Eleanor Farjeon in her poem "What is Poetry?":

What is poetry? Who knows?
Not the rose, but the scent of the rose;
Not the sky, but the light of the sky;
Not the fly, but the gleam of the fly;
Not the sea, but the sound of the sea;
Not myself, but something that makes me
See, hear and feel something that prose
Cannot. What is it? Who knows?

As these lines suggest, defining poetry is elusive. It is difficult to define what poets do that is different from most writers of prose, but that ineffable something makes all the difference. And, of course, the effect differs from poem to poem.

Poetry Is Personal

Remember that poetry is personal. What appeals to one person may not appeal to another. Observe the varied subjects, language styles, and patterning of the poems included in a poetry collection. You will need to share a wide variety of poems in your classroom to ensure that you eventually discover something that touches each student. Fortunately, there is such a variety of poetry available, you can present a tempting buffet with offerings designed for every appetite.

Poetry and young people belong together. Children respond naturally to rhythm and melody, and they soon learn to delight in the humorous narrative poems that some poets have written for them. Gradually, students can come to appreciate the imagery and wisdom in more sophisticated poems. And, they learn to appreciate poetry most fully when they create their own original poems.

As you share poetry, you are touching students in ways no textbook can match. You are adding a component to your curriculum that will lift it above the ordinary and make students glad to be in your classroom.

The Special Attributes of Poetry

Poetry has long been revered as the queen of literature. Somehow it stands above the novel, the drama, and the essay. A distinctive attribute of the poet is a love of language, for the compact nature of poetic forms requires choosing just the right words and polishing them. Each word must carry its share of the impact, its portion of the message. Poets are word merchants who select words carefully and share their creations. As Robert Frost, one of the best-known American poets, wrote, "Poetry is a performance in words."

Because poems are much shorter than most forms of prose, they are especially well adapted to teaching within the time constraints of the classroom. Of course, some poems are long, but more frequently they are no longer than 12 lines. Thus, you can easily present a poem in large print on a transparency or on one sheet of paper so that each student can have an individual copy. Many poems, like these lines from Mary O'Neill's "What Is Orange?," can serve as models for students' original poetry:

> Orange is a tiger lily,
> A carrot,
> A feather from
> A parrot,
> A flame,
> The wildest color
> You can name.

Poetry deals with a variety of subjects, so you can always find poems that are relevant to the different subjects you teach. Students may be surprised to find that a poet may write about such mundane topics as a bat or a road as well as love or joy. Poets may write in many different styles, too, ranging from an ode to a hero to an expression of observed beauty, from the chants of street vendors to jolly, foot-tapping jingles. Poets may choose sedate rhythms suitable for matters of life or death that are much different from the rollicking pace that is used for narratives about a humorous character or the lyrical rhythm of a love song. Poetry offers something for every taste or interest.

In presenting poetry to children, we will not attempt to teach them the technical labels for the stylized rhythms that can be found in traditional adult poetry. They don't need to deal with *dactyls* or *iambic pentameter*. Rather, we will invite them to respond to the rhythms and rhymes without knowing the scholarly terminology associated with meters and rhyme schemes. We also will not indulge in excessive analysis of the meaning of more sophisticated poems. Our purpose in engaging children with poetry is to encourage their enjoyment of language and literature. Poetry can enhance learning experiences related to any subject at all levels of education, which is what we will explore in this book.

What Poetry Communicates

The message of the poet is both emotional and intellectual, affective as well as cognitive. A poem usually conveys something of both, for it is difficult to isolate feelings or to be completely objective in presenting an idea expressed in poetic form. As Robert Frost wrote, "Poetry begins in delight and ends in wisdom."

In this section, we will examine some of the aspects of learning a poet shares that complement the curriculum we are expected to teach. Although we will often share poetry for pure enjoyment, as classroom teachers we want to take full advantage of all the possibilities of this form of literature. Therefore, we will justify taking time for poetry within the busy school day because it

- conveys a love of language and introduces new vocabulary,

- adds the creative component of humor to the learning process,

- helps students become aware of ways of knowing through different senses,

- provides the element of musicality to students' lives, and

- supports students' development of a sense of self-worth.

Poetry Conveys a Love of Language and Vocabulary

Poetry can communicate even if the language is not fully understood. Therefore, it is important that we share poems orally with children who cannot yet read them. Children delight in the rhythm of the language as you read. Their listening vocabularies—much larger than their speaking, reading, or writing vocabularies—enable them to comprehend new words and ideas presented in context. Therefore, they can often get the gist of the meaning from listening, although they may not be able to define every word.

Consider "City Pigeons" by Leland Jacobs, which paints a picture in words:

> In Herald Square,
> In Herald Square,
> I saw the pigeons gathered there,
> Talking, strutting with an air
> As if they owned all Herald Square,
> Standing on the hot concrete
> Having little snacks to eat.
> And I'd call

To your attention,
The pigeons hold
A huge convention
there
In Herald Square,
In Herald Square.

The rhythm of the words as they are read aloud carries the listener along, so that young children do not need to know the exact meaning of "Herald Square," which is a plaza in New York City. For most, it will be just an area where there is concrete in a city setting, perhaps similar to places they know. Children will probably get the feeling of strutting from your voice, and they can picture the flock of pigeons from personal experience without full knowledge of what it is to hold a convention. A casual explanation or discussion of a few keywords, however, will add interest to the poem and will help develop vocabulary in an effective way, as you say,

> Who knows what strutting is? The poet says the pigeons are strutting. Can you show us how to strut, Dan? That's the way—would you all like to try strutting? Strut like a proud pigeon.

> The poet says the pigeons were at a convention. I went to a convention last month. Who has some idea of what a convention is? Yes, a meeting of lots of people. Can you picture the pigeons looking like a meeting of people—strutting around, "talking," getting the latest news?

After this type of discussion, you can read the poem again: "Listen as I read the poem again. See if you can picture the convention of pigeons strutting around Herald Square." Then, make a point of inserting these words into the classroom dialogue later to reinforce the knowledge gained and to remind children of the enjoyable poetry experience you shared. Print the poem for a wall display that includes children's drawings to illustrate the meaning of the poet's words. In this way, you begin to build a poetry repertoire with your class.

Poetry Adds the Creative Component of Humor to Learning

Studies show that a sense of humor is an essential aspect of the creative process. Humor adds to the effectiveness of instruction and to the likelihood that students will learn what is presented. Poetry can provide opportunities for students to exercise their sense of humor.

Many poets delight in word play, nonsense, and gentle spoofs. Ogden Nash is a master of audacious plays on words to suit his witty observations that amuse both children and adults. In one funny example, he describes a panther as a leopard that "hasn't been peppered."

Edward Lear, whose name is almost synonymous with nonsense poetry, is especially known for comical limericks that often are based on sheer whimsy, as in this verse:

> There once was a man with a beard,
> Who said, "It is just as I feared."
> > Two larks and a wren
> > Three owls and a hen
> Have all made a nest in my beard.

Introduce other poets who are known for humorous verses, such as Charles Edward Carryl, "The Plaint of the Camel"; Lewis Carroll, "The Walrus and the Carpenter"; John Ciardi, "The Reason for the Pelican"; Jack Prelutsky, *The Gargoyles on the Roof*; and Shel Silverstein, *Where the Sidewalk Ends*.

Poetry Increases Awareness of the Different Senses

We are so accustomed to learning through visual methods that we may forget the importance of other senses. Poetry can provide students with a chance to use different senses to experience the world.

Poets appeal to all the senses as they strive for different effects. Consider the imagery in the short poem, "Down the Rain Falls," by Elizabeth Coatsworth. Or, introduce children to Christopher Morley's "Smells (Junior)," which focuses on a sense that is not as common in poetry as visual and sound images:

> My Daddy smells like tobacco and books,
> > Mother, like lavender and listerine;
> Uncle John carries a whiff of cigars,
> > Nannie smells starchy and soapy and clean.
> Shandy, my dog, has a smell of his own
> > (When he's been out in the rain, he smells most);
> But Katie, the cook, is more splendid than all—
> > She smells exactly like hot buttered toast!

Ask students to list smells they really like or ones that they especially remember. Help them make conscious use of their senses by passing around slices of lemon or a little cinnamon sprinkled on a paper towel to smell or taste. Share additional poems that deal with all the senses, especially those other than sight.

Poetry Adds Musicality to Students' Learning Experience

Musicality is an important aspect of the human existence. You can probably list several terms that are common to both music and poetry—rhythm, ballad, lyric, beat—the list becomes surprisingly long. Consider how these concepts fit into the contexts of both music and poetry. This connection will be discussed further in Chapter 7.

Combinations of words are often arranged in poetry to create rhythms that are pleasing to hear and appropriate to the subject of the poem. David McCord, for instance, conveys a foot-tapping beat, imitating the rhythm of train wheels in "Song of the Train." Students of any age will clap their hands as you read this poem aloud, particularly the words *click-ety-clack*.

Students of all ages will know songs they like to sing. Make them aware that the lyrics of songs are poems, too. Print one or more of them in poetry form so they can read the words they already know and like.

Poetry Supports Students' Sense of Self-Worth

The expression of personal feelings and thoughts, typical of many poems, reaches out to the reader. Students will find themselves sharing the emotion, feeling for and with the speaker, and identifying with the poet. They may become more aware of their own emotions and values. Sharing such literature may help them learn to accept their emotions and perhaps even to disclose them in a poem themselves.

"Keep a poem in your pocket...and you'll never feel lonely at night when you're in bed," writes Beatrice Schenk de Regniers. Loneliness and aloneness, two quite different feelings, are important emotions to be aware of. Older students may understand Walt Whitman's feelings as he writes of the sense of community he perceives as he sits alone thinking:

This moment yearning and thoughtful sitting alone,
It seems to me there are other men in other lands yearning and
thoughtful,

It seems to me I can look over and behold them in Germany, Italy, France, Spain,

Or far, far away, in China, or in Russia or Japan, talking other dialects,

And it seems to me if I could know those other men I should become attached to them as I do to men in my own lands,

O I know we should be brethren and lovers,

I know I should be happy with them.

The desire for a private place, a place for hiding precious belongings and one's self, is another feeling students may appreciate. Margaret Weddemer expresses this desire for privacy in "The Secret Cavern," in which she describes a dark, cavernous place that "None of all the other children know!" Ask students to describe a secret retreat. This would be a stimulating writing prompt for student journals.

Another feeling with which children can identify is the joy and appreciation of nature's beauty. "O world, I cannot hold thee close enough!" cries Edna St. Vincent Millay, as she glories in the beauty of the woods. On the following page is another of her poems that expresses her enjoyment of the outdoors.

In "Leisure," William H. Davies says, "What is this life if, full of care,/We have no time to stand and stare?" Bliss Carman's well-known lines share his enjoyment of the beautiful fall coloring in "A Vagabond Song." He describes his heart "like a rhyme with the yellow and the purple and the crimson keeping time."

Children need the opportunity to share dreams and feelings. They need to hear the poets speaking to them and to realize that poets are people like themselves.

The Contents of This Book

The intent of this book is to guide you in discovering the many possibilities for using poetry to enhance your teaching and to expand student learning in your classroom. Each chapter includes some ideas that are more suitable for the early school years, as well as others that are appropriate for upper elementary and middle school grades. Suggestions are provided for adapting activities for different levels of ability and interest. You will have to choose what poetry and activities best fit the needs of your students and the curriculum you are presenting.

Many full-length poems, songs, useful parts of poems, and significant lines are reproduced throughout the book so that you may try out the suggested

AFTERNOON ON A HILL

I will be the gladdest thing
    Under the sun.
I will touch a hundred flowers
    And not pick one.

I will look at cliffs and clouds
    With quiet eyes,
Watch the wind bow down the grass,
    And the grass rise.

And when lights begin to show
    Up from the town,
I will mark which must be mine,
    And then start down!

—EDNA ST. VINCENT MILLAY

activities and lessons immediately. Throughout each chapter and in the appendixes, I share additional recommended resources to assist you in locating the materials you need to work with poetry in your classroom. Lesson plans provided in Appendix A demonstrate how to work with some of the activities suggested. These plans serve as models for additional lessons you and your colleagues can design.

Conclusion

In this chapter, we have begun to explore what poetry has to offer both students and teachers in elementary and middle school grades. In Chapter 2, we will discuss the possibilities for teaching with poetry in elementary and middle school classrooms, along with specific ways to engage students with poetry as they learn across the total curriculum.

Be like the bird,

Halting in his flight

On limb too slight,

Feels it give way beneath him,

Yet sings,

Knowing he hath wings.

—Victor Hugo

Be Like the Bird:
Teaching With Poetry

"Poetry is the crown of imaginative literature. This form of writing does the most to open our minds and free our imaginations," writes Harold Bloom in *The Joys of Reading* (2001, p. 146). Because it is essential that children experience poetry throughout the elementary and middle school years, this chapter focuses on teaching and the teacher, providing an overview of how poetry can fit into your curriculum. We'll start by getting better acquainted with poets and their poetry. Then, we'll explore how to select poetry for the classroom and how to design lessons based on poetry. Finally, we will discuss some recommended teaching strategies.

Getting Acquainted With Poets and Their Poems

To share poetry with students and to use poems to enhance your teaching, you first need to know poetry. In this book you will meet many poets and their work, and you will read poems that are presented in lessons designed for you and your students.

Remember that poets are writing for you and the students you teach. They want you to enjoy their poems. Consider the words of children's poet Karla Kuskin (1979): "Instead of building a fence of formality around poetry, I want to emphasize its accessibility, the sound of rhythm, humor, the inherent simplicity" (p. 4). Although Kuskin is a winner of the National Council of Teachers of English Award for Excellence in Poetry for Children, she invites you to join the club and encourages you to present poetry naturally as an essential part of the daily experiences you plan for your students.

Poetry is meant to be shared and enjoyed. "You come, too," invites Robert Frost as he sets out to check the pasture spring in "The Pasture":

I'm going out to clean the pasture spring;
I'll only stop to rake the leaves away
(And wait to watch the water clear, I may):
I shan't be gone long—You come, too.

I'm going out to fetch the little calf
That's standing by the mother. It's so young
It totters when she licks it with her tongue.
I shan't be gone long—You come, too.

How can you resist such a warm invitation? Share this poem with children of all ages as you lead them to discover poetry and to make it part of their lives. (For a thorough treatment of this poem, see Thinking + Lesson Plan 1 in Appendix A.)

This is the kind of poetry you need to know. You need to know not only Robert Frost and his poetry, but also the writings of Harry Behn, Laura E. Richards, Christina Rossetti, Langston Hughes, and Robert Louis Stevenson. We can introduce students to wonderful lines from selected poems written by such noted poets as Emily Dickinson, Walt Whitman, Edna St. Vincent Millay, Ogden Nash, Edward Lear, Edgar Allan Poe, and even William Shakespeare and the great Japanese writers of haiku. These are the poets you probably read in English classes when you went to school. You also should be aware of works by more contemporary poets, who have written poetry especially suitable for young people. Here is a sampling of additional poets you may find in anthologies of poetry for young people:

Maya Angelou	Louise Erdrich	Patricia Hubbell
John Ashbury	Tom Feelings	John Keats
Stephen Vincent Benet	Lawrence Ferlinghetti	Karla Kuskin
William Blake	Syd Fleischman	Edward Lear
Gwendolyn Brooks	Douglas Florian	Myra Cohn Livingstone
Anne Carson	Louis Ginsberg	David McCord
John Ciardi	Nikki Grimes	Eve Merriam
Lucille Clifton	Florence Heide	Lilian Moore
Hart Crane	Mary Ann Hoberman	Pat Mora
e.e. cummings	Garrett Kaoru Hongo	Mary O'Neill

Jack Prelutsky	William Jay Smith	William Wordsworth
Adrienne Rich	Kaye Starbird	Jane Yolen
Theodore Roethke	Wallace Stevens	
Shel Silverstein	Judith Viorst	

Bringing Poets Into Your Classroom

Your knowledge of individual poets helps make them come alive for students as you present their poetry. Whenever you share a poem for which the poet is known—Carl Sandburg, Emily Dickinson, Jack Prelutsky, and so on—be sure to name the poet to give these writers credit for their work. After students have heard a poem and completed the activity you plan, write the poet's name and the title of the poem on the board so that students make a visual connection with this information. Students can also begin a list of poets and their poems in their Poetry Portfolios (see page 32).

You will usually find biographical data about noted authors in the public library's set of *Contemporary Authors* or other biographical dictionaries. The entries often contain interesting quotes that you could share with students as a way of demonstrating that poets are ordinary people who might live just down the street with their children, spouses, and pets. Authors have often prepared collective biographies that present selected writers that you will find useful for teaching and encouraging student research. One fine example is *Lives of the Writers: Comedies, Tragedies (and What the Neighbors Thought)*, edited by Kathleen Krull and illustrated by Kathryn Hewitt. Six poets are among the 19 authors presented in lively biographies and interesting full-page portraits that would appeal to young people. More biographies written for young people are discussed in Chapter 4 as books students might enjoy reading, but you are likely to find them highly informative and entertaining as well. Articles from sources such as *Elementary English* can be located by searching in the *Education Index* in a college or university library. Interviews with writers often appear in such professional journals as *Language Arts* and *The Reading Teacher*, which are covered by that index.

Make a point, too, of displaying photographs of poets that you introduce as often as feasible. Thus, these writers become real for the students. Students can mount copies of poetry on the bulletin board beside the poet's picture and any other information they may have obtained.

I have included photographs of selected poets in the next section to help you get started on developing a collection of photos of poets that you and your students will enjoy. Most publishers are happy to supply black-and-white publicity photographs of poets whose work they publish. You can plan a letter-writing lesson focusing on letters requesting copies of photographs for poets students are interested in. Ask your librarian to suggest reference books that list publishers' addresses. Or, search the Internet to find out which company publishes a specific poet's work and then locate the mailing address for that company.

Pictures of poets also can be located in biographies or collections of poetry by a single poet. Duplicate these pictures and enlarge them for display. You also might check *Education Index* to ascertain whether pictures of poets have been included with interviews or biographical sketches in journals such as *Language Arts*.

Over the year a class can compile a *Book of Poets We Like*, perhaps adding brief biographical information and favorite poems with the picture of each poet.

Knowing poets and their poetry, you will be able to help children enjoy the language, understand the message communicated, and appreciate the experiments of poets.

Poets and Their Audiences

An important aspect of knowing poets and their poetry is to know the audiences for whom the poets write. Some poets write strictly for children—for example, Douglas Florian or Jack Prelutsky—whereas others write primarily for an adult audience—for example, Lawrence Ferlinghetti and William Wordsworth. However, remember that many students in middle school will be reading at the adult level, so explore a variety of poetry as you select poems to share. We should always be leading the way, not merely keeping up with our students.

Lucille Clifton is one example of a poet who has written for both children and adults. Distinguished Professor of Humanities at St. Mary's College in Maryland, she teaches creative writing, poetry, and children's literature. This versatile and talented writer has written a number of narratives for young people, among them *Good Times*, a sensitive story about a family's grief when the father dies in the middle of a happy picnic. Older children will enjoy her charming book of poems about a young African American boy titled *Some of the Days of Everett Anderson*, which begins, "Being six/Is full of tricks." Her poetry for adults reflects other interests, for example, *Good Woman: Poems and a Memoir 1969–1980*, which was a finalist for the Pulitzer Prize, as were two other volumes of her poetry. Clifton's *Blessing the Boats: New and Selected Poems 1988–2000* won the National Book Award for poetry in 2000. Two

Lucille Clifton

of her poems are included in the "Archive" section of Poetry Daily's website at http://www.poetrydaily.org. She has done a number of recorded poetry readings that you could share with your class. You also might display the following quotation, which explains Clifton's view of poetry: "Poetry is important in the world and has the power to save lives from the inside out."

Pat Mora is another author who writes for varied audiences. She has written poetry, nonfiction, and children's books, including *The Bakery Lady: La Senora de la Panadería, This Big Sky, A Birthday Basket for Tía, Delicious Hullabaloo: Pachanga Deliciosa, The Desert Is My Mother: El Desierto es mi Madre, The Gift of the Poinsettia: El Regalo de la Flor de Nochebuena, Listen to the Desert: Oye al Desierto,* and *Love to Mama: A Tribute to Mothers.* Of special interest to our study of poetry is her compilation *My Own True Name: New and Selected Poems for Young Adults,* which was included in the New York Public Library's "2001–2002 Readings for the Teenage List." To be published soon is a book of poems for adults, *Adobe Odes,* as well as *A Library for Juana,* a picture book biography of Sor Juana Indés de la Cruz, Mexico's most famous female poet.

Pat Mora

For more information about Pat Mora, check her website: http://www. patmora.com. Note that her work, often in both Spanish and English, serves well in presenting an inclusive curriculum. Mora's work affirms positive identities for Mexican American children and other Latinos. For a sample lesson based on Pat Mora's work, see Thinking + Lesson Plan 2 in Appendix A.

Another interesting poet you might introduce to older students is Edgar Allan Poe, an author best known for his classic short stories that deal with horror and mystery. His life is reflected in such poems as "Annabel Lee" and "To Helen," but his best known poem is "The Raven," which includes the haunting line "Quoth the Raven, 'Nevermore.'" A handsome collection of his poems, *Poetry for Young People: Edgar Allan Poe,* was edited by Brod Bagert and illustrated by Carolynn Cobleigh. His poems are further discussed in Chapter 3 and in Chapter 7.

Selecting Poetry for Your Students

Edgar Allan Poe

Begin now to expand your knowledge of poetry by reading some of the many poems written for young people. Order books for your library that will introduce poets and their work to children, such as *A Brighter Garden: Poetry by Emily Dickinson,* collected by Karen Ackerman and illustrated beautifully by

Tasha Tudor. These poems are grouped according to the four seasons. Another attractive volume of Dickinson's poetry is *I'm Nobody! Who Are You?: Poems of Emily Dickinson for Children*, illustrated by Rex Schneider with an introduction by Richard Sewall. Both of these books include biographical information about this well-known American poet.

You'll also need a copy of Mother Goose poems and a good anthology of poems selected for children in grades K–8, but you should also choose at least one volume that includes some of the classics that older children will enjoy. Several volumes worth looking for in used bookstores include *America's Favorite Poems*, edited by Linda Ann Hughes; *Talking to the Sun: An Illustrated Anthology of Poems for Young People*, edited by Kenneth Koch and Kate Farrell; and *Mother Goose: The Original Volland Edition*, edited by Eulalie Grover and illustrated by Frederick Richardson.

Also look in the 808 section of the juvenile nonfiction in your public library to see what books you can borrow. You will find anthologies of suitable poetry to browse through as you become acquainted with the wealth of poems from which you can choose, for example, *The Children's Classic Poetry Collection*, compiled by Nicola Baxter and illustrated by Cathie Shuttleworth; *The New Oxford Treasury of Children's Poems*, compiled by Michael Harrison and Christopher Stuart-Clark; *The Golden Books Family Treasury of Poetry*, selected and with a commentary by Louis Untermeyer; *The Random House Book of Poetry for Children: A Treasury of 572 Poems for Today's Child*, selected by Jack Prelutsky and illustrated by Arnold Lobel; *The 20th Century Children's Poetry Treasury*, selected by Jack Prelutsky and illustrated by Meilo So Knopf. Many additional collections of poetry, especially those featuring writing by a single poet, are suggested throughout this book.

Facilitating Poet-Student Communication

Remember that no poet can speak to students in your classroom unless you decide to let him or her in. You must open the door. Poets cannot communicate with young children without the assistance of an "interpreter," someone to read poetry to children who cannot yet read the poems independently. Children's reactions to poetry at all ages will be influenced greatly by your presentation as their interpreter of poetry, for attitudes and values are reflected in your voice as you read, in the way you introduce the poem, and in your enthusiasm. Children will never learn to love poetry unless you convey a love for poetry and take time to share a variety of poems with them.

Eve Merriam describes this dependence of the poet and, indeed, the poem itself on a reader in " 'I,' Says the Poem." Her poem ends with an invitation to the reader: "I cannot speak until you come."

Your role then, as teacher, is to bring the poets, their poems, and students together. Your voice must become that of the poet who through you shares humor, joy, and wise commentaries on life. Through you students will experience poetry, and that may make a remarkable difference in their lives both now and later.

Designing Poetry Lessons

Effective poetry lessons don't just happen! They are planned carefully based on our knowledge of sound educational theory and practice. This section begins with an examination of research regarding the teaching of poetry in elementary and middle school classrooms. Following this discussion, a useful lesson plan form is provided, along with suggestions on how you may use it to design lessons that will engage your students in reading and writing poetry.

Research on Teaching Poetry to Children

A review of research related to the presentation of poetry in the elementary school classroom shows that there is not a large body of research about this form of literature. This might suggest a subject for action research by teachers at different levels. If interested, you might investigate the grants given annually for this kind of research by the National Council of Teachers of English.

An early study by Mackintosh (1924) found that teachers tended to choose traditional poems. This finding was corroborated by a later study by Tom (1969), who identified such choices as "Paul Revere's Ride," "Stopping by Woods on a Snowy Evening," "A Visit From St. Nicholas," "Casey at the Bat," "Little Orphan Annie," "Shadow," and "Hiawatha." Notice that no contemporary poets were included, nor were poets who write expressly for children.

Ann Terry's (1974) comprehensive study of poetry preferences in grades 4–6 concluded that poetry is a neglected form of literature in most elementary school classrooms. The report includes interesting findings regarding teachers' knowledge of and attitudes toward poetry. Also enlightening was the finding that teachers' tastes did not coincide with those of most children.

This study clearly indicated that teachers were not enthusiastic about poetry, as few teachers read poetry aloud on a regular basis. Most teachers reported that children seldom wrote poetry in their classrooms. In general, teachers also showed a lack of knowledge of poetry, which further explains why they didn't tend to use poetry in their teaching. This would certainly affect children's knowledge of poetry and their attitude toward it.

Terry's detailed study also demonstrated that children in the sample showed a clear preference for poems that were funny, had a story element, and were more contemporary in flavor. The poem received most enthusiastically by the sampling of 422 fourth, fifth, and sixth graders was "Mummy Slept Late and Daddy Fixed Breakfast" by John Ciardi from *You Read to Me, I'll Read to You*. This funny poem relates how the waffles resembled coal rather than anything edible.

The next 10 poems that these students ranked high in appeal were:

1. "'Fire! Fire!' Cried Mrs. McGuire" Anonymous; see page 36

2. "There was an old man of Blackheath" Anonymous

3. "Little Miss Muffett" by Paul Dehn

4. "There once was an old kangaroo" by Edward Mullin

5. "There once was a young lady of Niger" by Cosmos Monkhouse

6. "Hughbert and the Glue" by Karla Kuskin

7. "Betty Botter" Anonymous; see page 65

8. "Lone Dog" by Irene R. McLeod

9. "Eletelephony" by Laura E. Richards

10. "Questions" by Marci Ridlow

More than half of the 10 poems chosen are humorous—including three limericks—which supports the finding that children like humor.

Terry also found that children disliked haiku, free verse, and poems that contained extensive imagery (for example, Carl Sandburg's "Fog" and Patricia Hubbell's "Shadows") when they were presented orally without other activities. Therefore, it may be most effective to begin with poems that have the natural appeal of humor and rhythm, as we gradually help students understand and appreciate imagery. One way to instill an appreciation for imagery is through engaging children in writing poetry. Children who are creating images or trying free verse may be more interested in reading this kind of poetry.

In 1987, Michael Ford completed a doctoral study of the effect of a planned daily poetry program on changing children's concepts about and attitudes toward poetry. After presenting the program for a period of 4 weeks, he used a survey to determine if any changes had occurred. Not surprisingly, after so brief a time, he found little or no change.

In 1994, teacher Barbara Sepura, noting that her young students seemed to know little about poetry, reviewed Ford's study. She decided that a 4-week program was not sufficient to effect change. So, she replicated Ford's study using a full-year intensive study of poetry with a group of 27 second-grade students. Essentially, she read aloud one poem a day that she had printed on chart paper. These poems were then mounted on walls in the classroom and in the hall allowing students to see, hear, read, and write the poems presented.

Integrating the poetry into the curriculum, she might, for example, read a poem like Rose Fyleman's "Mice" (see page 137) to lead to the reading of Beverly Cleary's *The Mouse and the Motorcycle*. As Sepura observes, "When poetry is an integral part of the literary environment, children are empowered with rich language and beguiled by the beauty of poetry" (p. 278).

At the end of the year, Sepura administered the same surveys used by Ford to determine changes in students' knowledge about concepts related to poetry and changes in their attitudes toward poetry. Again, the results were disappointing. However, her conclusion was that the survey assessment tool used was too limited (what we assess doesn't always fit what we aim to teach). Her ethnographic study, on the other hand, recorded children's increased engagement with poetry over the year. Students' obvious enjoyment of this form of literature was revealed, for example, through their repeated requests to "read it again!" Sepura concluded that children respond actively to poems that are personally important to them and that providing familiar formats helped children to write poetry. She recommended that a planned poetry program include daily experiences with poetry as a natural part of the school day.

So, what do these research findings tell us? Clearly, the method of presentation is important, because Terry relied solely on poetry taped by a single reader for the sake of providing the same experience for every child. Furthermore, children listened to 10–12 poems in one day, hearing each poem twice; the children listened to 113 poems in a 10-day period. This method of sharing poetry can scarcely compete with an enthusiastic, timely reading of, for example, "A Song of Greatness," after reading Michael Doris's *Morning Girl* as part of a well-developed thematic study of the lives of Native Americans before Christopher Columbus arrived.

The way you present a poem obviously affects how well the poet is able to communicate, and children need to be exposed to varied forms and content selected with care. Also, it takes time for children to come to know poetry and to enjoy it. Certainly we will not avoid exposing children to Carl Sandburg or Patricia Hubbell, but their poems require more careful presentation. Throughout this book, appropriate methods of introducing a wide variety of poetry effectively to students of different levels and for different objectives are addressed.

A Lesson Plan Form

On the opposite page is a model lesson plan form you can use as you plan lessons that focus on poetry. Duplicate the form or scan it into your computer. This is the form used in presenting the lessons in Appendix A, which are referred to throughout the book.

Notice that this form is titled "Thinking + Lesson Plan Form." The "plus" is important because, first, it emphasizes the importance of consciously teaching specific thinking skills while students engage in language activities. However, it is also important to include feelings or emotions, the affective aspects of learning that are usually ignored in high-stakes testing. Howard Gardner (1999) and others have identified 11 kinds of intelligence. Poetry is more apt to engage the affective or personal side of learning, which may appeal to some students' kind of intellect more than expository prose. Notice, too, that this lesson plan begins with clearly stated outcomes expected for the lesson and ends with assessment in the form of student performance, not just a paper-and-pencil test. Thus, assessment is an integral part of planning.

The Thinking + Lesson Plans described throughout the book are presented for convenience in Appendix A as full-page examples that you can duplicate. For example, Thinking + Lesson Plan 3 focuses on the work of Mary O'Neill in *Hailstones and Halibut Bones*, a collection of her poems about colors. (One of these poems, "What Is Orange?," is included in Chapter 1.) O'Neill wrote these poems some time ago, but they are still delightful and can inspire students of all ages to talk about color and to observe color around them. Because of its popularity, this book will be found in most public libraries or university collections of children's literature, and it was reissued in a second paperback edition with new illustrations. The lesson based on this book will demonstrate to your students that they can write poetry, so it's a great one to start with.

A variety of techniques may be used with poetry—reading aloud, writing original poems, saying poems together, and dramatizing poetry. For example, middle grade students will enjoy acting out Oliver Herford's poem "The Elf and the Dormouse":

> Under a toadstool
> Crept a wee Elf,
> Out of the rain
> To shelter himself.
>
> Under the toadstool,
> Sound asleep,

THINKING + LESSON PLAN FORM

Title of Lesson: _____

Expected Outcomes

The learner will

    1. _____

    2. _____

    3. _____

Resources

Directions

  Step I:

  Step II:

  Step III:

Assessment

  1.

  2.

Sat a big Dormouse
    All in a heap.

Trembled the wee Elf,
    Frightened, and yet
Fearing to fly away
    Lest he get wet.

To the next shelter—
    Maybe a mile.
Suddenly the wee Elf
    Smiled a wee smile,

Tugged till the toadstool
    Toppled in two.
Holding it over him
    Gaily he flew.

Soon he was safe home
    Dry as could be.
Soon woke the Dormouse—
    "Good gracious me!

Where is my toadstool?"
    Loud he lamented.
—And that's how umbrellas,
    First were invented!

To act out this poem, have several children be toadstools with arms outstretched. An elf will be needed for each toadstool as well as a dormouse "all in a heap." The rest of the class can read the poem aloud, pacing it so the actors have time to make their moves. Children can change places for a second reading. Such dramatic interpretations can later be included in a presentation for another class. See Thinking + Lesson Plan 4 in Appendix A for a lesson based on this poem.

Adapting Plans for Different Levels

The lesson about Mary O'Neill's poems that explore color can be used at almost any grade level because the topic has general appeal and the language is not obscure. However, this is not true of all poetry. Thinking + Lesson Plan 5 in Appendix A features "wind" as the topic. A number of poets have written poems about this interesting phenomenon, but some poems would be better for younger children, for example, "Who Has Seen the Wind?," which I set to music, as shown in Figure 1.

Another poem titled "Wind" by Aileen Fisher describes the noises made by the wind. Other poems might appeal to more advanced students, for example, Robert Louis Stevenson's poem "Wind," or his poem "Windy Nights":

> Whenever the moon and stars are set,
>   Whenever the wind is high,
> All night long in the dark and wet,
>   A man goes riding by.
> Late in the night when the fires are out,
> Why does he gallop and gallop about?
>
> Whenever the trees are crying aloud,
>   And ships are tossed at sea,
> By, on the highway, low and loud,
>   By at the gallop goes he:
> By at the gallop he goes, and then
> By he comes back at the gallop again.

Recommended Teaching Strategies

Teaching strategies are discussed throughout this book, but I'd like to emphasize several basic strategies that are especially important as you work with poetry. Perhaps the most important is the rationale and technique for reading poetry aloud to students of all levels.

Reading Poetry Aloud

Why should you read poetry aloud? Reading any literature aloud has decided benefits for students of all ages. Poetry is especially well suited to reading aloud; it is meant to be heard. Through reading poetry aloud to your students you are

FIGURE 1
Who Has Seen the Wind?

- stimulating thinking,

- motivating students to read independently,

- providing amusement and entertainment,

- sharing feelings,

- providing support for slower students,

- sharing your enthusiasm for poetry,

- developing student language abilities,

- teaching listening skills,

- developing rapport with your students, and

- creating a sense of community.

The first rule in selecting a poem to share is to choose one that you really like, for your enthusiasm will carry over to the children through your voice and the expressions on your face. It is virtually impossible to project enthusiasm when you don't really feel it. If you have selected a poem to share, this presupposes that you have read the poem. Avoid falling into the trap of picking up just any book at the last minute; be sure you know many of the poems included in anthologies you have on your desk.

Sharing a poem offers the opportunity to provide much incidental as well as planned learning. To take advantage of these opportunities, however, you need to be prepared. Be sure you know the meanings of words used by the poet, for example, so you can explain them appropriately.

Another aspect of reading aloud is the follow-up. What happens after you read the poem? Discussion stimulated by your questions is a natural follow-up for most poems. You may, however, have more specific ideas in mind. After reading Dr. Seuss's poetic *And to Think That I Saw It on Mulberry Street*, for instance, you might want a group of second graders to begin a colorful mural based on the parade that Marco imagined. Following your reading of the story, you might ask the children to name all the interesting things that Marco imagined—reindeer, a chariot, a big brass band. Then, each child could choose something to paint in the parade. Almost anything would be appropriate.

How should one read a poem? How can you improve your effectiveness as a reader? Like most skills, you will learn to read well by practicing. Choose a poem that you enjoy. In a room by yourself—the empty classroom or your bedroom—read the poem aloud before an imagined audience. Read with a full voice, speaking clearly and stopping to show a picture, if that is appropriate.

Although you may sometimes read a poem to a small group of children, it is more common, as a teacher, to read a poem to the entire class. It is important, therefore, to consider the following aspects of reading aloud:

- Can you be heard easily by all the children, especially those at the back of the room?

- Does your reading flow pleasantly? Does it sound natural?

- Is the reading paced appropriately—not too fast?

- Can you use expression (varied intonation) to add to the effect?

- Do you feel at ease and able to really enjoy the experience of sharing a poem with children?

Listen to yourself as you read a poem aloud. You can actually hear yourself as you read aloud, and sometimes you will have the clear impression that you are coming across well. That impression, of course, will increase your self-confidence, and you will perform even more effectively. Another way of hearing yourself is to tape a series of poems on a cassette. You can note specific lines that you would like to read differently. Read the passage again as you consciously make the changes. When you read poetry to a real audience, you will read much more easily and effectively than if you had not practiced.

Teachers often have questions about reading poetry. Should I stop at the end of each line? Should I read poetry just as I would prose, stopping for commas and periods, and so forth? Most people advocate reading poetry much as you do prose. The poet inserted punctuation for a reason, so pause for periods. Avoid any affectation. Read naturally so the language of the poet can be heard.

Here are a number of books you might choose for reading aloud, grouped roughly into poems for young children and poems for older students. Notice that some of these titles will help affirm diversity in your classroom.

Younger Children

Did You Hear Wind Sing Your Name? An Oneida Song of Spring by Sandra DeCoteau Orie

The Sun Is So Quiet by Nikki Giovanni

Confetti: Poems for Children by Pat Mora

The Beauty of the Beast: Poems From the Animal Kingdom, edited by Jack Prelutsky; see also his *It's Raining Pigs and Noodles: Poems, The New Kid on the Block, Something Big Has Been Here*, and *A Pizza the Size of the Sun*

The Pig in the Spigot: Poems by Richard Wilbur

For variety, try a story poem like those by Calef Brown, who writes and illustrates exuberant stories. An earlier collection of his work is *Polkabats and Octopus Slacks: 14 Stories.*

Older Students

I Am the Darker Brother: An Anthology of Modern Poems by African Americans, edited by Arnold Adoff

Cool Salsa: Bilingual Poems on Growing Up Latino in the United States, edited by Lori M. Carlson

Poetry After Lunch: Poems to Read Aloud, edited by Joyce A. Carroll and Edward E. Wilson

I, Too, Sing America: Three Centuries of African American Poetry by Catherine Clinton

Come With Me: Poems for a Journey by Naomi Shihab Nye

For more on sharing poems orally, see Chapter 3.

Guiding Student Thinking About Poetry

As with teaching any form of literature, one of our aims is to stimulate student thinking abilities. Furthermore, it is important in reading poetry that students learn to move beyond the literal or factual level. As we work with poetry, we want students to make inferences as they deal with imagery and to move toward creative thinking as they begin to write original verse. Invite students to respond to the poem "White Sheep, White Sheep" using the worksheet on page 30. The music for this song appears in Figure 2.

Students will approach the poem at one of the following levels:

- Literal Level (Factual Knowledge): At the literal level, students may visualize a flock of sheep on the hill.

- Inferential Level: I like to tell students to look for "meaning the writer has hidden between the lines." Thus, after reading this poem, students may be able to see that the poet is talking not about sheep at all but the clouds in the sky. Some students will not see this immediately, so you may need to ask some leading questions to help them work through this beginning experience.

White sheep,

White sheep,

On a blue hill.

When the wind stops,

You all stand still.

When the wind blows,

You walk away slow.

White sheep, white sheep

Where do you go?

1. What are the white sheep in this poem?

_____

2. What else could clouds look like?

_____

FIGURE 2
White Sheep, White Sheep

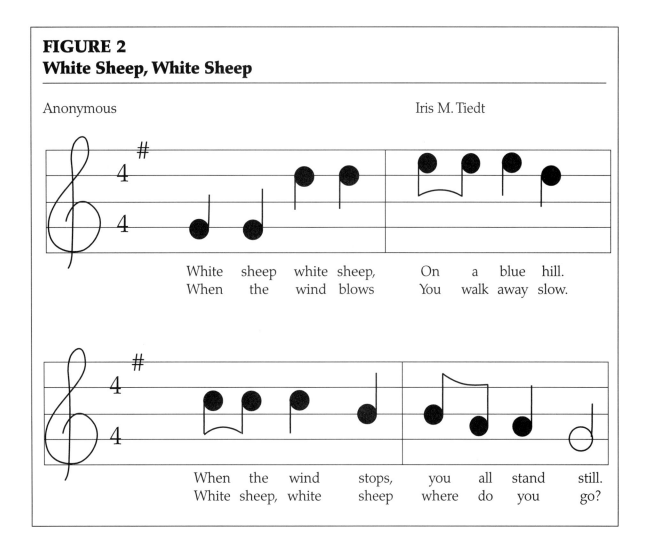

Anonymous   Iris M. Tiedt

White   sheep   white sheep,   On   a   blue   hill.
When   the   wind   blows   You   walk away   slow.

When   the   wind   stops,   you   all   stand still.
White   sheep, white sheep   where do   you   go?

- Creative Level: As students become more aware of imagery, for example, simile and metaphor, they may write a line or two that makes a pleasant creative leap and is personally satisfying.

We need to provide many experiences for students like this so that they are aware of these different ways of thinking. See Thinking + Lesson Plan 6 in Appendix A for a full treatment of this poem.

Teaching for Diversity

Don't forget the importance of addressing the many different groups represented in our multiculture. Students need to be able to identify with the learning activities and the literature you include during the daily lessons. Therefore, it is essential that multicultural education be in your mind as you design lessons to meet curriculum goals and student needs. In *Multicultural Teaching: A Handbook of Activities, Information, and Resources* (Tiedt & Tiedt, 2002), multicultural education is defined as follows:

> Multicultural education is an inclusive teaching/learning process that engages all students in (1) developing a strong sense of self-*esteem*, (2) discovering *empathy* for persons of diverse cultural backgrounds, and (3) experiencing *equitable* opportunities to achieve to their fullest potential. (p. 17)

In planning poetry lessons for a diverse classroom, we need to keep esteem, empathy, and equity clearly in mind as we plan activities and select literature for teaching. Feature poetry by poets who represent diverse backgrounds; for example, Pat Mora speaks directly to students who have close connections with Mexico, and Lucille Clifton and Langston Hughes serve as role models for African American children. Design a lesson around Walter Dean Myers's historically accurate book *Brown Angels*. Students of all ages will respond positively to the sepia tone turn-of-the-century family photographs depicting African American childhood that this talented author further interprets through gentle, caring poetry.

Using Poetry Portfolios

Have students create individual poetry portfolios in which they do all the writing related to poetry. Here, too, they will record information about poetry that you give them or something that they encounter independently that they choose to include. They can also include copies of poetry, again, that you give them or poems they especially like and want to copy for themselves. Keeping a poetry portfolio makes clear the importance of poetry as a special part of your curriculum. Periodically, you can make a point of telling students to complete an activity in the portfolio, for example, when writing original poetry. I refer to using the poetry portfolio throughout this book.

These portfolios can be developed in colorful three-ringed notebooks in which full sheets can be inserted readily, as needed. Or you may prefer to use spiral-bound notebooks. The main consideration is to have sufficient pages available so students have ample space for a full semester of work. Portfolios should be stored in the classroom in alphabetical order by student names in a large box to which students return them after completing their work. Students can make attractive covers for their portfolios, as described in Chapter 7.

Review students' poetry portfolios periodically. Schedule 5–10 minute individual conferences with each student about once a month while other students are busy with an independent reading activity. Before beginning these conferences, talk with the class about the conference process—how the conference will work, what you want to see in their portfolios, and the fact that they can tell you something special during the conference or ask you a question. Have students mark something they are especially proud of that they want you to see. This allows the children to take full advantage of these few minutes alone with you and helps you conduct effective conferences.

Sitting at a table beside the student, talk with him or her about poetry and look through the portfolio together. This kind of conference has multiple benefits for you and the individual learners. It is a time when you communicate directly with students, making it clear that you know them and that you are interested in how things are going for each child. Ask questions such as the following:

- What poem do you like best?

- How did you like that funny poem I read today?

- What would you especially like me to see in your portfolio?

Conclude the conferences by asking students if there is any way that you can help them, or if they have a question they would like to ask. (Give them time to think about that.) Then, say something like, "You're doing a good job, Jillian. Thank you for sharing your portfolio with me." It would be wonderful to follow up this conference by sending a note to the child's parents or guardians, saying something like, "This week Rashad and I had a conference to review his poetry portfolio. He will probably tell you about it. I especially liked his poem about playing soccer. He is really improving his reading and writing skills every day." Give these folded notes to the students to take home. Tell students you want them to read the note themselves and to bring it back signed by the person to whom it is addressed.

At the end of the semester, have students review their portfolios, preparing them for a final evaluation of their work with poetry. Talk with the class about what you might want to see in their portfolios as you review them, for example, some original poems that they wrote and a few poems that they added on their own. Ask students what they think should be in their portfolios.

Then, give the students time to go through their portfolios, tweaking them as they see fit. Having them make a table of contents for the portfolio will guide them to organize their work into a book about poetry that they can take home to keep. As a final entry in each portfolio, have students write an essay about their experiences with poetry during the past months, a type of summary of what they learned or enjoyed.

Your criteria for evaluating students' portfolios should be shared with them, making it clear how they can get a good evaluation. For example,

Outstanding

- Has a table of contents and is well organized
- Contains at least five original poems
- Contains at least five poems by other poets
- Contains information about writing poetry
- Has an attractive cover that includes a title and the poet's name

Good

- Has a table of contents
- Contains several original poems
- Contains one or two poems by other authors
- Contains all information shared in class about poetry

Poor

- Contains no original work
- Contains no poems by other authors
- Has no table of contents

With these criteria before them and class time allotted for reviewing their portfolios, no student should receive an assessment of Poor.

Using the Word Wall to Support Poetry Instruction

The word wall is a simple convention that involves developing an extensive list of words with students to support a reading or writing activity. To make them more flexible in use than the chalkboard, which eventually has to be erased, word walls are created on large sheets of butcher paper, which most schools buy in huge rolls that are available in the teachers' supply room. This same kind of paper is used for creating murals. I refer to using word walls throughout the book.

To create a word wall, mount a large sheet of butcher paper on a wall that all students can see. Then, invite them to begin a list of words related to the activity at hand. For example, in the lesson on onomatopoeia in Thinking + Lesson Plan 11 in Appendix A, I suggest listing words that sound like what they mean—*jingle, buzz, ring, plop, scratch, purr*. This list is left on the wall as long as students are working with it. Children should continue to print additional words on the wall themselves. Occasionally, you might review the words on the wall, taking the opportunity to explain the meaning of unusual words, thus adding to students' vocabularies and encouraging them to use onomatopoetic words in their writing to help make it more descriptive. The list on the wall suggests interesting words to use and helps students spell them correctly. This procedure supports the reading-writing process.

When you are finished with an activity and want to create a new word wall, take the current one down and roll it up. Print the subject along the side so you can locate it easily if you want to use it again. Over the year, you will accumulate a number of these rolls. At the end of the year, your students may find it interesting to examine some of these lists again as they review all the things they have done over the year.

Let me caution you about one thing: Students in a class learn a great deal through the use of these word walls, but each class must go through the generative process anew. Never save old word walls and bring them forth, ready-made, for a new class to use. Students will have missed the total learning process and will have no sense of ownership in a list made by a different class. Instead, let your students take these lists home at the end of the year, if they like, or simply throw them away.

Conclusion

In this chapter, we have explored some general teaching suggestions designed to help you get started with a poetry program. The ideas shared here will help you succeed as you incorporate this form of literature into your curriculum. In Chapter 3, we take a more in-depth look at sharing poetry orally, which is a great way to engage students in listening to poetry and speaking it aloud in different ways.

"FIRE! FIRE!" CRIED MRS. MCGUIRE!

"Fire! Fire!"
Cried Mrs. McGuire.
"Where? Where?"
Asked Mrs. Blair.
"All over town!"
Said Mrs. Brown.
"Get some water!"
Cried her daughter.
"We'd better jump!"
Said Mrs. Grump.
"That would be silly."
Replied Mrs. Minelli.
"What'll we do?"
Asked Mrs. LaRue.
"Turn in the alarm."
Said Mrs. Parm.
"Save us! Save us!"
Screamed Mrs. Davis.

The fire department
Got the call,
And the firemen saved them,
One and all!

— ANONYMOUS

CHAPTER 3

"Fire! Fire!" Cried Mrs. McGuire: Sharing Poetry Orally

P oetry is meant to be heard, so read poems aloud daily to your students. Then, encourage them to join you in reciting or singing poems that they have learned. In time, they will be receptive to saying poems in groups or dramatizing narrative poetry. Before you know it, your class will have acquired a considerable repertoire of poetry they enjoy sharing with one another or performing for others. Thus, students develop listening and speaking skills in a pleasant way that adds a nice variation to the usual classroom routine.

You may say that the idea of sharing poetry orally sounds great for primary grades, but what about older students? In fact, older students respond positively to this approach as well. Middle school teachers also need to emphasize oral language skills as a way of learning that we use much more than we do reading and writing. Furthermore, strong oral language development supports both reading and writing, and oral activities tend to enhance learning experiences at all levels. It's all in how you present this kind of lesson.

Reading Poetry Aloud at All Levels
Reading Poems to Prereaders

Reading aloud to students of all ages is important; however, reading aloud is especially important as a method of introducing literature to young children before they are ready to read. Keep several collections of poetry on your desk so that you can pick one up when there is a break in the day's routine. You could, for example, read a poem or two when most of the children are ready to move on to another activity, yet a few are still completing a task. You might enjoy these collections:

Winter Eyes by Douglas Florian. Quiet poems about winter.

It's Raining Laughter by Nikki Grimes with photographs by Myles C. Pinkney. Joyful verses about African American children.

Climb Into My Lap: First Poems to Read Together, compiled by Lee B. Hopkins and illustrated by Kathryn Brown. Poems for the very young.

Side by Side: Poems to Read Together, compiled by Lee B. Hopkins and illustrated by Hilary Knight. Follows the collection above.

Days Like This: A Collection of Small Poems, edited and illustrated by Simon James. Short poems about familiar topics.

Read-Aloud Rhymes for the Very Young by Jack Prelutsky. Short humorous poems.

Reading Poems to Independent Readers

Children who have become independent readers will still enjoy listening to poetry, and they will continue to learn through listening. Plan short poetry sessions, but also tuck in poems at odd moments during the day. Read a funny poem while children are in line waiting for the bell to ring at lunchtime or while students are getting ready for dismissal in the afternoon. Books you might like to have close at hand include the following:

Lemonade Sun and Other Summer Poems, written by Rebecca Kai Dotlich and illustrated by Jan Spivey Gilchrist. Light-hearted with attractive rhythms.

It's Raining Pigs and Noodles: Poems by Jack Prelutsky. A humorous collection.

Where the Sidewalk Ends by Shel Silverstein. Silverstein's original poems have long been popular with students because most are humorous.

In Daddy's Arms I Am Tall: African Americans Celebrating Fathers, edited and illustrated by Javaka Steptoe. Poets in this collection include Folami Biade, Angela Johnson, and Javaka Steptoe, who created the collage art and a poem to his father, John Steptoe, author of *Stevie* and other picture books.

Cornflakes: Poems, compiled and illustrated by James Stevenson. Look for other popular collections by this talented artist such as *Popcorn, Candy Corn*, and *Sweet Corn*.

Reading Poems to Older Students

Older students will enjoy humorous poems such as those by Robert W. Service, for example, "The Cremation of Sam McGee," which begins with these classic lines:

> There are strange things done in the midnight sun
> By the men who moil for gold;
> The Arctic trails have their secret tales
> That would make your blood run cold.

This long poem is presented in a handsome picture book illustrated by Yukon artist Ted Harrison. Service's poems also can be read as part of a study of the Gold Rush days.

Humor is always a good entrée for students whom you may expect to resist any study of poetry (humor is further discussed later in this chapter). Once students accept humorous poems, you can branch out to poems that treat more serious topics. Share poems, for example, that other students their age have written—poems about sports, poems about travel, and so forth. Work up to poems from collections such as the following:

Pass It On: African-American Poetry for Children, compiled by Wade Hudson and illustrated by Floyd Cooper. Poems by African American poets including Langston Hughes, Nikki Giovanni, Gwendolyn Brooks, and Eloise Greenfield. The attractive illustrations are in muted tones.

My Own True Name: New and Selected Poems for Young Adults by Pat Mora. Poems that speak especially to Latino students.

Choosing the Content of Poems

As you select poems for use in your classroom, think of your students and what they are likely to find interesting. It helps to start with humor, which has the greatest chance of success with beginning experiences.

Humor

Students of all ages enjoy nonsense rhymes or other humorous poems that you recite or read aloud to them. Some funny poems appeal to all ages. Notice that the following verse uses a quick, rollicking rhythm and the rhyme scheme of the limerick. Repeating the last line is just for fun!

> I went to the animal fair—
> The birds and the beasts were there.

The big baboon
By the light of the moon
Was combing his auburn hair.

The monkey he went plunk
Right on the elephant's trunk.
The elephant sneezed
And fell to his knees,
And what became of the monk, the monk,
And what became of the monk?

Introduce students to poets who write humorous verse. The poems of Lewis Carroll and Edward Lear are widely known. Ogden Nash and Dorothy Parker wrote funny commentaries on life that older students usually like. Also, Eve Merriam's funny parodies of Mother Goose rhymes (see Chapter 5) are entertaining. Contemporary poets such as Jack Prelutsky offer a variety of enjoyable funny poems you can share with students of all ages. In addition, these titles are worth examining:

The Beastly Feast, written by Bruce Goldstone and illustrated by Blair Lent. Funny poems about animals.

The Llama Who Had No Pajama, written by Mary Ann Hoberman and illustrated by Betty Fraser. Humorous verses for young readers.

Cat Up a Tree: A Story in Poems, written by Anne Isaacs and illustrated by Stephen Mackey. A continuous poem.

Imagine That! Poems of Never-Was, compiled by Jack Prelutsky and illustrated by Kevin Hawkes. A collection of 50 poems, including Lewis Carroll's "Jabberwocky" and Ogden Nash's "The Wendigo." Also included are poems by less familiar poets, for example, Florence Heide's "Before You Fix Your Next Peanut Butter Sandwich—Read This!" This book is especially useful for the middle school teacher.

Sharing Feelings

Poetry is especially suited to expressing feelings. Younger children will respond positively to these types of poems. However, older students, particularly boys, will need to work up to poetry about loneliness, love, or grief. You will need to develop a climate of trust and acceptance in a middle school classroom before introducing more sensitive topics. It's worth the effort, however, as children of that age particularly need this experience. Following are some books you might share with your students:

Some Things Are Scary, written by Florence Parry Heide and illustrated by Jules Feiffer. This is a poetic book about things that make children feel scared. Students could write poems about the feelings expressed here as they share their own version of scary things.

Little Feelings, written by Judy Spain Barton and illustrated by Benjamin Hummel. Barton's poems treat such topics as loneliness, a new baby, and making choices.

I Hate to Go to Bed!, written and illustrated by Katie Davis. This book also could be used to stimulate writing poems about things students hate.

Listening to Poetry

As a teacher, of course, you want to improve students' listening skills. Although we listen much more than we speak, read, or write, the teaching of listening is often ignored in the school curriculum. Therefore, you need to plan learning activities that will make students aware of listening—why and how to listen more effectively. We can have students listen to poetry as one way to help us achieve this goal. The teacher's reading aloud is effective, but students can also read to one another in cooperative learning groups. In addition, they can listen to poetry recordings at the listening center.

Students are accustomed to learning language through listening, as they have been doing so since birth. Listening is the easiest language skill for students to perform because they do not have to produce the language that is shared. Therefore, all students have larger listening vocabularies than reading and writing vocabularies. So, we begin by reciting or reading poetry aloud as students listen.

Here is one interesting activity that makes students aware of listening as a way of gathering data. Take children for a listening walk, as described in Thinking + Lesson Plan 7 in Appendix A. Give each of the children a piece of stiff cardboard on which a piece of writing paper is attached so that they can take notes as they walk. Have the children jot down all the things they hear—automobiles, birds, voices, a hammer, even the sound of their own feet. As part of this walk, have the children sit down, close their eyes, and "listen to silence."

When you return to the classroom, guide your students to compose a class poem that you might title "The Sounds of Silence" or "Listen!":

> The sounds we hear—
>> Birds singing,
>>
>> Children calling,
>>
>> Church bells ringing.

Or, you might focus on the season or time of the year, as in this example:

> The sounds of autumn—
>> Leaves rustling,
>>
>> Boys and girls playing in the schoolyard,
>>
>> A wedge of geese honking.

This activity could be extended to include all five senses as students observe what they see, hear, smell, feel, and taste. Each sense is developed into one stanza of a longer poem.

Identifying Special Effects

As you read favorite poems aloud, encourage students to listen and to respond through clapping or tapping their feet. Students will enjoy exploring the poet's use of sounds to create special effects, for example, alliteration and ono-matopoeia. Such poetic devices add to the music of poetry.

RHYTHM. Most children enjoy poems that have distinctive rhymes. Young children will clap eagerly in response to David McCord's "Song of the Train" as you read aloud the words he uses to imitate the sound of the wheels on the track: "Clickety, clack; clickety clack." Middle grade students will enjoy Laura E. Richards's funny poem "Antonio, Antonio," which is composed in limerick stanzas.

Jump-rope songs also have pronounced rhythms, as in "Down in the valley, where the green grass grows; there sat *Trina* as sweet as a rose." Ask students to recite songs they know as they all beat out the rhythm that imitates jumping feet.

A fast-paced poem that younger children like is the anonymous verse "The Squirrel," presented on the opposite page. You'll find a lesson based on this poem in Thinking + Lesson Plan 8 in Appendix A. Display this poem on the

THE SQUIRREL

Whisky frisky.
Hippety hop,
Up he scrambles
To the treetop.

Whirly, furly,
What a tail!
Tall as a feather,
Broad as a sail!

Where's his supper?
In the shell.
Snappity, crackity—
Out it fell!

— ANONYMOUS

bulletin board with one or more pictures of squirrels. The words move quickly, just as the animal does.

With older students, read Edgar Allan Poe's "The Bells," which compares the sounds made by four kinds of bells—sleigh bells, wedding bells, alarm bells, and iron bells (see Thinking + Lesson Plan 9 in Appendix A). The words Poe uses, such as *tintinnabulation,* reflect the different sounds, as in this first part of the poem:

> Hear the sledges with the bells—
> Silver bells!
> *What* a world of merriment their melody foretells!
> How they tinkle, tinkle, tinkle,
> In the icy air of night!
> While the stars that oversprinkle
> All the Heavens, seem to twinkle
> With a crystalline delight;
> Keeping time, time, time,
> In a sort of Runic rhyme,
> To the tintinnabulation that so musically wells
> From the bells, bells, bells, bells,
> Bells, bells, bells—
> From the jingling and the tinkling of the bells.

Practice reading this poem aloud before presenting all four verses to your class. Poe wrote "The Bells" to be read aloud, so take full advantage of his wonderful language. Encourage students to think about the stages of life Poe is describing, beginning with the merriment of childhood exemplified by the sleigh bells.

Additional poems that exhibit interesting rhythms include Rowena Bennett's "The Witch of Willowby Wood," Mother Goose's "The Noble Duke of York," and Mildred P. Merryman's "The Pirate Don Durk of Dowdee."

ALLITERATION. Alliteration is achieved by repeating a consonant sound in two consecutive words or more as in *luscious lollipops* or *pretty purple pansies.* Part of the music of poetry is achieved through the deliberate repetition of specific sounds. A classic example, written by Walter de la Mare, repeats the /s/ phoneme both at the beginning and end of words. In his poem "Silver," notice how frequently the word *silver* itself is included. Read this poem aloud to older students as they listen to the sound effects the poet achieves:

Slowly, silently, now the moon

Walks the night in her silver shoon;

This way, and that, she peers, and sees

Silver fruit upon silver trees;

One by one the casements catch

Her beams beneath the silvery thatch;

Couched in his kennel, like a log,

With paws of silver, sleeps the dog;

From their shadowy cote the white breasts peep

Of doves in a silver-feathered sleep;

A harvest mouse goes scampering by,

With silver claws, and silver eye;

And moveless fish in the water gleam,

And moveless reeds in a silver stream.

Have students repeat the first two lines to experience how the words slide across their tongues as they say them. Read the poem again as students listen for the feeling of the moonlight's sinuous movements as it silvers everything it touches. Notice also that this poem contains an example of another device used by writers: personification. Here, the poet gives the moon human attributes as she "walks," "peers," and "sees."

Of course, someone will ask, "What is *shoon*?" Ask if anyone can guess from the context. *Shoon* is an interesting example of an archaic plural form for "shoe." Only a poet would use this older plural form. However, even today we sometimes speak of "brethren," usually in church, and we all frequently use the similar old plural form of child, "children." If a few more advanced students become interested, you can encourage them to investigate the history of the English language.

Younger students will respond to the beginning alliterative lines and the rhythms used in Rowena Bennett's humorous poem "The Witch of Willowby Wood":

There once was a witch of Willowby Wood,

And a weird wild witch was she,

With hair that was snarled,

And hands that were gnarled,

And a kickety, rickety knee.

You or a student could tape this full poem for use at the listening center.

For a sample lesson plan focusing on alliteration, see Thinking + Lesson Plan 10 in Appendix A.

ONOMATOPOEIA. Onomatopoeia is achieved when poets deliberately use words that sound like what they mean, such as *jingle* or *swoosh*. In the poem "Galoshes," Rhoda Bacmeister uses both alliteration and onomatopoeia as she writes about Susie's galoshes that "splish and splosh," two invented words that fit the poet's need to describe walking in slippery slush. Next, she introduces *stamp* and *tramp*, which certainly sound like what they mean. She also uses "stuck in the muck and the mud," which through alliteration and onomatopoeia reminds us of experiences we may have had.

Onomatopoeia is an interesting word to say, but you may have to approach it slowly, syllable by syllable: *ah no mah toe pee' ah*, before your students can say it glibly. Thinking + Lesson Plan 11 in Appendix A focuses on onomatopoeia. Students can make a word wall list of examples of onomatopoeic words—for instance, *crack, thump, scream*. You might group the words into categories, for example: loud words, soft words, musical words, and so on. Then, encourage students to use such words as they compose original poetry (see Chapter 6). Note that effects like onomatopoeia add to the fun of saying poems aloud, which we will explore in the next section.

Saying Poems Aloud

The process of listening to poetry leads naturally to saying it aloud by chanting, reciting together as a voice choir, or singing lyrics. Such activities add an enjoyable element to the classroom routine. Spoken poetry also fits into learning experiences across the curriculum.

Sharing Poems Children Know

Ask students if they know any poems they can share. Even primary grade students will know quite a few—advertising jingles, songs, jump-rope songs, family sayings. After someone says a poem, ask others to join in if they know the poem, too. Soon most of the class will know some of the same poems so that the class can share them just as they might songs they know. Gradually, the class will develop a repertoire they can recite together.

Consciously build this repertoire by teaching poems to your class. For example, ask how many children know the following small verse, part of a much longer poem by Jane Taylor:

> Star, light; star, bright;
> First star I've seen tonight;
> Wish I may,
> Wish I might,
> Have the wish I wish tonight.

Repeat the poem with everyone joining in as much as they can. Then, help young children memorize the poem by saying phrases that children can repeat, for instance, "Star light." Talk about the meaning of the poem so that students in the English as a Second Language program fully understand the act of "wishing on a star." Also, note the repeated use of the rime *ight* and the repetition of the word *wish*. (See Chapter 4 for a discussion regarding building on such forms to support emerging reading skills.)

Introduce the following poem to young children. The repetition makes this poem an easy one for young children to learn, and of course, they will want to add actions.

> This is the way we wash our clothes,
> Wash our clothes, wash our clothes.
> This is the way we wash our clothes
> All on a Monday morning.

This rhyme continues with a different activity for each day, thus: Tuesday: This is the way we iron our clothes, (All on a Tuesday morning). Children can invent lines based on their school activities, which would have more meaning for them.

Use the following similar pattern to encourage young children to invent additional rhythmic verses that they can say together. Note that the first line can be about any action or place, but choose a word that presents a useful rime, for example, *store*, *park*, or *town*. Then, you can print the children's newly created verse so they can read it as they say it.

> Here we go for a walk in the park,
> Walk in the park, walk in the park.
> Here we go for a walk in the park
> So early in the morning.

Jump-rope songs are also a natural for students to share in the elementary grades. One of the most familiar rhymes, "Teddy Bear, Teddy Bear," goes something like this, although there are many different versions:

Teddy Bear, Teddy Bear, turn around.
Teddy Bear, Teddy Bear, touch the ground.
Teddy Bear, Teddy Bear, I am sick.
Send for the doctor, quick, quick, quick.
Teddy Bear, Teddy Bear, tie your shoe;
Teddy Bear, Teddy Bear, has much to do.
Teddy Bear, Teddy Bear, go upstairs;
Teddy Bear, Teddy Bear, say your prayers.
Teddy Bear, Teddy Bear, turn out the light.
Teddy Bear, Teddy Bear, say good night. (Jumper runs out.)

Many games children play have chants or songs attached that are fun for children to learn, for example,

Ring around the Rosie
A pocket full of posies.
Ashes! Ashes!
We all fall down.

Other game songs can be heard on the playground, including "A Tisket, a Tasket," "The Farmer in the Dell," and "London Bridge Is Falling Down." Again, print these poems on large sheets of paper or poster board and display them where students can "read" them from memory.

Older students might make a collection of these jump-rope jingles or game songs. They could publish the collection to share with primary grade teachers and interested parents. A group of students also could present a demonstration to show parents how these games are conducted. Many parents, particularly those from different cultures, do not know these rhymes, which come largely from European traditions.

Students also could invite children of different cultures to share similar songs and games that they are accustomed to playing. Including examples of these songs in a publication would make the collection a contribution to multicultural education in your school.

Funny Sayings, Games, and Riddles

Children learn funny rhymes like the following, usually from one another:

> Adam and Eve and Pinchme
>
> Went down to the river to bathe.
>
> Adam and Eve were drowned—
>
> Who do you think was saved? (Watch out!)

With the following rhyme, the child tells someone who doesn't know the poem to "Repeat after me."

> I am a gold key, (Second child repeats.)
>
> I am a lead key, (Repeat)
>
> I am a brass key, (Repeat)
>
> I am a silver key, (Repeat)
>
> I am a mon key. (Repeat)
>
> > Of course, you are!

Action Poems

Some poems lend themselves to being acted out. A favorite with the younger crowd is "I'm a Little Teapot," which also can be sung:

> I'm a little teapot, short and stout.
>
> Here is my handle; (Make a handle with one arm.)
>
> Here is my spout. (Form a spout with the other arm.)
>
> When I get all steamed up,
>
> Then, I shout,
>
> "Just tip me over
>
> And pour me out!" (Bend toward the spout side to
>
> > pour out the tea.)

The following verse has been developed into a clapping game for two players who sit facing each other. Feel free to adapt these directions. Have two students practice the directions ahead of time until they are sufficiently skilled so they can demonstrate the actions to the class.

Pease porridge hot, (Both persons first slap their knees, then clap their hands, and then clap the open hands of the other person.)

Pease porridge cold, (Both clap their own hands, slap their knees, and then clap the other person's hands again.)

Pease porridge in the pot, (Both clap the other's right hand, clap their own hands together, clap the other's left hand, and then clap their own hands together.)

Nine days old! (Each person slaps his or her own knees, both clap their own hands again, and then clap both open hands of partner for final beat.)

Verse 2

Some like it hot, (Motions same as above.)

Some like it cold,

Some like it in the pot

Nine days old!

Singing Poems for Fun

The poem on the opposite page is a favorite with kindergarten and primary grade children. However, older students who remember it from their earlier years are often pleased to join in when anyone begins to sing it. Give students copies so they can read the poem and illustrate it. This poem could then become part of their individual collections of favorite poems.

Hand motions accompany this song. You can probably create them by just using your imagination, and many children will already know them so they can demonstrate just how it is done. First, the spider inches up the spout (your hand is the spider climbing up). Then, the rain comes down (both hands make rain fall). To indicate the shining sun, circle your face and smile broadly. Of course, your hand (spider) climbs up the spout again.

A similar song that older students enjoy is the anonymous spoof "On Top of Spaghetti," which is sung to the tune of "On Top of Old Smokey":

On top of spaghetti,

All covered with cheese,

I lost my last meatball,

When somebody sneezed.

THE EENTSY, WEENTSY SPIDER

The eentsy, weentsy spider
Climbed up the water spout.

Down poured the rain
And washed the spider out.

Out came the sun
And dried up all the rain.

So eentsy, weentsy spider
Climbed up the spout again.

It rolled under the table,
And over the floor,
And then my old meatball,
Rolled out of the door.

It rolled into the garden,
And under a bush,
And then my poor meatball,
Was nothing but mush.

The mush was as tasty,
As tasty can be,
And early next summer,
It grew into a tree.

The tree, it was covered,
All over with moss,
It grew lovely meatballs
And sweet smelling sauce.

So, when eating spaghetti,
All covered with cheese,
Hold onto your meatball,
Should somebody sneeze!

Books That Feature Songs

Sometimes illustrators choose to create a picture book based on a familiar song. Look for these books to stimulate interest in reading as well as singing songs together. It's all part of building the experiential base for your students. Here are some examples:

I Know an Old Lady Who Swallowed a Fly, illustrated by Glen Rounds. The book features bold print presented with humorous, unconventional illustrations that fit this anonymous folk verse.

Old MacDonald Had a Farm, illustrated by Glen Rounds. The illustrator uses fat felt pen outlines to depict the rugged animal figures with individuality.

This Land Is Your Land by folksinger and guitarist Woody Guthrie. This attractive book presents Guthrie's famous song, which could be used in the social studies curriculum as well as music and art.

Tongue Twisters

Students will have fun with the language presented in poetry as they learn to say tongue twisters and other poems that include language play. Two well-known examples include the following:

> Peter Piper picked a peck of pickled peppers;
> A peck of pickled peppers Peter Piper picked.
> If Peter Piper picked a peck of pickled peppers,
> Where's the peck of pickled peppers Peter Piper picked?

> How much wood would a woodchuck chuck
> If a woodchuck could chuck wood?
> A woodchuck would chuck as much as he could chuck,
> If a woodchuck could chuck wood.

"Out and In" is another funny poem by an anonymous author that requires two readers (or speakers, once they learn the words):

> 1   There were two skunks,
> Out and In.
> When In was out,
> Out was in.
> One day Out was in
> And In was out.
> 2   Their mother
> Who was in with Out,
> Wanted In in.
> "Bring In in,"
> She said to Out.
> 1   So Out went out
> And brought In in.
> 2   "How did you find him
> So fast?" asked Mother.
> 1   "Instinct," he answered.

The Voice Choir

The group recital of poetry is an excellent technique for enriching the oral language program and encouraging all children to speak. Sometimes called ensemble speaking, this approach permits a group to share their appreciation of a poet's work. There is a wide range of poetry suitable for this activity. What is presented here is just a sampling. Thinking + Lesson Plan 12 in Appendix A also focuses on building a class repertoire of poems the students can say together.

You might begin with a short humorous verse that appeals to young students as well as upper elementary students, for example, a limerick. Stress clarity of enunciation, and a long questioning pause indicated by the comma after *reason*, as students say this poem:

> A sleeper from the Amazon
> Put nighties of his gra'ma's on—
> The reason, that
> He was too fat
> To get his *own* pajamas on!

An occasional tongue twister adds spice to language arts activities and increases children's awareness of word play. Students need to concentrate and to speak deliberately as they share this verse:

> I saw Esau sawing wood, (pause)
> And Esau saw I saw him. (quickly)
> Though Esau saw I saw him saw, (pause)
> Still Esau went on sawing!

The following limerick is a great example of word play:

> A tutor who tooted the flute
> Tried to tutor two tooters to toot.
> Said the two to the tutor,
> "Is it harder to toot, or
> To tutor two tooters to toot?"

Verses known to children, such as jump-rope songs, provide good rhythmical chants for ensemble work, for example,

Not last night, but the night before,
Twenty-four burglars at my door,
I went downstairs to let them in;
They hit me over the head
With a rolling pin!

Students enjoy the rhyming and the excitement included in the poem at the beginning of this chapter, "'Fire! Fire!' Cried Mrs. McGuire!" Read this poem aloud to your class. Then, assign a couplet to individual students, as marked here:

1   "Fire! Fire!
      Cried Mrs. McGuire.

2   "Where? Where?"
      Asked Mrs. Blair.

3   "All over town!"
      Said Mrs. Brown.

4   "Get some water!"
      Cried her daughter.

5   "We'd better jump!"
      Said Mrs. Grump.

6   "That would be silly."
      Replied Mrs. Minelli.

7   "What'll we do?"
      Asked Mrs. LaRue.

8   "Turn in the alarm."
      Said Mrs. Parm.

9   "Save us! Save us!"
      Screamed Mrs. Davis.

ALL   The fire department
      Got the call,
      And the firemen saved them,
      One and all!

Thus, nine individuals have an assigned role, and the entire class gets to chime in with the final lines. Repeat the poem several times, so everyone gets a chance to speak a special couplet.

A poem that tells a story lends itself to clear enunciation and varied intonation. Read the poem to the students first, then work stanza by stanza as they learn the lines. Later, ask them for suggestions about how to say different lines. With second or third graders, try "The Secret" by an anonymous poet:

> We have a secret, just we three,
> The robin, and I, and the sweet cherry tree.
> The bird told the tree, and the tree told me,
> And nobody knows it, but just we three.
>
> But, of course, the robin knows it best,
> Because she built the—I shan't tell the rest;
> And laid the four little—something in it.
> I'm afraid I shall tell it every minute.
>
> But if the tree and the robin don't peep,
> I'll try my best the secret to keep.
> Though I know when the little birds fly about,
> Then the whole secret will be out!

In planning a celebration of poetry, as suggested in Chapter 8, you might include a number of ensemble poems presented by a large choir. For variety, include poems done by small groups of students, duets, and solos. Older students will enjoy the humor and the actions of "A Tragic Story" by William Makepeace Thackeray, which several students could act out as a narrator or the choir presents the background information:

> There lived a sage in days of yore,
> And he a handsome pigtail wore;
> But wondered much and sorrowed more,
>   Because it hung behind him.
>
> He mused upon this curious case,
> And swore he'd change the pigtail's place,
> And have it hanging at his face,
>   Not dangling there behind him.
>
> Said he, "The mystery I've found—

I'll turn me round:
—And he turned him round,
        But still it hung behind him.

Then round and round, and out and in,
All day the puzzled sage did spin;
In vain—it mattered not a pin—
        The pigtail hung behind him.

And right and left, and roundabout,
And up and down, and in and out,
He turned, but still the pigtail stout
        Hung steadily behind him.

And though his efforts never slack,
And though he twist, and twirl, and tack,
Alas! Still faithful to his back,
        The pigtail hangs behind him!

Two students could prepare a duet using a poem that includes an amusing conversation as in "You Are Old, Father William" by Lewis Carroll. Edward Lear wrote a funny conversation between a table and a chair that could also be prepared as a duet. Note that you will find two more verses for "The Table and the Chair" in most anthologies:

Said the Table to the Chair,
"You can hardly be aware,
How I suffer from the heat,
And the chilblains on my feet!
If we took a little walk,
We might have a little talk;
Pray let us take the air!"
Said the Table to the Chair.

Said the Chair unto the Table,
"Now you know we are not able!
How foolishly you talk,

When you know we cannot walk!"
Said the Table, with a sigh,
"It can do no harm to try,
I've as many legs as you,
Why can't we walk on two?"

So they both went slowly down,
And walked about the town
With a cheerful bumpy sound,
As they toddled round and round.
And everybody cried,
As they hastened to their side,
"See! The Table and the Chair
Have come out to take the air!"

An occasional solo offers variety and an opportunity for a talented student. Someone might recite the old favorite "Mr. Nobody," which many parents may recognize from their schooldays:

I know a funny little man,
    As quiet as a mouse,
Who does the mischief that is done
    In everybody's house.
There's no one ever sees his face,
    And yet we all agree
That every plate we break was cracked
    By Mr. Nobody.

'Tis he who always tears our books,
    who leaves the door ajar.
He pulls the buttons from our shirts,
    And scatters pins afar;
That squeaking door will always squeak
    For, prithee, don't you see,
We leave the oiling to be done
    By Mr. Nobody.

He puts damp wood upon the fire,
    That kettles do not boil;
His are the feet that bring in mud,
    And all the carpets soil.
The papers always are mislaid,
    Who had them last, but he?
There's no one tosses them about
    But Mr. Nobody.

The finger marks upon the door
    By none of us are made;
We never leave the blinds unclosed,
    To let the curtains fade.
The ink we never spill.
    The boots that lie around, you see
Are not our boots; they all belong
    To Mr. Nobody.

Conclusion

In this chapter, we have covered ways of developing the essential language skills of listening and speaking while at the same time enjoying a variety of poems. Poetry will help you engage students in using these aural/oral language abilities with pleasure as they expand their thinking and learn more about poetry as a form of literature. In Chapter 4, we will focus on integrating poetry into your reading program.

THE EAGLE

 He clasps the crag with crooked hands;
Close to the sun in lonely lands,
Ringed with the azure world, he stands.

The wrinkled sea beneath him crawls;
He watches from his mountain walls,
And like a thunderbolt he falls.

— ALFRED LORD TENNYSON

Like a Thunderbolt: Infusing Poetry Into Your Reading Program

Poetry belongs in reading programs at all levels. Using language experience methods, you can engage beginning readers naturally with reading poems they can already say. More able readers can be introduced to poems suitable to their abilities and interests. More advanced students should continue perusing the writings of poets, perhaps making discoveries of their own, as they move ahead into adult literature.

Learning to Read With Poetry

Poetry should be an integral element of an early reading program. Long before children face the printed word, poetry is part of their lives. Most preschoolers are singing songs and chanting jingles before they come to school. The skillful teacher will use children's natural enjoyment of rhyming and poetry to support the reading program.

Emerging Reading Skills

Beginning readers learn to recognize rhyming in most basic reading programs. They learn to observe rimes or phonograms as patterns that recur in English spelling. (Note that recent reading textbooks are using the variant spelling of rime for this purpose rather than the more common Greek spelling of *rhyme*, which is still used in discussions of poetry.) Building phonemic awareness skills, children learn "If you can read *dog*, then you can read *log, fog,* and *hog.*" In this case, *og* is the rime. Then, they extend these skills by constructing lists of rimes on a continually growing word wall, which serves as a sort of dictionary to which they can refer for help with reading and writing.

We need to be conversant with this approach to reading instruction so that we can see how it fits with engaging students with poetry within the reading program. Note, too, how this emphasis on patterns in English spelling supports children's learning to spell words according to accepted conventions.

Reading Poetry Aloud

As mentioned previously, reading literature aloud to children provides the foundation for a strong reading program. Children need to hear poetry, and they need to see poetry as they begin to read. Thus, they make the connection between spoken and written language. For example, display the anonymous poem "A Kite" in the classroom with kites that children have made. Read the poem aloud, and have children read it with you as you point to the words:

> I often sit and wish that I
> Could be a kite up in the sky,
> And ride upon the breeze and go
> Whichever way I chance to blow.

Bring in books of poetry and share poems daily as children develop their emerging language abilities. In addition to Mother Goose, there is a large body of other poetry for children that you can introduce in this way. As mentioned in Chapter 3, there are jump-rope songs and folk songs, verses by anonymous poets that many of us seem to know, puzzles, and games. Many poets have delighted in writing poems especially for younger children. Teachers need to read such poems aloud and encourage children to share the ones they know. For example, "Rain, Rain, Go Away" is one by an unknown poet that we all may recite on occasion and some children may know:

> Rain, rain, go away.
> Come again some other day.
> Little Johnny wants to play.

Keep several collections of poetry on your desk so that you can use a few minutes before recess to share a poem or two. Refer to the lists included at the beginning of Chapter 3 (see pages 38–40). Here are a couple of additional suggestions:

The New Oxford Treasury of Children's Poems, compiled by Michael Harrison and
  Christopher Stuart-Clark

The Golden Books Family Treasury of Poetry, compiled by Louis Untermeyer and illustrated by Joan Walsh Anglund

Remember to display copies of the poems you read aloud as you continue to reinforce the connection between oral and written language.

Developing Reading Ability

While enjoying poetry with students in different ways, we can support their growing reading abilities. Reproduce poems from collections such as those suggested throughout this book. Make poetry visible in your classroom with displays and by bringing in books that students can read.

Poetry Books for Primary Grade Students

If we want children to read poetry, then we must expose them to poetry in print. We must bring in books that contain poems especially written or selected for younger children, books that may contain poems that they already know and therefore will be able to read. Here is one that may be in your public library or local bookstore:

Kids Pick the Funniest Poems, written by Bruce Lansky and illustrated by Stephen Carpenter

Poems about food are popular with young children. Look for these for children in grades K–3:

Eats by Arnold Adoff

What's on the Menu?, written by Bobbye Goldstein and illustrated by Chris Demarest

Munching: Poems About Eating by Lee Bennett Hopkins

Yummy: Eating Through a Day by Lee Bennett Hopkins

Poetry Collections for Teachers and Parents

Many poetry collections are suitable for both teachers and parents. You could prepare a list of books that parents might share with their younger children.

One excellent suggestion is *Animal Crackers: A Delectable Collection of Pictures, Poems, and Lullabies for the Very Young,* collected and illustrated by Jane Dyer. In this attractive oversize book, Dyer includes a few verses from Mother Goose, some favorite jump-rope rhymes, and selected poems by known poets, for example, David McCord's "Song of the Train" and A.A. Milne's "The End." She also includes a nice selection of lullabies. Among them are the familiar "Golden Slumbers" by Thomas Dekker, which has been set to music, and the old German lullaby, "Sleep, Baby, Sleep." Less common lullabies are the Brazilian song "Cradle Song of the Elephants" by Adriano del Valle, and an African folk song, "African Lullaby," which begins, "Someone would like to have you as her child/But you are mine."

The Runaway Bunny by Margaret Brown is another example of free verse that children enjoy. Brown is also the author of *Good Night, Moon,* which has had considerable impact on the world of young children. First published in 1900, it remains in print and is a popular gift for a new baby. Older students might enjoy rereading these books, perhaps sharing them with a toddler they know.

Following are additional selections:

A Little Book of Poems & Prayers by Joan Walsh Anglund

The Sun Is So Quiet, written by Nikki Giovanni and illustrated by Ashley Bryan

Poems for Fathers, edited by Myra Cohn Livingstone and illustrated by Robert Casilla

Confetti: Poems for Children, written by Pat Mora and illustrated by Enrique O. Sanachey

Poems for the Very Young, written by Michael Rosen and illustrated by Bob Graham

Sing a Song of Popcorn, written by Beatrice Schenk de Regniers, Eva Moore, and Mary Michaels White, and illustrated by nine Caldecott winners

Developing Reading Skills

Even older students will benefit from some of the techniques suggested for primary grades. Such teaching ideas will especially benefit slower learners or students who are learning English as a second language. In this section, additional ideas are presented, such as reinforcing sound-symbol relationships and having students read about poets.

Reinforcement of Sound-Symbol Relationships

The following poem emphasizes the sound /b/, but it also illustrates the importance of varying vowel sounds. This type of tongue twister is intriguing, and it may serve to strengthen students' awareness of spelling patterns.

> Betty Botter bought some butter,
> But, she said, "This butter's bitter;
> If I put it in my batter,
> It will make my batter bitter,
> But a bit of better butter
> Will make my batter better."
> So she bought a bit of butter
> Better than her bitter butter,
> And she put it in her batter
> And the batter was not bitter.
> So 'twas better Betty Botter
> Bought a bit of better butter.

Alliteration is an aspect of poetry that supports student knowledge of sound-symbol relationships. Observing alliteration in a poem like this helps reinforce student knowledge of these relationships, as does writing examples of alliterative phrases, as suggested in Chapter 6.

Display Poetry Around the Room

If we want to promote poetry in the classroom, then we need to make poetry visible. Make a point of displaying poetry in your classroom. After reading a poem aloud, be sure to post a printed copy of that poem, because many students will be interested in reading a poem they have just heard. Students can help you make an enlarged copy of a poem that you have shared by using the computer and decorating the copy they have made.

Share the following poem with your class and display it on a poster. The poem emphasizes the alphabet, but it also includes interesting vocabulary that older students might enjoy. You could use it as a model for more advanced students, who might enjoy playing with this form as they create new ABC poetry to share.

A   was once an Apple Pie.

B   Bit it,

C   Cut it,

D   Divided it,

E   Earned it,

F   Fought for it,

G   Got it,

H   Had it,

I   Inspected it,

J   Jumped for it,

K   Kept it,

L   Longed for it,

M   Mourned for it,

N   Nabbed it,

O   Opened it,

P   Peeked at it,

Q   Quartered it,

R   Ran with it,

S   Sang for it,

T   Took it,

U   Upset it,

V   Viewed it,

W   Wanted it,

X, Y, and Z

All had a great big slice and toddled off to bed!

Elementary students also will enjoy reading the repetitive verse "There's One Wide River to Cross" about Noah and all the animals he saved in the ark. Display the first verses together with animal figures cut from magazines. Of course, this is a kind of counting rhyme, too. Students can create additional verses, making up their own rhyming lines for "five by five," "six by six," and so forth. When completed, this verse is an effective chant to perform in chorus.

Old Noah he did build an ark.

He built one out of hickory bark.

There's one wide river to cross.

The first animals went two by two,
The elephant and the kangaroo.
There's one wide river to cross.

Some animals walked three by three,
The big baboons and the chimpanzees.
There's one wide river to cross.

Then animals marched four by four
Until the hippopotamus blocked the door.
There's one wide river to cross.

Poetry to Read Independently

Every classroom library should include a number of books of poetry that students can peruse at their leisure, familiar friends that they come to know as they search for verses they enjoy. To supplement this collection, bring in 20 or more titles from the library, particularly if you plan to emphasize reading or writing poetry. This circulating library might include titles such as the following:

Jumbo's Lullaby, written by Laura Krauss Melmed and illustrated by Henri Sorensen. Mother Elephant sings a lullaby to her baby. Each verse describes a different animal and its sleeping habits, then ends with a chorus: "Shusha, shusha, little Jumbo,/Mama's love will hold you tight. [Each line varies]." The book is based on the story of Jumbo, a real elephant that lived in the London zoo until Barnum brought him to the United States in 1882. The author imagines Jumbo recalling his days with his mother on the African savannah.

I Look Like a Girl by Sheila Hamanaka. "I look like a girl, but…"—imagination carries this child afar with the animals "to free what is wild" so I can be "me, just me."

In November, written by Cynthia Rylant and illustrated by Jill Kastner. Beautiful art presented across the pages in imaginative ways enhances Rylant's poetic imagery. She describes fall and the approach of winter in the country, saying, for example, "In November, at winter's gate, the stars are brittle." Students also might enjoy reading Rylant's autobiography, *Best Wishes*, which tells about her life in Ohio and how she writes.

Falling Up by Shel Silverstein. Another collection of funny poems that everyone enjoys. Students who know *Where the Sidewalk Ends* will welcome this volume.

Alphabestiary: Animal Poems From A to Z, written by Jane Yolen and illustrated by Allan Eitzen. This is an entertaining book for all ages. Although it is an attractive picture book and uses the ABC format, it includes poems for all ages, for example, Irene R. McLeod's "Lone Dog," which begins, "I'm a lean dog, a keen dog, a wild dog, and lone."

Reading About Poets

For older students, bring in biographies about poets. Students will be especially interested in reading about people whose poetry they have read. There aren't too many biographies available, because they tend to be written about writers who are no longer living. However, you might locate some of the following:

To Remember Robert Louis Stevenson by Alice Cooper Bailey. This biography is unusual in that it is based on what people told the author about the Robert Louis Stevenson they knew. Following the Stevenson trail, Cooper tells of the various places the poet and his family lived.

All the World's a Stage: A Pop-up Biography of William Shakespeare by Michael Bender. This charming book tells of Shakespeare's life from his birth in Stratford-upon-Avon to his death in 1616. Pop-ups cleverly illustrate this book with various stagings and a mock-up of the Globe Theatre.

Robert Frost: America's Poet, written by Doris Faber and illustrated by Paul Frame. This book tells the life story of the poet who was first to present a poem at a U.S. presidential inauguration. He amazed the crowd by reciting the poem from memory when the wind blew away his copy. When Frost died at 88, President Kennedy said, "He had promises to keep and miles to go, and now he sleeps."

Carl Sandburg by Jeffrey H. Hacker. Written in simple expository prose, this biography provides a series of images of Sandburg as a poet and author. However, we also learn that Sandburg was a folksinger and a newspaperman. The book is illustrated with outstanding full-page photographs of Sandburg that show him in his various roles at different times of his life. Samples of his poetry are interspersed throughout the text.

Edgar Allan Poe: Genius in Torment by William Jay Jacobs. This famous poet began life as the ward of a wealthy merchant, was well educated, and at one time went to West Point. Yet, he ended his life at 40, a tortured alcoholic who produced amazing short stories and beautiful, memorable poetry.

Kipling: Storyteller of East and West by Gloria Kamen. This biography presents Kipling more as a storyteller than a poet, but it does tell about his parents and early life, as well as his development as a writer.

Love: The Story of Elizabeth Barrett Browning, written by Mary Logue and illustrated by Peter Kavanagh. Although this is a picture book, the content is for more advanced readers. Focusing on the topic of love, the author blends the story of Browning's life with this theme, which is discussed in boxed asides. She also includes a study guide with answers and a chronology of Elizabeth Barrett Browning's life.

Maya Angelou: Journey of the Heart by Jane Pettit. This biography begins with Maya Angelou's delivery of her poem "On the Pulse of the Morning" at U.S. President Bill Clinton's inauguration. Then it goes back to tell the reader of the long struggle that led to that auspicious moment for this African American poet.

Paul Laurence Dunbar: Portrait of a Poet by Catherine Reef. The author includes a number of photographs, a chronology, and other resources in addition to the story of this African American poet's life. One famous line from his poetry is "Hats off! The flag is passing by!"

Langston Hughes by Jack Rummel. Part of the Black Americans of Achievement series, this biography is introduced by Coretta Scott King. The story of this poet's life is amplified by a fine collection of black and white photographs.

Bard of Avon: The Story of William Shakespeare, written by Diane Stanley and Peter Vennema and illustrated by Diane Stanley. Based on historical research, this beautiful biography is amplified by wonderful full-page paintings.

Note that often biographies fit with social studies themes. Robert Frost, for example, typifies New England, and Maya Angelou could be used to introduce a thematic study of African Americans: Then and Now. Students also could write short biographical sketches of other poets they like, basing their work on library research, for example, entries in reference books such as *Contemporary Authors*. You might like to order the following collections of interviews with contemporary poets for your school library:

Speaking of Poets: Interviews With Poets Who Write for Children and Young Adults, edited by Jeffrey S. Copeland

Speaking of Poets 2: More Interviews With Poets Who Write for Children and Young Adults, edited by Jeffrey S. Copeland and Vicky L. Copeland

Reading Poetry on a Specific Theme

Have students compare several poems about the same topic. Many poets have written or collected poems about a particular theme that interests them, for example, animals, trains, or a special holiday like Halloween. Poetry can also be included as part of a broad thematic study, for example, Living in Africa, Beasts of Burden, Transportation, or Holidays Around the World.

Animals in Our World

We begin with animals around the house and branch out to include less common beasts:

Cats Are Cats, compiled by Nancy Larrick and illustrated by Ed Young. The illustrations are especially effective, depicting cats of various ages doing what cats do—often just sleeping or looking wise. Larrick and Young created a second beautiful book, *Mice Are Nice*. Included in this book is a variety of work by well-known poets.

It's About Dogs, compiled by Tony Johnston with paintings by Ted Rand. A collection of poems about canines.

Eric Carle's Animals Animals, edited by Laura Whipple and illustrated by Eric Carle. Carle has created wonderful animals of tissue paper and paint to illustrate this collection of poems. Recognizing the ornery reputation of the camel, Rudyard Kipling wrote "Commissariat Camels":

> We haven't a camelty tune of our own
> To help us trollop along.
> But every neck is a hairy trombone,
> Ru-ta-ta-ta! Is a hairy trombone,
> And this is our marching song:
> > Can't! Don't!
> > Shan't! Won't!
> Pass it along the line!
> Pass it along the line!

The Very Lonely Firefly, written and illustrated by Eric Carle. This book tells of a firefly's search for a friend. Finally he meets a whole group of fireflies flashing their lights back at him. The fireflies really do twinkle on the last page, much to the reader's delight and surprise.

One Sun Rises: An African Wildlife Counting Book by Wendy Hartmann. This book is unique in its illustrations by Nicolaas Maritz from Cape Town. The counting lines do not rhyme; nonetheless, they read like free verse that begins and ends with "One sun rises over Africa."

Butterfly House, written by Eve Bunting and illustrated by Greg Shed. Shed's full-page spreads show the different stages of the butterfly transition from larva to a winged beauty. Bunting describes the butterfly that emerges from the chrysalis as "all spotted, orange, black, and brown as if someone had shaken paints and let the drops fall down."

Dinosaurs and Other Fearsome Creatures

Children are intrigued by dinosaurs such as the stegosaurus and tyrannosaurus rex. Bring in a variety of poems about dinosaurs and other fearsome creatures. Share them on a large bulletin board where children can display their drawings with copies of poetry they like. Books that will help develop this interest include the following:

Tyrannosaurus Was a Beast, written by Jack Prelutsky and illustrated by Arnold Lobel. Prelutsky provides a poem for each of fourteen different dinosaurs. He begins with the giant beast of the Cretaceous period and works his way to the Seismosaurus, which lived in the Jurassic period. For each, realistic illustrations are accompanied by basic information about size and location, as well as the pronunciation of each name.

Bone Poems, written by Jeff Moss and illustrated by Tom Leigh. This unusual collection of poems is about the dinosaurs and similar creatures whose bones are now in the museum. The book is based on the holdings of the American Museum of Natural History.

Good Night, Dinosaurs, written by Judy Sierra and illustrated by Victoria Chess. Sierra imagines just how the many different dinosaurs might have interacted as families, with special emphasis on going to bed. Although the drawings have some scientific basis, their appearance is freely interpreted. Her poetry might stimulate the thinking of students as they try writing poems about these extinct creatures and how they might have lived.

There's a Zoo in Room 22, written by Judy Sierra and illustrated by Barney Salzberg. In this creative collection of poems, Sierra has written an alphabet of classroom pets for Miss Darling's room, beginning with Amanda Anaconda.

Eric Carle's Dragons Dragons & Other Creatures That Never Were, compiled by Laura Whipple and illustrated by Eric Carle. Eric Carle has had fun painting fantastic pictures to illustrate a collection of poems. Students will enjoy the poems and add to their knowledge about such fantasy creatures as mermaids and minotaurs. Students may try to create their own pictures using Carle's art technique, which combines colored tissue paper and paints. The book includes a wonderful four-page foldout of the Chinese dragon.

Trains

Trains have always held a certain fascination for people of all ages. This topic brings in history, the romance of railway travel, and the sounds made by trains of different kinds. You might begin with David McCord's "Song of the Train" and then share Rowena Bennett's "A Modern Dragon," which presents a marvelous metaphor (and ties in with the dinosaurs and dragons theme):

> A train is a dragon that roars through the dark.
> He wriggles his tail as he sends up a spark.
> He pierces the night with his one yellow eye,
> And all the earth trembles when he rushes by.

Another favorite is Emily Dickinson's "I Like to See It Lap the Miles," which likens the train to a horse (see page 88). Edna St. Vincent Millay wrote a poem about the allure of trains as they invite us to take to the "road," which is reproduced on the opposite page.

Halloween

Halloween offers an opportunity to share scary poems about witches, goblins, and other interesting characters. You might plan a Halloween Readers Theatre presentation to share with students in other rooms. Following is a sampling of the varied poems you can share with your students. You'll find many more in your local library.

TRAVEL

The railroad track is miles away,

And the day is loud with voices speaking,

Yet there isn't a train goes by all day

But I hear its whistle shrieking.

All night there isn't a train goes by,

Though the night is still for sleep and dreaming,

But I see its cinders red on the sky,

And hear its engine steaming.

My heart is warm with the friends I make,

And better friends I'll not be knowing,

Yet there isn't a train I wouldn't take,

No matter where it's going.

— EDNA ST. VINCENT MILLAY —

Scared Silly: A Book for the Brave by Marc T. Brown. A collection of poems, riddles, jokes, stories, and more.

Some Things Are Scary, written by Florence Heide and illustrated by Jules Feiffer. A kind of free verse about a different type of scariness that extends beyond Halloween.

Boo! Halloween Poems and Limericks, written by Patricia Hubbell and illustrated by Jeff Spackman. A collection of poems about spooky topics including bones and skeletons, cemeteries and ghouls, witches and bats, and other ghostly creatures.

Halloween Poems, edited by Myra Cohn Livingstone and illustrated by Stephen Gammell. A variety of poems that cross grade levels.

It's Halloween, written by Jack Prelutsky and illustrated by Marylin Hafner. Poems by Prelutsky for the younger set.

Creating Personal Poetry Collections

Students need to hear and read a wide variety of poems. As they are exposed to more poetry, they will naturally identify favorites, asking to hear them again and again. Encourage students to read a wide range of poems by bringing in lots of books for them to explore. Suggest then that they create their own book, perhaps titled *My Favorite Poems*. Selecting poems to put in these personal anthologies leads students to compare poems and to establish informal criteria on which to base their selections.

Children can print or write each poem they select on a page, decorating it artfully. Some students may use the computer for printing their poems with varied fonts to add interest, such as in the treatment of "The Little Turtle" in Figure 3.

Encourage students to look through the collections of poetry in the classroom for types of art they might want to use to decorate their poems, or plan a trip to the library where they can look through more books for ideas. Also, point out picture books like the following:

The Bookworm's Feast: A Potluck of Poems by J. Patrick Lewis. Includes lots of word play and onomatopoeia to delight readers.

Wake Up House: Rooms Full of Poems, written by Dee Lillegard and illustrated by Don Carter. Includes illustrations of thick paint on foam board and plaster to decorate short, pithy verses.

FIGURE 3

The Little Turtle

There was a little turtle.
He lived in a box.
He swam in a puddle.
He climbed on the rocks.

He snapped at a mosquito.
He snapped at a flea.
He snapped at a minnow.
And he snapped at me.

He caught the mosquito.
He caught the flea.
He caught the minnow.
But he didn't catch me!

Vachel Lindsay

Talk with students about materials you could make available to facilitate their plans for presenting individual poems—colored paper, colored pens, crayons, paints, papers with varied textures, and so on.

Reading Both Poetry and Prose

Most reading programs include good literature, both poetry and prose. Point out characteristics that these forms of writing share. For example, poetic language is not found only in poems. Many writers use lyrical language as they describe a landscape, tell a story, or share information. Encourage students to share examples of descriptive language that sounds like poetry that they find when reading prose.

Beautiful Images

A delightful way to introduce children to the use of poetic imagery and also to the varied beliefs of people around the world is through books created by Natalie Belting. *The Sun Is a Golden Earring,* illustrated by Bernarda Bryson and an Honor Book for the Caldecott Award, compares ideas that are related to the heavens and might fit nicely with a study of astronomy. An example of the imagery contained in this book is the following metaphor:

> The moon is a white cat
>
> that hunts
>
> the gray mice of the night.

Belting's *Calendar Moon* relates ideas about the calendar or year. *The Earth Is on a Fish's Back* shows children many explanations of how the earth began. *Whirlwind Is a Ghost Dancing* presents the lore of North American Indian tribes. In each of these books, the editor, author, and illustrator have worked hard to combine the poetic prose with outstanding art so that the books are truly lovely. Although they are short picture books, these books should be introduced to older children as well as younger children, for they are too good to miss. They contain wonderful examples of similes and metaphors that will be useful in developing these concepts with your students.

Extending the Comparison of Poetry and Prose

To extend students' understanding of the differences between poetry and prose, have them compare two versions of the same narrative. For example, you can present an interesting lesson based on the comparison of a fable written in prose and the same fable written in poetry.

The fable is a distinctive form of folklore designed to demonstrate a moral or lesson. Each fable consists of two parts: the narration, which presents a brief story, and the moral, which states the conclusion succinctly. The characters in a fable are usually animals, although occasionally inanimate or human figures may be used.

Fables are closely related to proverbs, which may actually be the moral statement that accompanies a fable. One example is, "Never count your chickens before they've hatched." Fables, as we know them today, have their roots in Oriental and Greek literature. Some of the most famous, attributed to the Greek slave Aesop, date back to the 5th century B.C. Much later, in the 17th century, poet La Fontaine adapted many of Aesop's fables and also wrote original ones. Here is one of Aesop's most familiar fables, "The Ant and the Grasshopper," as retold in prose by Joseph Jacobs in *The Fables of Aesop*:

> In a field one summer's day a grasshopper was hopping about, chirping and singing to its heart's content. An ant passed by, bearing along with great toil an ear of corn he was taking to the nest.
>
> "Why not come and chat with me," said the grasshopper, "instead of toiling and moiling in that way?"
>
> "I am helping to lay up food for the winter," said the ant, "and I recommend that you do the same."
>
> "Why bother about winter?" said the grasshopper. "We have plenty of food at present."
>
> But the ant went on its way and continued its toil. When the winter came, the grasshopper had no food, and found itself dying of hunger, while it saw the ants distributing every day corn and grain from the stores they had collected in the summer. Then the grasshopper knew—
> *It is best to prepare for the days of necessity.*

Older students can compare this same fable with the poem "The Grasshopper and the Ant" as retold by La Fontaine in *A Hundred Fables*:

> A grasshopper gay
> Sang the Summer away,
> And found herself poor
> By the winter's first roar.

Of meat and of bread,

Not a morsel she had!

So a-begging she went,

To her neighbor the ant.

    For the loan of some wheat,

    Which would serve her to eat

Till the season came round.

    "I will pay you," she saith

    "On an animal's faith,

Double weight in the pound

'ere the harvest be bound."

The ant is a friend

(And here she might mend)

Little given to lend.

"How spent you the summer?"

Quoth she, looking shame

At the borrowing dame.

"Night and day to each comer

I sang if you please."

"You sang! I'm at ease;

For 'tis plain at a glance,

Now, Ma'am, you must dance."

Ask students which form of the story is easiest to understand, and ask if they found any lines difficult. Students should find it interesting to observe how La Fontaine has interpreted the original story. He literally starts with the end of Aesop's story and focuses on what happens after summer is past. Note, too, how the poet has developed the ant's character in just a few pointed words.

Challenge some of your talented older students to try their hand at writing poetic versions of folktales or other stories that intrigue them. Bring in collections of folktales, for example, one of these attractive collections of Chaucer's tales, which are presented in modern English:

Canterbury Tales by Geoffrey Chaucer; selected, translated, and adapted by Barbara Cohen and illustrated by Trina Schart Hyman

The Canterbury Tales, edited by Geraldine McCaughrean and illustrated by Victor G. Ambrus

Found Poetry

"Found poetry" is poetry you find in unexpected places—writing that was not intended to be poetry. Many fine writers use language so rhythmically as they describe a setting, for example, that we suddenly realize we are not reading the usual cadences of expository writing. Or, they write a descriptive paragraph with such colorful imagery that it reads more like poetry than prose.

Many authors of picture books present their stories in beautiful poetic sentences. One example is Cynthia Rylant's *When I Was Young in the Mountains*, an autobiographical story about living with her grandparents in the mining country of West Virginia. The repetition of "When I was young in the mountains" adds to the lyrical quality of the text. Even older students can appreciate this author's work, which presents a model they can emulate.

Passages in any narrative writing may suggest a poem. For instance, I found a poem in the attractive picture book, *Stuartship*, written by Ryan Collay and Joanne Dubrow and illustrated by Sydney Roark. This clever book tells children about the importance of taking care of our planet—the importance of stewardship, which the main character thinks is spelled "Stuartship," because his name is Stuart. One of the characters is a wise gnome named Mr. Kenneth, who lives in a treehouse that is old—"Not old in a musty, dusty way, but old as a burnished stone step or polished handrail shows use and age." Mr. Kenneth tells Stuart about stewardship in these words:

> Well, stewardship is the idea
> That we take care of things,
> Think about our actions
> And look ahead to see the effect
> Of our choices.
> We need to design with foresight.
> We need to plan for the future.
> We must always remember
> That we are caretakers.

Poetry may be found in unexpected places. One author discovered poetry in the short stories of Edgar Allan Poe. Brod Bagert edited a collection of Poe's poetry that includes several selections from Poe's wonderfully horrifying mystery stories. Here is one found poem that comes from "The Pit and the Pendulum." This is a man's response on hearing his sentence to death:

> The sentence—the dread sentence of death—
> Was the last which reached my ears.
> I heard no more
> Yet, for a while I saw.
> I saw the lips of black-robed judges,
> Thin to grotesqueness,
> Thin with the intensity of their firmness,
> Of immovable resolution,
> Of stern contempt of human torture.
> I saw the decrees of Fate still issuing from those lips.
> I saw them writhe with deadly locution.
> I saw them fashion the syllables of my name
> And I shuddered.
> Then my vision fell upon the seven tall candles upon the table.
> At first they seemed white slender angels who would save me,
> But then the angel forms became spectres,
> With heads of flame,
> And I saw that from them there would be no help.
> And then the figures of the judges vanished.
> All swallowed up in a mad running descent...
> Then silence,
> And stillness,
> And night were the universe.

Illustrations by Carolynn Cobleigh portray the grim image of the judges and the spectral candles. This book will give students some excellent ideas for presenting found poetry.

Thus, poetry fits into the reading program as we link poetry and prose in interesting ways. In the next section, we will explore ways of presenting poetry through Readers Theatre.

Poetry and Readers Theatre

Because poetry is a shorter form of literature, it lends itself especially well to use in a Readers Theatre presentation. Select poetry around a theme or choose a collection of poems that will be familiar to the audience, for example, the Parent Teacher Association. The ideas that follow will get you started.

How Readers Theatre Works

Readers Theatre is a strategy that stimulates students to explore and share literature that can be related to any subject of study. It engages students in reading literature, poetry in this case, and then presenting it orally. Students usually work in groups as they plan a presentation, selecting and preparing the material to be presented, rehearsing the production, and then making the presentation before an audience. Of course, we are emphasizing poetry, but poems can be combined with other forms of literature, if that is appropriate to your curriculum. People have different ideas regarding Readers Theatre, but I recommend engaging students in the full thinking and learning process as they go through the following steps.

PLANNING A PRESENTATION. Readers Theatre is a strategy for making a presentation. Usually, there are no props or costuming. Readers may sit on stools or chairs. This strategy can be used with any topic or theme and with different purposes in mind. A poetry presentation might be planned to

- share poetry with primary grade children,

- present a holiday program for parents,

- share the works and life story of a single poet, or

- summarize a unit of study.

SELECTING MATERIALS. If, for example, you decide to participate in a school program on Halloween for parents, students would need to find material suitable for that topic. This could include poems, songs, factual information about superstitions, and original writing by students. Visit the library as groups work to locate material they can use. Note that throughout this process, the teacher's role is that of a symphony conductor, orchestrating but not playing the music. Students are learning by doing—evaluating, making decisions, and producing.

PREPARING THE SCRIPT. Students will need to copy the poems and other material they select. Then, they will need to decide how each poem will be presented, whether as an individual reading one poem, a two-part poem, or something for the full voice choir. Remember throughout that this is a reading process, not memorization. The group also will need to decide who will do what and make sure that each person has an equitable role. At this stage they should consider their audience in terms of pacing and variety in the presentation, for example, following a serious poem with some short, hilarious ones. Copies of the material to be read for one presentation can be placed in colored folders that all members of the troupe hold.

REHEARSING THE PRODUCTION. Once student assignments are clear, each student needs to practice the material he or she is to read. Then, the whole group rehearses the entire presentation to see how it fits together. One student should be appointed as director to make suggestions or to raise questions that the group needs to address. Each group can rehearse before the rest of the class as it gets close to a full presentation. Thus, class members can also make suggestions designed to improve each presentation.

MAKING THE PRESENTATION. After groups have rehearsed and feel they are ready, one group or several might present to another class or two. Then the presentation might be included as part of an assembly or shared with parents.

Humorous Poems for Readers Theatre

Funny poems are sure to please an audience of students or adults. Suggest short verses by Ogden Nash, limericks, even the "Pinchme" verse on page 49, but also introduce students to longer poems that have a rollicking rhythm like Edward Lear's "The Jumblies," a nonsense poem which begins like this:

> They went to sea in a Sieve, they did,
> In a Sieve they went to sea:
> In spite of all their friends could say,
> On a winter's morn, on a stormy day,
> In a Sieve they went to sea!
> And when the Sieve turned round and round,
> And everyone cried, "You'll all be drowned!"
> They called aloud, "Our Sieve ain't big,

But we don't care a button! We don't care a fig!

In a Sieve we'll go to sea!"

Far and few, far and few,

Are the lands where the Jumblies live;

Their heads are green, and their hands are blue,

And they went to sea in a Sieve.

The poem has a fast-paced rhythm, so it moves along quickly. Also, remember that students are reading these poems, so they don't have to memorize a long verse. Adding to the musical effect of Lear's poem, each verse ends with a chorus of four lines that students will soon memorize, so they can look up at their audience. (Note that choruses allow all students to participate, so sometimes you may suggest that students create a refrain for a longer poem.) When you share "The Jumblies" with students, they may want to know what a sieve is, so bring one in from your kitchen. For a performance, students could flourish a variety of sieves. (The teacher as conductor can make suggestions or provide tips occasionally!)

Other humorous verse students might consider include the following:

"Eletelephony" by Laura E. Richards

"Fire! Fire!" Cried Mrs. McGuire (see page 36)

"Habits of the Hippopotamus" by Arthur Guiterman

Limericks

"Little Miss Muffett" by Guy Wetmore Carryl

"Pollution" by Tom Lehrer (and other songs by Lehrer)

"Poor Old Woman"

Classic Works for Readers Theatre

Parents will be pleased to hear poems they read when they were in school, so a second grouping might feature a potpourri such as the following:

"The Highwayman" by Alfred Noyes

"Sea Fever" by John Masefield

"Silver" by Walter de la Mare (see page 45)

"Sweet and Low" by Alfred Lord Tennyson (could be spoken, then sung)

Many parents will know and appreciate the poem "Loveliest of Trees" by A.E. Housman, which could be read by a solo voice:

> Loveliest of trees, the cherry now
>
> Is hung with bloom along the bough,
>
> And stands about the woodland ride
>
> Wearing white for Eastertide.
>
> Now, of my threescore years and ten,
>
> Twenty will not come again,
>
> And take from seventy springs a score,
>
> It only leaves me fifty more.
>
> And since to look at things in bloom
>
> Fifty springs are little room,
>
> About the woodlands I will go
>
> To see the cherry hung with snow.

Parodies for Readers Theatre

Parodies are spoofs that might be an interesting addition to a Readers Theatre presentation. Usually a writer is simply having fun, but sometimes the writer may be making fun of another person's writing (as students would need to explain in presenting parodies). This was apparently the case when Kenyon Cox wrote a poem titled "The Octopussycat," which sounds remarkably like the poem "I Love Little Pussy" by Jane Taylor. Compare the two:

The Octopussycat

> I love Octopussy, his arms are so long;
>
> There's nothing in nature so sweet as his song.
>
> 'Tis true I'd not touch him—no, not for a farm!
>
> If I keep at a distance, he'll do me no harm.

I Love Little Pussy

I love little Pussy,
Her coat is so warm.
And if I don't hurt her,
She'll do me no harm.
So I'll not pull her tail
Nor drive her away,
But Pussy and I
Very gently will play.

Lewis Carroll was also poking fun at another writer when he wrote the parody "How Doth the Little Crocodile," which appears in *Alice's Adventures in Wonderland*:

How doth the little crocodile
    Improve his shining tail;
And pour the waters of the Nile
    On every golden scale!

How cheerfully he seems to grin,
    How neatly spreads his claws,
And welcomes little fishes in,
    With gently smiling jaws!

The poem he was mimicking was written by Isaac Watts and published in *Divine and Moral Songs for Children*. The poem attempts to teach a lesson to the children to whom it would be read:

How doth the little busy bee
    Improve each shining hour,
And gather honey all the day
    From every opening flower.

How skillfully she builds her cell!
    How neat she spreads the wax!
And labors hard to store it well
    With the sweet food she makes.

In works of labor or of skill
I would be busy too;
For Satan finds some mischief still
For idle hands to do.

In books, or work, or healthful play,
Let my first years be past;
That I may give for every day
Some good account at last.

More ideas about parodies are included in Chapter 5.

Readers Theatre is a wonderful, versatile strategy to use in stimulating students' thinking as they read widely and engage in making a presentation. As you use it with students, you will discover ideas for expanding its possibilities. Next, we will explore another special attribute of the poet's writing—imagery. Here, too, we will aim to encourage students to exercise creative ways of thinking.

Exploring the Imagery of Poetry

Fresh, vivid images distinguish good poetry from the mediocre. Begin a search for lines and full poems that develop interesting images, for example, similes and metaphors. Remember that both images compare two objects, but the simile expresses the relationship in explicit terms, as in "the sun is like a huge orange ball" or "that man is as sly as a fox." Conversely, in the metaphor the relationship is direct with no use of *like* or *as*. An example is "My friend is a rock on whom I can lean."

Many expressions have been used so frequently they have become trite, as in the example "as sly as a fox." Write some of these similes on the board, asking students to fill in the blanks:

As cold as _____   As blue as the _____

As busy as a _____   As quiet as a _____

You may be surprised to see how many students will easily come up with the same answers—ice, bee, sky, mouse. (However, be aware that this knowledge may be limited to native English speakers.)

Then take one of the comparisons, and challenge your students to suggest fresh images, such as the following, as you create a free verse poem together:

> As quiet as...
> A hummingbird at rest,
> A kitten dreaming,
> A house when all are sleeping.

Repeat the first line as you collect ideas for a second stanza and a third, if you like.

Share examples of similes and metaphors in poetry with your students. Maude E. Uschold develops a pleasant simile in her poem, "Moonlight":

> Like a white cat
> Moonlight peers through windows,
> Listening, watching.
> Like a white cat it moves
> Across the threshold
> And stretches itself on the floor;
> It sits on a chair
> And puts white paws on the table.
> Moonlight crouches among shadows,
>> Watching, waiting,
>> The slow passing of night.

Tennyson's well-known poem "The Eagle," presented at the beginning of this chapter, develops a powerful image that ends suddenly with a simile as the eagle dives toward the earth "like a thunderbolt." See Thinking + Lesson Plan 13 in Appendix A for a sample lesson focusing on similes based on this poem.

The metaphor achieves a similar effect, but it is more subtle than a simile. The poet presents one thing as another, sometimes without telling you; that's when you have to infer the meaning, as in these examples:

> Night gathers itself into a ball of yarn.
> Night loosens the ball and it spreads...
>> From "Night" by Carl Sandburg

I LIKE TO SEE IT LAP THE MILES

I like to see it lap the miles,

And lick the valleys up,

And stop to feed itself at tanks,

And then, prodigious, step

Around a pile of mountains,

And, supercilious, peer

In shanties by the sides of roads,

And then a quarry pare.

To fit its sides, and crawl between,

Complaining all the while

In horrid, hooting stanza,

Then chase itself down hill

And neigh like Boanerges—

Then, punctual as a star,

Stop—docile and omnipotent—

At its own stable door.

— EMILY DICKINSON —

Skins of lemons are waterproof slickers...
From "Skins" by Aileen Fisher

In the morning the city
Spreads its wings...
From "City" by Langston Hughes

A metaphor can be extensive, as in Emily Dickinson's "I Like to See It Lap the Miles," which is reproduced on the opposite page. She describes a train in terms of a horse that "feeds itself," "neighs," and finally stops at "its own stable door." Don't tell students about the comparison; rather, challenge them to figure out what Dickinson is describing in such an unusual way.

In another example of metaphor, Kaye Starbird compares December and breakfast cereal in the poem at the beginning of Chapter 1. See Thinking + Lesson Plan 14 in Appendix A for a sample lesson plan focusing on metaphors.

Working with imagery in this way stimulates student thinking. Your students will tap their creativity as they generate new images. Have them share their ideas so that they all begin to understand this way of playing with words.

Conclusion

In this chapter, we have explored various ways of working with poetry to stimulate thinking within the reading program. Thus, while students develop their reading abilities, they will acquire a love for poetry inspired by an enthusiastic teacher. In the next chapter, we will examine ways of ascertaining that all children know Mother Goose rhymes.

SIMPLE SIMON

Simple Simon met a pieman
Going to the fair.
Said Simple Simon to the pieman,
"Let me taste your wares."

Said the pieman to Simple Simon,
"Show me first your penny."
Said Simple Simon to the pieman,
"Indeed, I have not any."

— MOTHER GOOSE

CHAPTER 5

Simple Simon: Exploring Mother Goose Rhymes Across the Grades

Mother Goose rhymes and common folk verses often are familiar to students, who may have heard them recited, sung, or read by their parents from their earliest years. However, we cannot assume that all children in the primary grades or even in upper elementary or middle school know these verses. The rhymes are such an integral part of our literary heritage, however, that it is important that all children be introduced to them before they leave school.

I begin this chapter with activities for using Mother Goose in the primary grades. Then, I suggest specific ways of introducing these verses into language arts activities for older students to ensure that all students recognize this common heritage.

Mother Goose in the Primary Grades

The rhymes and jingles of childhood need to be part of every child's experiential background. Reading Mother Goose rhymes and other familiar verses appropriate for young children should be part of the daily lesson plan so that all children know such characters as Old King Cole, Mary and her lamb, Old Mother Hubbard, Little Bo-Peep, and many others.

Introducing Mother Goose

Sharing these verses with children gives adults an opportunity to enjoy them again, too. What a rich source of language, imagery, and story content! To take full advantage of this form of poetry, we need to read it and to have books on hand to which we can refer as we plan lessons.

Every teacher should own at least one good collection of Mother Goose rhymes to use in the classroom. The following collections should be readily available in public libraries or bookstores:

Jack and Jill and Other Nursery Rhymes by Lucy Cousins

A Child's Treasury of Nursery Rhymes by Kady Macdonald Denton

Tomie dePaola's Mother Goose by Tomie dePaola

The Glorious Mother Goose by Cooper Edens

The Random House Book of Mother Goose: A Treasury of 306 Timeless Nursery Rhymes by Arnold Lobel

Here Comes Mother Goose, edited by Iona Opie

My Very First Mother Goose, edited by Iona Opie and illustrated by Rosemary Wells

For the beginning teacher's basic resource, I suggest purchasing an inexpensive hardbound edition of Mother Goose rhymes published in 1992 by Barnes & Noble. This is a new edition of *The Real Mother Goose*, which was illustrated by Blanche Fisher Wright in 1916.

Browse through one of these volumes, refreshing your memory of the Mother Goose verses. Choose a group of the more familiar ones to use at first with primary grade children, for example,

Baa, Baa, Black Sheep	Little Miss Muffett
Humpty Dumpty	Old King Cole
Jack and Jill	Old Mother Hubbard
Little Bo-Peep	Peter, Peter, Pumpkin Eater
Little Boy Blue	Simple Simon
Little Jack Horner	The Old Woman Who Lived in a Shoe

Some artists have chosen to feature a single verse in a picture book, illustrating the events in one of the longer poems. Paul Galdone, for example, created the following illustrated Mother Goose rhymes, which are especially good for young children:

The History of Simple Simon	*The Old Woman and Her Pig*
The House That Jack Built	*Tom, Tom, the Piper's Son*
Old Mother Hubbard and Her Dog	

Developing Oral Language Skills

Begin by reciting or reading Mother Goose rhymes aloud to young children. As you recite or read poetry aloud to children, remember that you are teaching listening skills. Through this kind of listening, children are learning the same comprehension skills they will use as they read independently. They are also learning vocabulary, sentence construction, and different forms that poems can take. Notice what students are learning as they hear and repeat this verse:

> There was a crooked man,
> And he went a crooked mile,
> He found a crooked sixpence
> Against a crooked stile.
> He bought a crooked cat,
> Which caught a crooked mouse,
> And they all lived together
> In a crooked little house.

First, they are learning to enjoy a funny whimsical poem about a man, a cat, and a mouse. The repetition of the word *crooked* ties the poem together. After repeating this verse aloud, ask children what *crooked* means in this verse (not straight). They will enjoy drawing pictures, perhaps a mural, of all the crooked things named in this poem. You will need to explain the words *sixpence* (an English coin) and *stile* (steps over a fence). If your collection of Mother Goose verses contains an illustration of the poem, this will help children envision these less familiar objects.

Print the poem so students can read it. Then, they can add the rimes (*ile* and *ouse*) included in this poem to their lists if they haven't been encountered previously. See Chapter 4 for an explanation of the use of rimes in supporting emerging reading.

Supporting the Beginning Reading Program

Although this is not our primary purpose in bringing poetry into the classroom, poems can be used to teach children how to read. Using Language Experience Approach methods, we draw something from the children's experience (familiar poems they have been saying) to demonstrate the connections between what they say and what they can read.

For example, print a Mother Goose rhyme on a large poster or a tablet mounted on an easel. Thus, students see a poem in print that they have heard you read and have learned to say together, perhaps, "Jack and Jill." As you read the poem aloud, point to the words you are speaking. Then, invite the class to "read" the poem aloud with you as you again point to the words.

After reading the verse aloud, you can help students observe relationships between the sounds they hear and the letters printed on the poster. For example, in "Jack and Jill," presented on the opposite page, students could listen to the sounds heard at the beginning of these two names. Ask, "Do you know other names that begin with this same sound /j/?" Students might name John, Jerry, or Judy. If one of the children has an appropriate name, you can designate this phoneme as "Joe's sound." (Be careful about names like José or Johan, however, which come from different languages and represent different phonemes in English, /h/ and /y/, respectively. If less common spellings occur, be prepared to explain briefly that occasionally the letter *J* can stand for a sound other than /j/.)

Then, you might write the names Jack and Jill on the board, asking if anyone knows a word that rhymes with *Jack—back, crack, pack, sack—*and then listing rimes for *Jill—bill, hill, kill, will.* Draw students' attention to the use of *hill* in the poem to rhyme with *Jill.* The children can add these rimes to their word wall. In this way, you help students expand their phonemic awareness. Be careful not to overdo this work with any single poem, however, as your first objective in presenting poetry in the classroom should be to have students enjoy the verses you share.

As mentioned previously, vocabulary is another aspect of poetry that may require an explanation. In "Jack and Jill," for example, children may not recognize the word *fetch.* Encourage them to guess the meaning based on the context; perhaps someone will suggest "get" as a meaning. We do sometimes use this word today. We may, for instance, tell a dog to "fetch the ball." This kind of incidental exposure to words adds to vocabulary growth over time.

Singing Mother Goose Rhymes

Traditional melodies have been passed down through the generations for many Mother Goose rhymes. The traditional way of singing "Baa, Baa, Black Sheep" is depicted in Figure 4. We'll never know which mother first crooned this song to her young child.

Ask your music consultant for help in locating the melodies of additional verses. Singing these songs together forms a nice sense of community among the children. Of course, it also reinforces their love of poetry and their knowledge of this form of literature, part of our shared heritage.

JACK AND JILL

Jack and Jill
Went up the hill
To fetch a pail of water.

Jack fell down
And broke his crown
And Jill came tumbling after.

FIGURE 4
Baa, Baa, Black Sheep   **Traditional**

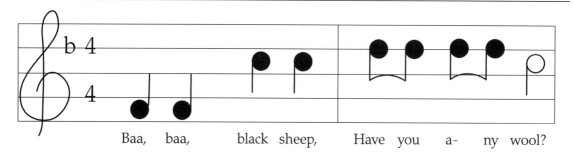

Baa, baa, black sheep, Have you a- ny wool?

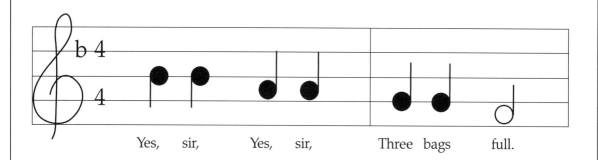

Yes, sir, Yes, sir, Three bags full.

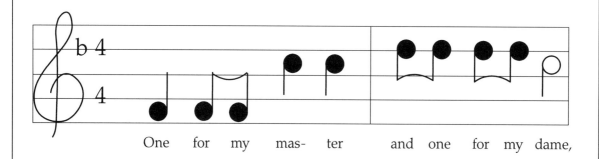

One for my mas- ter and one for my dame,

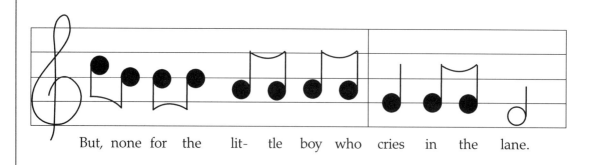

But, none for the lit- tle boy who cries in the lane.

Introducing Mother Goose Rhymes to Older Students

We often assume that everyone knows Mother Goose because the lines are so familiar as we read them. However, you may be surprised to discover what a small percentage of students in the upper elementary grades or middle school can recite these verses. If your students haven't met Jack and Jill, Georgie Porgie, Little Boy Blue, and all the other members of Mother Goose's varied family, make sure they have that experience before they leave your classroom. The trick is to provide an acceptable reason for their reading and reciting these intriguing verses.

Assessing Student Knowledge

First, find out what your students know about these verses. Ask them to supply the next line for each of the following, for example,

1. A diller, a dollar...

2. Peter, Peter, pumpkin eater...

3. Diddle, diddle, dumpling, my son John...

4. Tom, Tom, the piper's son...

5. Hush-a-bye, baby...

6. Mary, Mary, quite contrary...

7. Georgie, Porgie, pudding and pie...

8. Higgledy, piggledy, my black hen...

9. Wee Willie Winkie runs through the town...

10. There was an old woman who lived in a shoe...

Answers

1. a ten-o'clock scholar,

2. had a wife and couldn't keep her.

3. went to bed with his stockings on.

4. stole a pig and away did run.

5. on the treetop,

6. How does your garden grow?

7. kissed the girls and made them cry.

8. she lays eggs for gentlemen.

9. upstairs and downstairs in his nightgown.

10. she had so many children she didn't know what to do.

You may want to have students write the next lines for each verse as you read the beginning words aloud. Then, you can collect the papers to see what individual students know. Don't worry about spelling or even if the words are not exactly the same, because versions of these rhymes do vary. Any reasonable answer will show you if the student is fairly familiar with a specific verse. Remember that this preassessment is meant simply to help you plan your teaching.

Even students who know these verses well will enjoy and benefit from the activities suggested in this chapter. For students who show a complete lack of knowledge of the verses, you may need to provide small-group work designed to give them broader exposure to this literature. This would be particularly helpful for students who are slower readers or those who are learning English as a second language. Having some of your gifted students tape a selection of the most familiar verses would provide supportive material for use at a listening center (and provide yet another reason for engaging students with these rhymes).

Planning a Presentation of Mother Goose Rhymes

Your first task is to devise a worthwhile project that will give older students an acceptable reason for learning Mother Goose rhymes. One such project is the presentation of a selection of these verses to a group of kindergarten or first-grade students. (See Thinking + Lesson Plan 15 in Appendix A for more on this activity.) Explain to your students the importance of having all young children know these verses, which are an important part of our national heritage. (Forget the fact that they need to know them, too. That will be a natural result of developing the presentation.)

Divide the class into cooperative learning groups of three to five students each. Bring in a quantity of books that present Mother Goose rhymes. Borrow them from the library for a sufficient length of time so students have time to pore over them. The first job of each group is to read a number of verses, taking turns reading them aloud to one another. Then, each group should select three verses to present in creative ways. Brainstorm ideas for different ways of presenting a verse, for example,

- dramatizing (in costume or not),

- singing,

- a series of pictures,

- puppets, or

- putting on a skit including a verse or two.

After the students have practiced and then made a presentation to several different groups, they will have learned many of the most familiar verses. They may have so much fun making these presentations that they will want to share their talents with other audiences, for instance, the Parent Teacher Association or an assembly of upper-grade students.

Mother Goose Teachings

Mother Goose verses cover a wide range of topics and forms. You may be surprised to discover some of the poems that are attributed to Mother Goose in a comprehensive collection. Verses may be puzzles, mnemonic devices, games we play with babies, wise sayings, and more. For example, I think we all know the verse that helps us remember the number of days in each month:

> Thirty days has September,
> April, June, and November.
> All the rest have thirty-one
> Except February alone,
> Which has twenty-eight
> Until Leap Year gives it one day more!

Middle school students may be familiar with some of the lullabies and traditional verses that we use with young children to entertain them, such as this one we play with the child's toes:

> This little pig went to market;
> This little pig stayed home.
> This little pig had roast beef;
> This little pig had none.
> And, this little pig went, "Wee, wee, wee!"
> All the way home!

Here are two examples of a verse that sets up a riddle:

> Little Nancy Etticoat
> In a white petticoat,
> Has a red nose.
> The longer she stands,
> The shorter she grows.
> (A candle)

> Daffy-down-dilly
> Has come into town
> In a yellow petticoat
> And a green gown.
> (The daffodil)

A verse that reminds us of a sailor's way of predicting the weather goes like this:

> Red sky at night—
> Sailor's delight.
> Red sky in the morning—
> Sailors take warning.

Another couplet predicts rain based on a cock's crowing:

> If a rooster crows, when he goes to bed,
> He's apt to get up with rain on his head.

Older students can work together to make a collection of riddles and/or predictive verses. Illustrated poems can then be displayed on a bulletin board, preferably one in the hall where other students and parents can see them. Pairs of students could present riddles to classes of younger children.

The History of Mother Goose

Although the identity of Mother Goose lies hidden in history, older students might speculate as to who was Mother Goose. Boston claims that Dame Goose lies at rest in the Old Granary Burying Ground in the heart of the city, a claim based only on legend. The name Mother Goose appears to have been first used in a French publication, *Contes de Ma Mere l'Oye (Mother Goose Tales)*, by Charles Perrault in 1697, when he published a collection of famous fairy tales, including "Sleeping Beauty."

Whatever their origin, these jingles have endured over time and have consistently been favorites of young children. Frequently in popular literature, for example comic strips, there are references to these tales. The joke can only be understood if you know the verse or character, for example, Humpty Dumpty or Little Boy Blue.

Hundreds of collections of Mother Goose rhymes have been compiled and illustrated by fine artists. Some go back to the beginning of the 20th century, for example, Randolph Caldecott's *Hey Diddle Diddle Picture Book* and Leslie Brooke's *Ring O'Roses: A Nursery Rhyme Picture Book*. Following are a few later examples by noted illustrators, which are still available in many public libraries:

A Mother Goose ABC: In a Pumpkin Shell, illustrated by Joan Walsh Anglund

Marguerite de Angeli's Book of Nursery and Mother Goose Rhymes, illustrated by Marguerite de Angeli

Mother Goose: The Old Nursery Rhymes, illustrated by Arthur Rackham

The Tenggren Mother Goose, illustrated by Gustaf Tenggren

Mother Goose, illustrated by Tasha Tudor

Brian Wildsmith's Mother Goose, illustrated by Brian Wildsmith

If a few gifted middle school students become especially interested in finding out more about Mother Goose, you might refer them to the thick volume of research by William S. Baring-Gould and Ceil Baring-Gould under the title *The Annotated Mother Goose: Nursery Rhymes Old and New, Arranged and Explained*. This book has long been out of print, but I found a copy in a second-hand bookstore. Your library may have a copy. These authors present a compilation of information about the origins of the amazing potpourri of verses that appear in publications attributed to Mother Goose. They go through many of the verses, pointing out changing versions and the meanings behind some of the allusions that escape most of us. I have attempted to convey to some extent in this chapter the variety of content and purpose represented by these many rhymes and jingles, but it is impossible to treat them all. In general, we just have to accept them for what they are and enjoy them with children.

Writing Parodies

Some writers have enjoyed writing takeoffs on familiar rhymes that might inspire older students to join in the fun. Bruce Lansky produced a collection of such rhymes in *The New Adventures of Mother Goose: Gentle Rhymes for Happy Times*. Note that to write parodies, students need to know the original poems very well. Read one or two of Lansky's examples, first the original verse and then Lansky's variation, so students get the idea. In his version of "Little Miss Muffett," for example, Miss Muffett is eating an ice-cream cone instead of the traditional "curds and whey"; when the spider sits down beside her, she tells him to "go get his own." Instead of "blind mice," it becomes "kind mice." Little Boy Blue is told to "stop blowing his horn," because he will wake the neighbors.

Eve Merriam wrote another collection of parodies, titled *Inner City Mother Goose*. Merriam played with the format and content of each Mother Goose rhyme, giving it a sardonic twist and an urban setting. In one short rhyme based on "the crooked man" in the verse discussed earlier in this chapter, for example, she interprets the word *crooked* as many of us would. Her conclusion is a wry comment that he "did very well."

Challenge students to try a parody of a given verse, for example, "Sing a Song of Sixpence," which is presented on the opposite page.

Writing parodies might follow the activity of making a presentation to primary grade students. Thus, your students would be familiar with a variety of rhymes on which to base their work. Students could publish their own collection of parodies, perhaps titled "Fooling Around With Mother Goose."

Continuing the Familiar Stories

Occasionally, an author has created a picture book based on a given poem that he or she has continued, developing events according to the author's imagination. Look for Kin Eagle's *Humpty Dumpty*, which was illustrated by Rob Gilbert. The author's amusing continuation of the familiar rhyme could inspire older students to write additional adventures for Humpty Dumpty. Small groups of students might collaborate on producing similar continuations of other verses, for example, "Simple Simon" or "The Old Woman Who Lived in a Shoe."

Creating Poetry Posters

Stimulate students' artistic abilities and add a little variety to your language arts curriculum by having students create large poetry posters for their favorite Mother Goose rhymes. Display these posters in the multipurpose room or the school hall where all students can read them.

SING A SONG OF SIXPENCE

Sing a song of sixpence,
A pocket full of rye;
Four-and-twenty blackbirds
Baked in a pie!

When the pie was opened,
The birds began to sing;
Wasn't that a dainty dish
To set before the king?

The king was in his counting-house,
Counting out his money;
The queen was in the parlor
Eating bread and honey.

The maid was in the garden
Hanging out the clothes;
When down came a blackbird
And snipped off her nose!

LITTLE BOY BLUE

Little Boy Blue,
come, blow your horn,

The cow's in the meadow,
the sheep's in the corn;

But where is the little boy
tending the sheep?

He's under the haystack
fast asleep.

Will you wake him?
No, not I!
For if I do,
he's sure to cry.

Bring in picture books that feature Mother Goose poems to provide ideas that students might emulate. Some possibilities are listed earlier in this chapter. Another attractively illustrated collection is Celia Barker Lottridge's *Mother Goose: A Sampler*. Canadian illustrators donated their art for this book, which benefits the Parent-Child Mother Goose Program in Toronto. The interesting art and page design should stimulate student interest in producing similar poetry posters for use with young children. See the work, too, of other fine artists in books mentioned earlier in this chapter. Encourage students to select familiar poems like "Little Boy Blue," presented on the opposite page.

For more ideas about working with Mother Goose with older students, refer to my book *Teaching With Picture Books in the Middle School* (2000).

Conclusion

In this chapter, we explored using Mother Goose rhymes in different ways through the grades. We discussed the familiar use of these rhymes in primary grades, then looked at the importance of reviewing (or introducing) these rhymes at the middle school level. In the next chapter, we will focus on writing original poetry, including free verse, patterned poetry, and various rhymed forms.

SWIFT THINGS ARE BEAUTIFUL

Swift things are beautiful:
Swallows and deer,
And lightning that falls
Bright-veined and clear,
Rivers and meteors,
Wind in the wheat,
The strong-withered horse,
The runner's sure feet.

—ELIZABETH COATSWORTH

CHAPTER 6

Swift Things Are Beautiful: Writing Original Poetry

n this chapter, we will look at a variety of poetry forms that elementary and middle school students can write. Some forms are easier than others, for example, unrhymed listings and rhymed jingles, so even young students will be able to write them successfully. Other forms, for instance, acrostics and haiku, require more mature thinking and are better left for older or more able students. The chapter begins with unrhymed poetry and patterned verse forms and then moves into different kinds of rhymed poetry. Some special forms, for example, concrete and found poetry, are discussed in other chapters. Most teachers find that children enjoy creating poetry and that they produce delightful verses. Such successful writing experiences add to each learner's self-esteem, thus motivating further learning. The following activities are designed to help you achieve this goal.

Prewriting Activities

Read aloud some poems that children have written, perhaps taken from your school publications, the local newspaper, or such magazines as *Cricket* and *Stone Soup*. Many published collections of poetry written by young people are available, too. Consider purchasing copies of some of the following books for your school library:

Here I Am! by Virginia O. Baron

The Voices of the Children, compiled by June Jordan and Torri Bush

Rose, Where Did You Get That Red? by Kenneth Koch

Stuff, edited by Herbert Kohl and Victor H. Cruz

Male and Female Under 18 by Eve Merriam and Nancy Larrick

Have You Seen a Comet? Children's Art and Writing From Around the World, edited by Pellowski et al.

As young people come to know poetry and to see the variety of form and content that is possible, they will also come to perceive poetry as something they can produce. They will feel at home with poetry and will be able to conceive of themselves as poets. The development of this image is the key to stimulating students to compose poetry. Notice, too, how this ties in with supporting children's feelings of self-esteem.

Be ready to take advantage of natural opportunities that arise. When a child expresses a thought or an apt bit of imagery, say, "I like the way you said that. Let's write your words on the board so everybody can enjoy them." Some teachers keep strips of manila paper on which phrases or sentences can be printed quickly with a felt pen so that students' words can be recorded and displayed on a bulletin board. Beneath the caption "Pleasing Words," a teacher might display, for instance,

Quiet as a flea at work—Sally

Soft, secret sound—Phil

Our earth is round,
all water and ground.—Carlos

The bear clumped and humped,
thumped and bumped.—Katisha

As a teacher, you need to be aware of the possibilities for poetry as it occurs in natural form. When Tonya brings a frog to school and calls it "my funny, funny frog," the mere repetition of her phrase could lead children to create a spontaneous class composition. You could take advantage of this moment by saying, "'My funny, funny frog.' That sounds like a poem. Who can add another line?" As you write these words on the board, someone suggests "Hippety, hippety, hop," and another child adds excitedly, "Will he ever stop?", and there you have a poem to read and enjoy together.

My funny, funny frog,
Hippety, hippety, hop.
Will he ever stop?

You cannot, of course, wait for the unplanned experience in composing poetry to just happen. We must plan experiences that seem as natural and desirable as those that may be initiated in the manner just described, and we must provide the stimulus. A sequence of experiences in the writing of poetry can be readily developed beginning with the least complicated types of poetry.

Enjoyment should remain the emphasis in the writing of poetry, as was true with the reading of poetry. Elementary and middle school students who are steeped in poetry from an early age will find writing original verse a natural means for expressing their thoughts.

Unrhymed Verse

Unrhymed verse is usually easier for students to write successfully. Many teachers find free verse, for example, highly successful with children who have had little experience with writing poetry. Beginning poets may write only one line, whereas the more able or experienced child may write two, three, or more lines. In this section, we focus on beginning activities that K–8 students might find appealing as they learn to express their thoughts in writing. Even the youngest students, with your assistance, will be able to compose poetic lines successfully.

Beginning Experiences With Free Verse

Why is free verse especially suited to inexperienced writers? The key word is *freedom*, for in free verse there is

- no rhyming to lend artificiality;

- no set pattern of rhythm or meter;

- free variation in length of lines, form, and content;

- emphasis on the thoughts expressed; and

- greater attention to language.

Because free verse may consist of one or many lines, it accommodates individual abilities. The child for whom writing is laborious finds success in composing one line, whereas the child for whom writing comes with ease may extend ideas into 10 lines. For this reason, the following suggestions for motivating the writing of free verse may be used at any level.

PICTURES. Display a large picture of a boy and girl. Ask some provocative questions: "What are these children doing? What are they thinking? Can you imagine that you are the boy or girl in this picture?" Pretending that he or she is one of the figures in the picture, each student then writes the thoughts that person might be thinking. Suggest that each thought begin on a new line, thus:

> I wish that I could get a new bike,
> Then, I'd go like the wind—
> Down Madison Street,
> Across the highway—
> No place would be too far for me
> If I had a bright shiny new bike.

THE SENSES. Use the senses to motivate the writing of poetry by providing an object that is concealed within a box or a large paper bag. To feature the concept of softness, for example, use a piece of fur or velvet. After students have felt the concealed article, ask them how it felt. When someone mentions the word *soft*, ask the question, "What is soft? How would you tell someone what you mean by softness?" Have each student write ideas on paper as they try to think not of how many thoughts they can jot down, but of how interesting or unusual each thought is. Students can write a class or an individual poem, something like this:

> What Is Soft?
> Soft is a feeling,
> Soft is velvety fur.
> Soft is a small kitten's paw,
> Soft is my mother's cheek.

Thus, in a natural way, students are creating interesting images that could lead to creating metaphors.

POETRY MODELS. Read poems to students in the upper elementary and middle school grades that are written by poets who do not always use rhyme, such as Hilda Conkling, Carl Sandburg, e.e. cummings, and Walt Whitman. This passage from Whitman's *Song of Myself* describes a handsome stallion. It could serve as a model for student poems about an animal they know. Guide students to observe that this poem is a single, long sentence.

A gigantic beauty of a stallion, fresh and responsive to my caresses,
Head high in the forehead, wide between the ears,
Limbs glossy and supple, tail dusting the ground,
Eyes full of sparkling wickedness, ears finely cut, flexibly moving,
His nostrils dilate as my heels embrace him,
His well-built limbs tremble with pleasure as we race around and return.

THE WEATHER. Write these words on the board: Rain is.... (Use this idea on a rainy day for best results. As appropriate, try "Snow is..." or "Sunshine is....") Then ask the class what rain means to them. Have them write their ideas on paper, beginning each new idea on a fresh line. When completed, each child will have a poem of varied length about rain. Display the poems on large raindrops as shown in Figure 5.

FIGURE 5
Sample "Rain Is..." Poems

Rain is...
Patter on the roof,
A day for hiding
behind the sofa,
The flower maker.

Rain is...
The producer
of umbrellas.
The washer
of leaves,
The frizzies!

Listing Poems

Introduce students to the listing poem as an interesting way of exploring a topic. Note that this activity is adaptable for any school-age child. You might begin by printing on the board a word to which most children can respond, for instance, *circus*, or create a word wall. If your students are not likely to have experienced a circus, you might need to use a film or other pictures to provide some common basis for discussing this topic. Ask students to think of all the words or phrases they associate with the circus. Go around the room quickly, writing the words as they are suggested:

horses	wagons	ladies in fancy dresses
tigers	sideshows	a parade
big elephants	monkeys	funny clowns
colorful tents	trapeze	the ringmaster

After you have a long list of suggestions, begin to write a group poem together. You might begin this way:

> The circus is coming to town—
>> A parade of horses and funny clowns,
>> The band playing jolly music.
>> Colorful tents and circus wagons,
>> Big elephants performing tricks—
> The circus is coming to town!

Continue to create another verse based on ideas suggested. Beginning readers can use this type of material for reading. Older students can follow this model to compose a poem on a topic of their choice. This kind of activity allows students to become acclimated as they see what they can do with poetry. See Thinking + Lesson Plan 16 for more on this activity.

Many poets have composed listing poems, although some have chosen to rhyme the lines. When using such poems as models, make it clear that the lines in a poem don't have to rhyme, as many children may have this misconception (as do some adults). You might like to post a sign in your classroom: Poetry doesn't have to rhyme!

The poem "Swift Things Are Beautiful" by Elizabeth Coatsworth at the beginning of this chapter is a good example of a listing poem. Use it as a model with older students, noting how the poet names something that is swift and then describes it in a few words. (Note that this verse makes up only half the poem, but this is sufficient for your purposes.) Another excellent example (which also uses rhymes) is Arnold Shapiro's "I Talk, I Say, I Speak." Some students may want to use rhyme in writing their poems, but again make it clear that poetry doesn't always have to rhyme.

Mary O'Neill's poetry about colors (see the example in Chapter 1 on page 4) includes additional examples of listing poems that rhyme. Students will enjoy writing similar poems. For more on this activity, refer to Thinking + Lesson Plan 3 in Appendix A.

Many picture books also can be used to stimulate the writing of listing poems. Judi Barrett provides a number of examples in her *Things That Are Most in the World*. She introduces superlatives in a humorous way that will appeal to students of all ages. John Nickle provides funny illustrations to accompany each idea. Students could write list poems about any of the topics covered in the book.

You might also explore the following picture books for other possibilities:

Up North at the Cabin, written by Marsha W. Chall and illustrated by Steve Johnson

If I Were Queen of the World, written by Fred Hiatt and illustrated by Mark Graham

Jessie's Island, written by Sheryl McFarlane and illustrated by Sheena Lott

All the Places to Love, written by Patricia MacLachlan and illustrated by Mike Wimmer

Roxaboxen by Alice McLerran

Listing poetry can be written about a variety of topics, for example,

- I remember...

- What I love about summer

- When I grow up, I will...

For an additional activity focusing on listing poems, see Thinking + Lesson Plan 17 in Appendix A.

Continuing the Exploration of Free Verse

The term *free verse* does not mean "anything goes," as some people maintain. The poet who writes free verse still may include definite rhythms, beat, or other poetic devices that set the poem apart from ordinary prose. Try the following activities based on poetry by poets who write free verse.

HILDA CONKLING. Have students observe the way Hilda Conkling uses questions in this short poem she wrote when she was very young:

> Little Mouse in gray velvet,
>
> Have you had a cheese-breakfast?
>
> There are no crumbs on your coat.
>
> Did you use a napkin?
>
> I wonder what you had to eat,
>
> And who dresses you in gray velvet?

Students could begin a poem just as Conkling did, starting with a question such as, "Where are you going today, Mr. Fox?" Bring in an assortment of animal pictures so students can observe the animal they are addressing as they work to complete the poem. The poems can then be mounted on a bulletin board with the pictures. For another activity based on Conkling's poetry, refer to Thinking + Lesson Plan 18 in Appendix A.

CARL SANDBURG. Carl Sandburg is another poet who was fond of using free verse. "Fog," which likens the fog to a cat overlooking the city, can be understood by students of all ages. Fond of the Great Lakes, he also wrote a haunting passage that describes the sound of a boat's whistle on a foggy night, "Desolate and Lone." You can find many examples of Sandburg's work that are suitable for use with upper elementary and middle school students. Look for his well-known poem about Chicago, which begins "Hog butcher for the world" and includes many images of this proud city, for example,

> Fierce as a dog, with tongue lapping for action, cunning as
> a savage pitted against the wilderness,
>> Bareheaded,
>>
>> Shoveling,
>>
>> Wrecking,
>>
>> Planning,
>>
>> Building, breaking, rebuilding...

WALT WHITMAN. Walt Whitman also chose free verse for much of his poetry. See his poem "I Hear America Singing," presented in full-page format at the beginning of Chapter 7. Also see his description of a stallion earlier in this chapter. Older students who are studying the theme of freedom will enjoy Whitman's "Song of the Open Road," which includes these lines:

> I think heroic deeds were all conceiv'd in the open air,
> > and all free poems also,
> I think I could stop here myself and do miracles,
> I think whatever I shall meet on the road I shall like,
> > and whoever beholds me shall like me,
> I think whoever I see must be happy.

Following this model, students will naturally engage in making statements that support their own feelings of self-esteem. You'll find many additional lines regarding esteem that you may wish to use in your teaching in Whitman's *Leaves of Grass*.

ADVICE FOR YOUNG POETS. Help your students write more powerful poetry by talking with them, particularly the more advanced ones, about how they can improve their poetry. Poet and poetry consultant Tina Demerdjian (2001) offers the following guidelines that you might share:

- Use few words to express your ideas.
- Record observations from your five senses.
- Show; don't tell.
- End each phrase with a strong word.
- Express a strong premise (what do you think?).
- End the poem when it needs to end; not just when you get tired.
- Rewrite to make it stronger.
- Respect your work. (p. 4)

After students have composed free verse successfully, they will be easily guided to explore different forms of poetry. In the next section, we will look at a number of simple patterns that help students frame their thoughts.

Following Poetry Patterns

From free verse, it is natural to move on to introduce unrhymed poetry patterns. Children of all ages can produce enchanting cinquains. Then, I introduce forms that I invented: the diamante, septolet, quinzaine, and quintain. Haiku, which is also an unrhymed pattern, is discussed in the section on activities related to social studies and the study of Japan and Japanese Americans in Chapter 7.

Cinquain

Cinquains (sank′ ens) are poems comprised of five lines. (*Cinq* is the French word for *five*.) Although there are many varieties possible for five-line poetry—the limerick is one—the cinquain is a form more akin to haiku. The emphasis is on the thought to be expressed, but the unrhymed lines fit specific guidelines. Two forms of the cinquain are presented here.

COUNTED WORDS. The specifications for this cinquain, which is easier for young students to write, include the following:

> Line 1: One word (which may be the title)
> Line 2: Two words (describe the title)
> Line 3: Three words (an action)
> Line 4: Four words (a feeling)
> Line 5: One word (refers to the title; may be a synonym)

Here is an example:

> Rainbow—
> Sky's umbrella
> Turned upside down.
> Lovely splash of color—
> Aftermath.

COUNTED SYLLABLES. This cinquain form has been attributed to Adelaide Crapsey, a minor American poet, author of *Verse*. The form follows these specifications:

> Line 1: Two syllables
> Line 2: Four syllables

Line 3: Six syllables

Line 4: Eight syllables

Line 5: Two syllables

Here is an example of the cinquain written in syllabic format:

Funny—

People can seem

So different to me

Especially when far away—

Distanced.

Diamante

After my fourth-grade students worked successfully with cinquains and then haiku, I wondered if there were other patterns that students might try. As I wrote in 1970 (Tiedt et al., 2001),

> If you become enthusiastic about having students write poetry, as I have been, you will find yourself searching for additional patterns to challenge students who have become involved in the composition of poetry. It was this search that led to my creating four new poetry patterns that have proved to be very successful frames for ideas. While lending some structure, a pleasant patterning, the framework is not dominant or confining. (p. 1082)

The diamante, which many teachers have used successfully with elementary school children, is a seven-line diamond-shaped poem that follows this set of specifications:

Line 1: Subject, a noun (1 word)

Line 2: Adjectives (2 words)

Line 3: Participles, ing form (3 words)

Line 4: Nouns, a transition from noun above to noun below (4 words)

Line 5: Participles, ing form (3 words)

Line 6: Adjectives (2 words)

Line 7: Noun, opposite of subject (1 word)

Notice that this poem creates a contrast between two opposite concepts and that Line 4 has to create a transition from one to the other, as in this example:

<blockquote>

Breeze,

Balmy, soft,

Floating, wafting, soothing.

Wind, gust, gale, storm—

Twisting, howling, tearing,

Wet, threatening,

Hurricane.

</blockquote>

To make it easy for students to create the diamond shape of the diamante, provide a form like that on the opposite page. Here's a tip: If you type students' diamantes (or have students do it) with a computer, set the lines for centering, which automatically creates a diamond-shaped pattern.

Septolet, Quinzaine, and Quintain

The septolet, quinzaine, and quintain are the three other patterned forms I created. How and why I chose these names will become clear as the three patterns are described.

The septolet consists of seven lines of 1, 2, 3, 2, and 1, 2, 3 words (14 words in all) with a break in the pattern as indicated in this sample model:

<blockquote>

Kitten

Padding stealthily

Among green grasses

Most intent.

Bird

Ascends rapidly

Causing great disappointment.

</blockquote>

The quinzaine (kan'zen) consists of 15 syllables in 3 lines (7, 5, 3) that make a statement followed by a question, thus,

<blockquote>

Boys shouting in the distance—

When will silence drop

On the night?

</blockquote>

Diamante Form

_____

Title

_____

_____

_____

_____

_____

_____

By_____

119

The quintain (kwin'ten) is a syllabic progression of 15 words: 2, 4, 6, 8, 10, as illustrated here:

> Novel,
> Read secretly—
> Flashlight glowing brightly
> Beneath blankets' warm security—
> Creaking staircase extinguishes the light!

Students might like to invent patterns for poetry, too. Anyone can play the game!

Exploring Forms of Rhymed Poetry

Now, let's look at various rhyming forms of poetry that children can chant or sing, read and write, or just plain enjoy. We first need to teach children about rhyming as part of auditory discrimination as we focus on effective listening, and as a skill that supports their ability to read and to spell. We also need to make them aware of rhymes and how poets use them in poetry. Then, they can attempt their own original couplets, triplets, limericks, and quatrains.

Rhyming as a Poetic Skill

Encourage children to share poems they know—you'll find most of their favorite jingles will rhyme. Read aloud Mother Goose rhymes, beginning with the most familiar, but also introducing an occasional less familiar verse, such as "Molly, My Sister, and I Fell Out!":

> Molly, my sister, and I fell out,
> And what do you think it was all about?
> > She loved coffee,
> > And I loved tea,
> And that was the reason we couldn't agree.

Talk about the rhymes in this poem or any other you choose to introduce. Have several ready on transparencies that you can display so students not only hear the rhymes but also see the rhyming words. Then use the following activities to help students become adept at rhyming before they attempt any extensive writing of rhymed poems.

RHYMING. Depending on the ages and abilities of your students, ask them what they know about rhymes and rhyming. You can compile a list of such understandings as the following:

1. Rhymes are based on the sound, not the appearance (spelling) of a word.

>   day, neigh, lei, prey
>
>   theme, dream, seem
>
>   sane, gain, reign, vein

2. Not all words have rhymes, for example, *silver*.

3. You need to pronounce a word correctly and listen carefully to determine if words really do rhyme, for example,

>   sand, tan   few, too   kind, fine

A RHYMING DICTIONARY. Make a class rhyming dictionary. Two to three students can work together with one phonogram, for example,

ing	ale	ight	or	at
ad	ine	ar	it	ame
ig	ag	ord	ate	ote

Add other endings as students need them. A page in the dictionary might look like this:

Rhymes for: ite/ight		
bite	fight	
rite	right	
site	sight	
kite	light	
mite	might	
spite	tight	
	night	
	knight	Others: height

Notice what students are learning by compiling such pages of rhymes. The words in this list are grouped according to the two most common spellings with one irregular spelling noted at the side. Obviously, students are observing varied spellings, but they are also acquiring new vocabulary as they check the dictionary for different words to add to their lists. For instance, what is a *mite* or a *rite*?

RHYMING SKILLS. Older students may become adept at making rhyme lists. They probably soon will realize that in searching for rhymes, you simply go through all the consonant sounds in alphabetical order. Forget the vowels! Point this out to those who haven't yet formalized this knowledge by writing the alphabet on the board and discussing the sounds represented by each letter. This may be helpful to slower students. The discussion provides insight into English spelling.

Begin a rhyming word wall with the letters of the alphabet:

a b c d e f g h i j k l m n o p q r s t u v w x y z

First, mark out the vowel letters (*a, e, i, o,* and *u*) because they don't help to make new rhymes. The letter *c* is useless because it represents either /k/ or /s/. Print a *u* beside the *q* because in English they are inseparable, representing /kw/. *G* need only represent what some of us learned to call the "hard sound" or /g/ because /j/ will pick up the other possible rhymes. And *x* is of little use, because it is tied in with /z/ and /ks/. So, we have cut down considerably the number of sounds to consider, making the rhyming task more efficient.

Then, some brilliant student may observe that we could also make a list of the common blends of consonants that begin many words. So, we add a list like this to the rhyming word wall:

bl/br

cl/cr

dr

fl/fr

gl/gr

pl/pr

sk/sl/sm/sn/sp/st/sw

tr/tw

And last, we have a few blends that combine three sounds:

scr/spr/str

Someone may suggest or question why we don't include *ch*, *sh*, and *th*. We can explain that these are perfectly good sounds to include, but they go in a special class by themselves called *diphthongs*.

SPELLING. As students work with these rhyming lists, they will make all kinds of interesting discoveries about alternative spellings for sounds in English, for example, the Greek *ph* in *phone* or the tricky spellings *gn* and *kn*. This is a marvelous way for students to become aware of interesting spellings. As students make new discoveries, add the information to your word wall.

Work on such lists makes interesting homework, which will probably get parents involved in suggesting different kinds of words, too. It's all part of the learning process!

As groups finish their pages, duplicate them and collate the pages to create 10–15 copies of these rhyming dictionaries. Place the dictionaries at your classroom poetry center so students can refer to them readily as they write rhymed poems. No list should be considered complete and the class should continue to add to these lists. New editions of the dictionary can be produced as needed. Students can also decorate the covers, providing an outlet for different talents.

Refer also to the discussion about using rimes with emergent readers in Chapter 4. At that level, the rhyming dictionary would be displayed as lists on the wall.

Note that each class needs to experience the entire discovery process as a way of learning. Therefore, discard dictionaries created by previous classes or give them to those students to take home. Create a new dictionary with each new group of children.

Couplets

After students are comfortable with rhyming, introduce the couplet, a set of two rhyming lines. Try some of the following activities.

WRITING RHYMING LINES. Have students practice composing couplets at the oral level by providing some possible first lines, for example,

> Flowers now are growing…
> A blizzard came to town last night…
> My favorite pet is a cat…
> In our backyard is an oak tree…

Write one of the lines on the board. Ask students to suggest interesting rhyming lines. Accept any that end with an appropriate rhyme, printing them on the board:

> Flowers now are growing
> And the grass is showing
> Gentle winds are blowing
> And the grass needs mowing
> Baseballs we are throwing

This is just a practice exercise, so move on to another first line, until you fill your board space. To help students get the feel of writing couplets, you may want to have each student write a couplet, choosing the rhyming line that he or she likes best for each of the several lines you have worked with or writing original lines. This would be an especially helpful task for younger students or those who are learning English as a second language. Students can read their poems to one another in small groups.

A CLASS COMPOSITION. Try a class composition based on a theme—the month, the season, the weather, a state, an event, a person. For a beginning experience, you might provide lines related to Halloween.

Early in October, introduce the subject of Halloween through a discussion about the holiday or by singing Halloween songs. Then say, "Let's write a poem about Halloween. Will you help me?" For this activity, you need to prepare a set of first lines for couplets based on the selected theme for which students can supply rhyming lines as they did in the previous activity. Make sure that each line you provide ends with an easily rhymed word. I've supplied a sample set of lines for a Halloween poem that you might try. Imagined student lines suggested by middle school students have been inserted to show how it might work:

> It's Halloween. It's Halloween! (Teacher's first line printed on the
>   board.)
> Come, Sarah, let's join the happy scene! (A student's suggestion
>   printed below.)
>
> Ghosts and goblins are all around. (Teacher's line, continuing the
>   poem.)

An owl is hooting with mournful sound. (Another student's
   suggestion.)

There are devils and demons and cats of black (Teacher's line.)
And each one carries a great big sack. (Student's suggestion.)

Aren't you afraid to be out this night? (Teacher's line.)
For devils are fearsome, and cats might bite! (Student's suggestion.)

Oh, no, not I, for don't you know, (Teacher's line.)
The cat is Susie, and that devil is Joe! (Student's suggestion.)

Here are some hints for group compositions:

1. Have several possible lines suggested each time before selecting the most interesting one to be written on the board. Say, "These are great ideas. Suppose we use Tim's line this time."

2. Select lines by different people each time so that as many as possible have contributed to the finished product. You may also have two (or more) poems produced at the same time so more than one student line can be used each time. Simply work on two boards with a student helping by writing in the lines for the second poem. Thus, twice as many students will get to contribute.

3. Children can learn to tap out the rhythm of the given line as they try to produce rhythm in the second line similar to the first line of each couplet—the beginnings of meter.

Triplets

The triplet, an intriguing verse form that is not widely used, offers interesting possibilities as a rhymed form that children can create. These three-line poems may tell a brief story or paint a picture. Two lines may rhyme or all three may rhyme.

Look for examples of poems that are written in triplets. David McCord uses a variation of the triplet in "This Is My Rock." Lew Sarett wrote a fine poem about "Four Little Foxes" using triplets that asks Spring to be gentle to the little foxes whose mother has died. Joseph Auslander's "A Blackbird Suddenly" is also written in triplets. Your class may enjoy the following activities.

PAIRED RHYMING. Have the students work in pairs. Give each pair a rhyme list or have them create a new rhyme list. They could, for example, choose a word from suggestions printed on the board: *plane, jet, train, car, swim, fish, play, book, sky, ride, game, sing, box, fort, eat, dog, cat, ball, sea*—all easy to rhyme. The word chosen is then written at the top of the page, and a rhyme list is created for that word, which is the subject of the triplet. The students select three related words on which to base their rhyming lines as in the following example:

> Standing silent before the sea,
> I thought the water talked to me,
> Then laughed aloud with sudden glee.

TRIANGULAR TRIPLETS. An interesting variation developed to add to the enjoyment of writing triplets is the triangular triplet. As in the following example, the reader may begin reading this poem at any point of the triangle. The poem must be composed so that the lines may be read in any order.

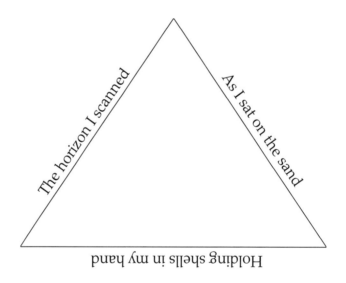

Limericks

The limerick, which consists of a triplet and couplet, is a form of verse that students usually enjoy. The form has consistently been used for humorous nonsense, which probably explains its appeal for young people. Engage your students in writing limericks with some of the following activities.

READING LIMERICKS. Read aloud a selection of limericks just for fun. The humor of most can be readily understood the first time they are heard, as in the anonymous verse "A Young Farmer of Leeds," which paints a funny picture:

> There was a young farmer of Leeds
> Who swallowed six packets of seeds.
> > It soon came to pass
> > He was covered with grass,
> And he couldn't sit down for the weeds!

A second limerick is a kind of tongue twister:

> A flea and a fly in a flue
> Were imprisoned, so what could they do?
> > Said the fly, "Let us flee."
> > Said the flea, "Let us fly."
> So they flew through a flaw in the flue.

Introduce students to Edward Lear, whose name is synonymous with the limerick. Share a number of his poems, which are included in any collection of poetry for children. You might also read the poem "How Pleasant to Know Mr. Lear," in which the poet pokes fun at himself.

Many other poets have composed limericks with equal effect, for example, this whimsical verse by Gelette Burgess:

> I wish that my room had a floor;
> I don't care so much for a door.
> > But this walking around
> > Without touching the ground
> Is getting to be quite a bore.

Look also for Cosmos Monkhouse's "There Once Was a Lady From Niger."

THE LIMERICK FORM. Copy a limerick on a transparency so that students can examine the form followed by the poet. They will, of course, discover that the limerick is a combination of a triplet and a couplet. Also, they can clap out the definite beat that changes in lines 3 and 4. Because the subject of the limerick is always humorous, the rhythm is jingly, and the rhymes made freely, students in grades 4–8 can compose them readily. (See Thinking + Lesson Plan 19 in Appendix A for a sample lesson on composing limericks.) Here is one example composed by a group of fourth graders:

> There once was a doggy named Rover,
> Who rolled in a patch of green clover.
> His master came out
> And cried with a shout,
> "Look! Rover's got clover all over!"

Have students compile a class book of limericks titled "Lively Limericks!" Within limits, you can allow interested students to contribute as many as they like. They may even get their families involved in the fun.

Quatrain

The quatrain or four-line verse is probably the most frequently used form of rhymed poetry, perhaps because of its versatility. You can readily find examples of varied rhyme schemes—aabb, abab, abcb, and others. (The *a* refers to the first phonogram introduced; the *b* to the second; the *c* to the third. Two *a*'s indicate that those two lines rhyme; two *b*'s identify a second pair of rhymes, and so on.) Collect examples from any collection of poetry for young people. Note that a quatrain may have only one group of four lines, or two sets, or three, but occasionally poems go on and on; it's entirely up to the poet.

Try the following activities with your students.

THE QUATRAIN FORM. Present examples of short quatrains on transparencies that you can use for teaching students about the varied ways of rhyming when poets work with four-line verses. Here are two funny examples:

> I eat my peas with honey;
> I've done it all my life.
> It makes the peas taste funny,
> But it keeps them on my knife!

> The rain it raineth on the just
> And also on the unjust fella;
> But chiefly on the just, because
> The unjust steals the just's umbrella.

Read the poems aloud as students read along with you. Then, examine one of the poems, asking students to identify the rhyming words. Note the rhyming pattern. Have students define the quatrain according to their observations, compiling a statement to put on the classroom wall as follows:

1. A quatrain contains four lines.

2. The lines are of similar length.

3. There is rhyming.

4. The rhyme pattern may vary from poem to poem.

READING QUATRAINS ALOUD. Have students go through collections of poetry to select a quatrain to share with the group. Reading a poem aloud gives students a reason to practice their reading skills as well as their delivery in terms of intonation and enunciation. You might require them to record their reading aloud on a tape recorder set up at a center for that purpose. This will give each student realistic practice, and it also will create a recording that you could use at the listening center to assist students who are less able readers.

A POETRY BOOK REPORT. Have students work in cooperative learning groups to compose a quatrain about a book they have been reading together. Require that their quatrain contain two or more verses. Be sure they understand that once they choose a rhyme scheme, it must be the same in all verses in the poem. Writing such a poem is a more creative way of reporting on a book than the sterile forms with blanks to fill in that are used in some classrooms.

SETTING POEMS TO MUSIC. Encourage students to set a poem they like to music, which they can create. Bring in a small xylophone or a piano for that purpose. Their music might be something like that I composed for Robert Louis Stevenson's "The Swing" (see Figure 6). A group of older students who play instruments might like to play this melody while others sing. They could present the song to a group of younger children.

Other Poetry Genres

There are many other poetry forms that students might enjoy. It's impossible to cover all of them, but let's look at the acrostic and the epitaph.

FIGURE 6
The Swing

Robert Louis Stevenson   Iris M. Tiedt

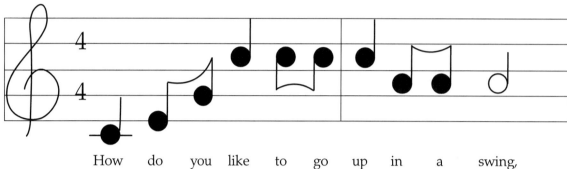

How do you like to go up in a swing,

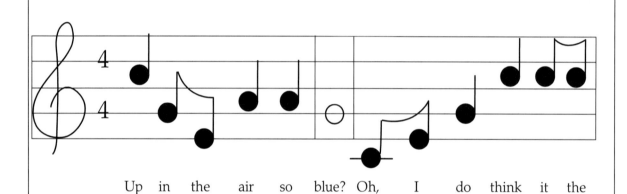

Up in the air so blue? Oh, I do think it the

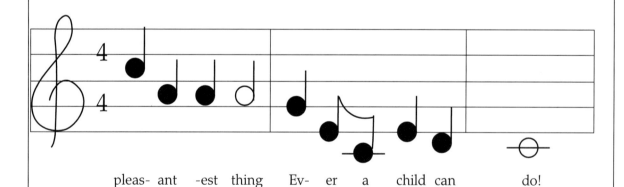

pleas- ant -est thing Ev- er a child can do!

Verse 2
Up in the air and over the wall,
Till I can see so wide,
Rivers and trees and cattle and all
Over the countryside.

Verse 3
Till I look down on the garden green,
Down on the roof so brown—
Up in the air I go flying again,
Up in the air and down!

Unrhymed Acrostics

The first letters of each line of the acrostic poem spell a word vertically. Try one of the following activities to engage your students with this form of poetry:

ACROSTIC NAMES. This is an excellent "get acquainted" activity for upper grade students in September. Have each student print his or her name vertically on a sheet of paper. Then, students print wonderful adjectives beside each letter of their names as follows:

> R adiant,
>
> A dorable,
>
> C ool,
>
> H ealthy,
>
> E ffervescent,
>
> L ovely!
>
> That's Rachel!

Notice that this also is a listing poem. Composing this acrostic will send students to the dictionary to discover intriguing adjectives.

Collect the poems and redistribute them. Then, have students introduce each other by reading someone's poem aloud and bowing to that classmate, who can stand to the applause of the group.

ANIMAL ACROSTICS. Author Seven Schnur wrote acrostics in a different way. In his *Autumn: An Alphabet Acrostic,* illustrated by Leslie Evans, he has written an acrostic sentence poem for each letter of the alphabet. For example, to represent the letter *h* Schnur uses *horse* and an acrostic that relies on words in a sentence that describes a stallion facing a storm. Students can create similar poems about different animals, for example, tiger, zebra, rhino, kitten, snake, and so on. Each sentence acrostic makes a statement about the animal, as in this example:

> Teeth bared, they
>
> Inch forward,
>
> Growling softly,
>
> Eager to
>
> Reach the
>
> Succulent zebra dinner.

Note that to create this acrostic, I had to refer to the dictionary for a perfect word or two. Encourage students to use their dictionaries to search for words they need. It's fun to read through all the *T* words, for instance, *tantalize, tempest, torturous*. Demonstrate this creative process to students by working on the board and discussing what you are doing.

Epitaphs

The epitaph is a special kind of epigram or short pithy saying that usually appears on a gravestone. Robert Louis Stevenson wrote a short poem that includes the epitaph placed on his monument in Samoa:

> Under the wide and starry sky
> Dig the grave and let me lie.
> Glad did I live and gladly die,
> > And I laid me down with a will.
>
> This be the verse you grave for me:
> *Here he lies where he longed to be;*
> *Home is the sailor, home from sea,*
> > *And the hunter home from the hill.*

Some epitaphs have been deliberately humorous, perhaps to deny the seriousness of a person's death. What was the occupation of the person whose remains lie beneath this epitaph?

> Stranger, approach this spot with gravity;
> John Brown is filling his last cavity.

We can presume that Mr. Merideth, a jolly fellow, composed this clever verse for his gravestone:

> Here lies one blown out of breath,
> Who lived a merry life, and died a Merideth.

Older students might enjoy composing epitaphs, perhaps funny ones like this:

> Here lies Herbie.
> I told you I was sick!

They might also compose more serious epitaphs for their favorite authors or poets or for noted figures from history.

Conclusion

In this chapter, we have explored various ways of engaging K–8 students with composing poetry. We began with unrhymed poetry, moved to various poetry patterns, and concluded with poetry that rhymes. Once students begin writing poetry, they seem to enjoy it. You'll likely enjoy it as well, taking pride in what your students produce. In the next chapter, we will investigate how poetry can be integrated into the study of subject areas such as art, mathematics, music, physical education, science, and social studies.

I HEAR AMERICA SINGING

I hear America singing, the varied carols I hear

Those of mechanics, each one singing his as it should be, blithe
and strong,

The carpenter singing his as he measures his plank or beam,

The mason singing his as he makes ready for work, or leaves off work,

The boatman singing what belongs to him in his boat, the deckhand
singing on the steamboat deck,

The shoemaker singing as he sits on his bench, the hatter singing as
he stands,

The wood-cutter's song, the ploughboy's on his way in the morning,
or at noon intermission or at sundown,

The delicious singing of the mother, or of the young wife at work,
or of the girl sewing or washing,

Each singing what belongs to him or her and to none else.

— WALT WHITMAN

CHAPTER 7

I Hear America Singing: Infusing Poetry Into the Total Curriculum

I n this chapter, we focus on ways of including poetry as you teach different subject areas of the curriculum. I covered language arts and reading in some detail in the other chapters. Here I suggest poetry activities for the general categories art, mathematics, music, physical education/health/recreation, science, and social studies (in alphabetical order). The ideas presented suggest how you can integrate poetry into any area that particularly interests you. Also, keep in mind possibilities for infusing poetry across the curriculum as you read the other chapters of this book.

Art

Art and poetry can be brought together within any formal art class in the middle school. Art will also enhance the study of poetry as part of language arts and reading instruction. In addition, art activities will add much to lessons in other curriculum areas such as social studies and science. As Dale Schneider (2001) says in "Something Beautiful: Reading Picture Books, Writing Poetry," "One of the great pleasures of teaching is sharing poetry art with students. The many wonderful picture books that combine poetry and art are treasures" (p. 67). You might try some of the following art activities with your students.

Illustrating Poetry

Have older students select lines of poetry to illustrate on large sheets of tagboard. These posters can be displayed in the hall to be enjoyed by other students and visitors. Your students might enjoy illustrating lines like the following:

Tiger! Tiger! Burning bright
In the forests of the night...
  —William Blake

He gained a world; he gave that world
Its grandest lesson: "On! Sail on!"
  —Joaquin Miller

That which we call a rose
By any other word would smell as sweet.
  —William Shakespeare

I must go down to the seas again,
To the lonely sea and the sky.
  —John Masefield

My heart leaps up when I behold
A rainbow in the sky...
  —William Wordsworth

A thing of beauty is a joy forever:
It's loveliness increases; it will never
Pass into nothingness...
  —John Keats

To suggest ideas for the illustrations, have students examine books of poetry to see how the poetry is presented. One attractive volume is an older collection, *Edna St. Vincent Millay's Poems Selected for Young People*, which features handsome woodcuts by Ronald Keller. The woodcuts are presented in blue tones, sometimes accented with black, against the white page. The striking detail may inspire some students to try wood or linoleum cutting to enhance the words of a favorite poet.

A more recent collection of poetry that contains beautiful quilt art is *Pieces: A Year in Poems & Quilts* by Anna Grossnickle Hines. The colors in the quilts fit the seasons described.

George Hornby chose to illustrate his collection of poetry with handsome pieces of porcelain sculpture—a kitten, heron, and plant, among others. His *Poems for Children and Other People* is an oversized book that children will enjoy.

As editor of *Elementary English*, which became *Language Arts*, I invited children to illustrate Rose Fyleman's whimsical poem "Mice," presented on the opposite page. Several of the best illustrations were published in an issue of the journal.

MICE

I think mice
Are rather nice.

    Their tails are long,

    Their faces small,

    They haven't any

    Chins at all.

    Their ears are pink,

    Their teeth are white,

    They run about

    The house at night.

    They nibble things

    They shouldn't touch

    And no one seems

    To like them much.

But, I think mice
Are rather nice.

— ROSE FYLEMAN

Students of all ages would enjoy participating in a similar schoolwide activity. Just send out an invitation to the students in your school, and provide copies of this poem to all teachers. Arrange for a committee of students and teachers to judge the illustrations submitted, and then publish a number of the best ones, perhaps displaying them on a large bulletin board near the entrance to your building.

See Thinking + Lesson Plan 20 in Appendix A for a sample lesson focusing on creating a class collection of illustrated poems. The following books provide suggestions that students can emulate as they illustrate their own collections of favorite poetry:

Voices: Poetry and Art From Around the World by Barbara Brenner. Art is varied, ranging from sculpture to modern paintings, folk art, and photography.

A Child's Calendar by John Updike. Luminous illustrations by Trina Shart Hyman earned this book a Caldecott Honor Award.

Mammabilia by Douglas Florian. Creative art accompanies each poem in the collection.

Students also could prepare poetry posters like the one presenting Emily Dickinson's poem "Morning," shown in Figure 7. This kind of poster can be framed and presented as a gift for a family member.

FIGURE 7

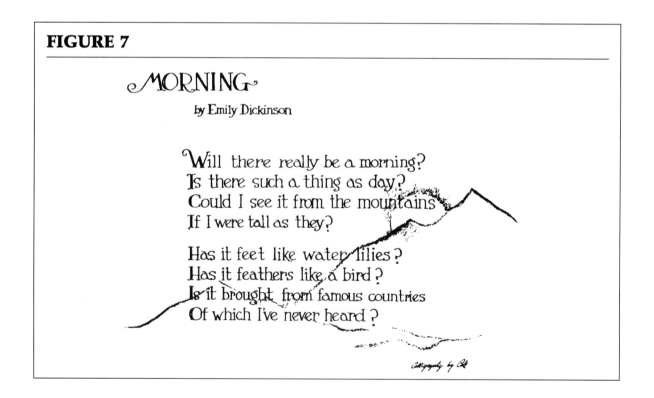

eMORNING

by Emily Dickinson

Will there really be a morning?
Is there such a thing as day?
Could I see it from the mountains
If I were tall as they?

Has it feet like water lilies?
Has it feathers like a bird?
Is it brought from famous countries
Of which I've never heard?

Calligraphy by Cat

Making Covers for Poetry Books

A front cover is an important aspect of the individual student's personal poetry anthology (see page 164). A front cover also adds to any group collection made in the classroom. Suggest the following techniques to create attractive covers.

MARBLEIZED PAPER. This technique is a favorite with author/illustrator Ezra Jack Keats. Bring in some of his books such as *The Snowy Day*, which won the Caldecott Award for illustrations, or *In a Spring Garden*, the book of haiku he illustrated for Richard Lewis. Keats explains how to do marbleized paper in *Ezra Jack Keats* (Scholastic, 1970), a documentary film by Weston Woods.

SCRATCH DESIGNS. In this technique, the paper is prepared by first creating patches of color with bright-colored crayons. Then, the sheet is painted over with black tempera. A picture or design is scratched with something sharp like the end of a paper clip into the black paint, and the color shows through attractively.

Visualizing Artistic Images

Some poetry has words that paint a picture you can see in your mind's eye. Encourage students to visualize the scene that Emily Dickinson provides in this visually stimulating poem titled "Autumn":

> The morns are meeker than they were,
> The cherry's cheek is plumper,
> The nuts are getting brown;
> The rose is out of town.
>
> The maple wears a gayer scarf,
> The field a scarlet gown.
> Lest I should be old-fashioned
> I'll put a trinket on.

Students could paint a picture that includes all the elements mentioned in the poem.

After reading "The Purple Cow" by Gelett Burgess, children could draw their version of the purple cow, as shown in Figure 8.

FIGURE 8

I never saw a purple cow;
I never hope to see one,
But I can tell you anyhow;
I'd rather see than be one!

Additional poems that suggest interesting artistic interpretations include the following:

"Brooms" by Dorothy Aldis

"Watching Clouds" by John Farrar

"People" by Lois Lenski

"The Balloon Man" by Rose Fyleman

"A Modern Dragon" by Rowena Bennett

"I'd Like to Be a Lighthouse" by Rachel Field

Creating Concrete Poetry

Concrete poetry is verse in which the poet tries to combine the words of a poem with a physical shape that further explicates or adds to the meaning of the poem. The poem may contain one or more words. Each poem is distinctly different as you see in the examples of one-word poems shown in Figure 9.

FIGURE 9

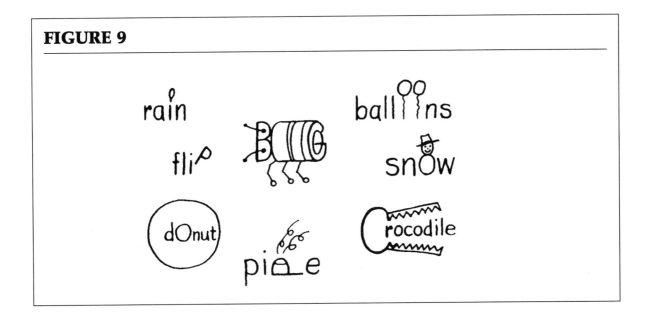

The following books contain more models for concrete poetry that may stimulate your students' imaginations:

Flicker Flash, written by Joan B. Graham and illustrated by Nancy David

Touch the Poem, written by Joan B. Graham and illustrated by Lisa Desimini

Mathematics

People don't usually associate mathematics with literature, and especially not with poetry. The creative teacher may discover that an occasional poem enhances his or her teaching. Consider some of the following activities to get you started.

Counting Rhymes

Counting rhymes are usually suitable for children in the preschool or primary grade years. "One, Two, Buckle My Shoe" is a familiar counting rhyme:

> One, two,
> Buckle my shoe;
>
> Three, four,
> Shut the door;

Five, six,
Pick up sticks;

Seven, eight,
Lay them straight;

Nine, ten,
A big fat hen!

Many authors have presented counting rhymes in picture book format. An unusual book is *Give the Dog a Bone,* in which Steven Kellogg illustrates the song that begins with this line in the first verse, "This old man, he played one." The title of the book comes from the refrain that ends each verse: "Nick-nack, pad-dy whack, give the dog a bone. This old man came rolling home." In this book, you'll find counting, a song, and art by an award-winning artist.

Older students may find it interesting to create original counting rhymes, particularly those that deal with larger numbers like the googol.

Creative Ideas

There are many creative ways to link poetry with your mathematics curriculum. For instance, the whimsical limerick "Relativity" deals with a mathematics concept:

There once was a lady named Bright,
Who traveled much faster than light.
She set out one day
In a relative way
And returned on the previous night.

Middle school students may be delighted to discover what a famous poet thought about arithmetic. Carl Sandburg presents interesting images of numbers in his poem "Arithmetic." For example, he sees numbers as pigeons that fly in and out of your head. Students can add lines to go with those of Sandburg as they consider what arithmetic means in our world—buying tickets for a jazz festival, flying an airplane, figuring out temperatures in Fahrenheit and Celsius, and so on. This creates a wonderful listing poem.

Finding Connections Between Math and Poetry

Challenge students to find out how many connections they can find between mathematics and poetry. Have students present their discoveries to the class. Then, add each one to a display titled Math/Poetry Connections. You can begin with the ones presented in this section. Then, ask if anyone can find on the Internet mathematicians who wrote poetry. Remember, too, that mathematics is related to the writing of music, how we keep score in sports, and scientific experimentation. All these topics can be expressed in the form of poetry.

Music

Poetry and music have much in common, beginning with vocabulary and common elements such as rhythm, movement, and singing. The lyrics of the songs we sing are poetry, and conversely, many poems have been set to music. The activities described here, as with art, can be integrated into other curricular areas as well.

Characteristics in Common

Poetry has often been compared to music, and it is easy to substantiate this comparison. Ask upper elementary and middle school students to help you create a word wall of musical words. Keep adding to this list as you continue your study of poetry together:

ballad	rhythm	stanza
lyric	measure	tone
beat	line	mood
song	verse	refrain
theme	pattern	chorus
compose	composer	repetition

The traditional beat (called meter) of formal poetry can be found in many poems that older students will enjoy. Robert Frost employs the strong beat identified as *iambic* meter in "Stopping by Woods on a Snowy Evening." Beat it out as you speak these lines, and you will discover four beats in each line. Have students do this, too, as they become more aware of specific rhythms. Each beat consists of an unaccented syllable followed by an accented syllable, for example, "The woods."

The woods are lovely, dark and deep,

But I have promises to keep,

And miles to go before I sleep.

Students can check the rhythms in their own lines of poetry. If the rhythm seems to be "off," they may add a word or rearrange their words so they achieve a definite beat.

Learning the technical vocabulary found in adult references about poetry is not appropriate for most elementary and middle school students. Our emphasis should remain on understanding and enjoying poetry. However, if an occasional advanced eighth-grade student observes such distinctive rhythms and wants to know more about them, you can certainly suggest books about poetry such as those listed in Appendix B.

Poetry We Sing

The lyrics of the songs we sing are, of course, poetry. The words may have first been written as a poem and later set to music. Print these lyrics so that students can read them. Sometimes this clarifies the meaning of words that have been sung over the years without real thought. You often hear jokes about children's mistaken interpretations of the words to "My Country 'Tis of Thee."

Following are discussions of different types of songs your students may enjoy.

PATRIOTIC SONGS. The U.S. national anthem, "The Star-Spangled Banner," began as a poem that was composed by Francis Scott Key as he watched the battle between two ships in Boston Harbor. Later, this poem was set to music.

Another favorite patriotic song, "America the Beautiful," also began as a poem and was set to a number of different tunes before one finally became accepted. The story of this song is told in *Purple Mountain Majesties: The Story of Katharine Lee Bates and "America the Beautiful,"* written by Barbara Younger and illustrated by Stacey Schuett. Younger tells of Bates's love of writing, her schooling at Wellesley College, and her being hired there to teach English. However, it was a trip west to teach one summer in Colorado that inspired the lines that became "America the Beautiful." On the way to Colorado, she visited the World's Fair in Chicago where she saw the "alabaster cities," then traveled across the "amber waves of grain" of the Great Plains, and finally arrived in the "purple mountains" of Colorado. Two years later, she completed her poem, which was published in a Fourth of July issue of *The Congregationalist* and soon after was set to music.

ROUNDS. Students of all ages enjoy singing rounds like "Row, Row, Row Your Boat" or "Are You Sleeping, Brother John? (Frere Jacques)." One of the loveliest of the rounds is "White Coral Bells," a song about the lily of the valley. The music for this traditional song appears in Figure 10.

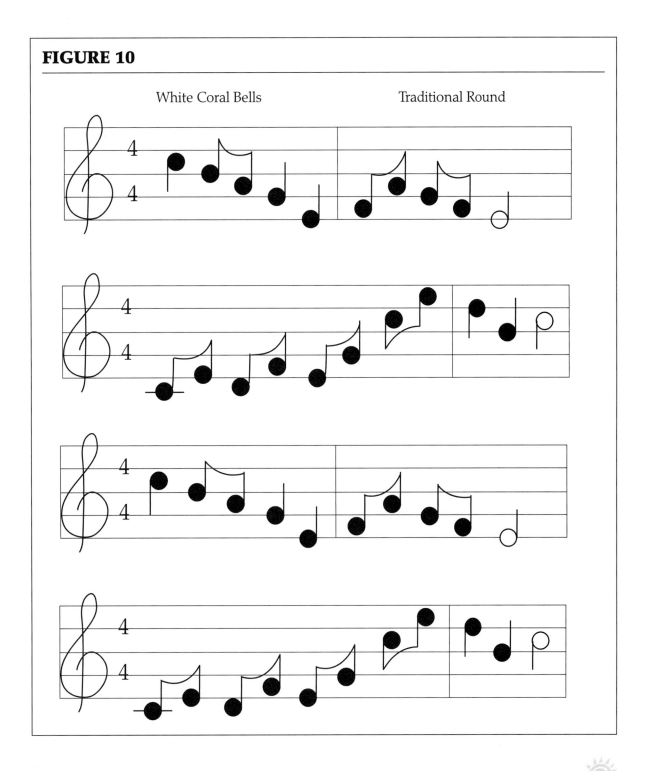

FIGURE 10

White Coral Bells   Traditional Round

LULLABIES. Several lullabies are included in most Mother Goose collections, for example, "Rock-a-by, Baby." A favorite lullaby with middle elementary school students is this one sung by a father who has funny ideas about what is appropriate for his baby girl. The repetitious pattern adds to the appeal and makes it easier for children to learn:

> Hush, little baby, don't say a word,
> Papa's gonna' buy you a mockingbird.
>
> If that mockingbird won't sing,
> Papa's gonna' buy you a diamond ring.
>
> And, if that diamond ring turns brass,
> Papa's gonna' buy you a looking glass.
>
> And, if that looking glass gets broke,
> Papa's gonna' buy you a billy goat.
>
> And, if that billy goat won't pull,
> Papa's gonna' buy you a horse and cart.
>
> And, if that horse and cart breaks down,
> You'll still be the prettiest girl in town!

The melody for the two lines appears in Figure 11.

Primary grade children will enjoy singing such Mother Goose rhymes as "Mary Had a Little Lamb," "Baa, Baa, Black Sheep," or "Little Bo-Peep." Older students might learn these songs to share with younger children, perhaps at home or when babysitting. (See page 96 for the music for "Baa, Baa, Black Sheep.")

SETTING A POEM TO MUSIC. At times, you and your students might choose to create a melody for a poem that you know. Students can pick out a tune on the piano (that's my method) for a short poem that appeals to them. A simple xylophone would also be handy and easier to bring to the classroom. This activity would be especially good for a student who plays the guitar and perhaps also sings. Students could work in pairs or small groups to produce a set of songs to entertain other children in the school. Students might also set their own poems to music. Encourage them to develop creative connections between poetry and music. If needed, ask for help with writing music for simple melodies. Don't hes-

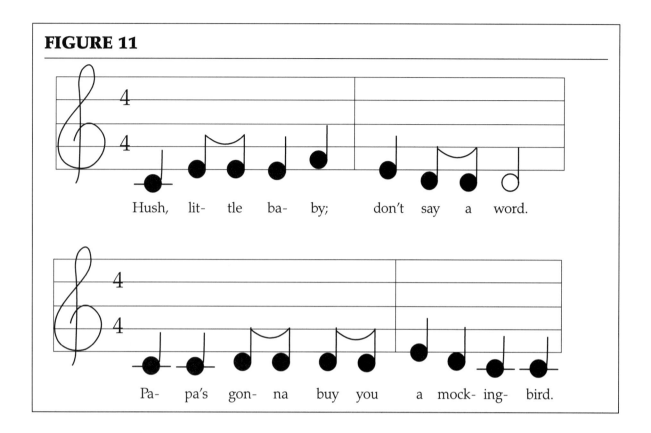

FIGURE 11

itate to use such ideas in the middle school classroom. Middle school students need this kind of stimulus to add interest. Such ideas may also help you reach students who don't always respond to paper-and-pencil activities.

FOLK SONGS. Students usually enjoy singing folk songs, for example, "I've Been Working on the Railroad," "The Erie Canal," or such spirituals as "Swing Low, Sweet Chariot." Again, print the words of the songs so that students can read the lyrics. This is highly motivating for slower readers or students who are learning English as a second language, especially in upper elementary and middle school classrooms.

A popular folk song that has been presented in a picture book is Woody Guthrie's *This Land Is Your Land*, with paintings by Kathy Jakobsen. Guthrie wrote both the words and the music, which is included in the book. Students will enjoy singing this song about the United States, which invites guitar accompaniment. The following books suggest additional possibilities:

Give the Dog a Bone: Stories, Poems, Jokes, and Riddles About Dogs by Joanna Cole and Stephanie Calmenson

And the Green Grass Grew All Around by Alvin Schwartz

Dominic Catalano provides another model in his book *Frog Went A-Courting: A Musical Play in Six Acts*. This well-known folk song is presented as an animated movie. Your students might act out this play, following Catalano's work. They could also choose to act out another folk tune, for example, "John Henry," or perhaps a long narrative poem such as "On the Road to Mandalay" by Rudyard Kipling. Talented students could create a multimedia presentation using the computer.

Music enhances the total curriculum. It adds a liveliness to learning that all children appreciate, and it touches a different kind of intelligence in our students.

Physical Education, Health, and Recreation

Poets write about any topic that interests them, so many have chosen sports, health, and recreational activities as subjects. Such poetry may provide a way of interesting some students in reading or acting out a poem, thus opening the door to a broader exposure to the work of poets. Students may be surprised to find that sports vocabulary has a valid place in a poem that they write. Sometimes, we need to begin where students are, choosing topics that interest them as we select poetry to use in the classroom.

Athletics

"The outlook wasn't brilliant for the Mudville nine that day"—a touch of humor adds much to the study of a subject, so don't forget such poems as "Casey at the Bat," a ballad about a famous baseball player by Ernest Thayer. First published in the San Francisco *Examiner* in 1888, it remains a classic. Some of your students will be especially pleased to have you share this poem about baseball, and all will enjoy it.

An unusual edition of Thayer's poem is presented by Christopher Bing, who uses a variety of newspaper clippings, pictures, and artifacts to illustrate the lines of the poem. Students might emulate Bing's work to present a poem that they especially enjoy.

Making a Sports Collage

Have students make a sports collage about any sport that interests them. They can include clippings from magazines and newspapers. The only requirement is that they also include a poem about the sport, one they have found or one they have written. Following are several collections of poems about sports (unfortunately, mostly about basketball) that you might consider for your library:

The Basket Counts, written by Arnold Adoff and illustrated by Michael Weaver

Sports Pages, written by Arnold Adoff and illustrated by Steve Kuzma. This book explores what it takes to be an athlete. Adoff's children inspired much of this poetry.

Slam Dunk: Poems About Basketball, written by Lillian Morrison and illustrated by Bill James. Poems about basketball designed for young athletes.

Rimshots: Basketball Pix, Rolls, and Rhythms by Charles R. Smith

Short Takes: Fast-Break Basketball Poetry by Charles R. Smith

Take It to the Hoop, Magic Johnson, written by Quincy Thorpe and illustrated by Shane Evans. An unusual presentation of court jive in poetic language simulating the movements of this ballplayer in an ode to Magic Johnson.

Individual poems that students might find in anthologies include the following:

"The Diver" by W.W.E. Ross

"Pitches" by Robert Francis

"The Base Stealer" by Robert Francis

"Under the Goal Posts" by Arthur Guiterman

"The Passer" by George Abbe

"The Double-Play" by Robert Wallace

Some students will be highly motivated to collect poetry about sports and other aspects of physical education. They might write original listing poems about their favorite sport or sports figure.

Science

Science is a broad subject area that includes diverse topics such as animals, experiments, medicine, and rocks, as well as scientific methods such as observation and collecting data. Again, interesting subject matter may provide an entrée to a more extensive study of poetry. Poetry can also introduce provocative ideas to the science classroom and suggest different modes of expressing findings related to scientific study.

Stimulating the Imagination

To stimulate your students' imaginations, share a poem like this one:

> If all the seas were one sea,
> What a *great* sea that would be!
> If all the trees were one tree,
> What a *great* tree that would be!
> And if all the axes were one axe,
> What a *great* axe that would be!
> And if all the men were one man,
> What a *great* man that would be!
> And if the *great* man took the great axe,
> And cut down the *great* tree,
> And let it fall into the *great* sea,
> What a splish-splash that would be!

Point out that creativity and imaginative thinking have often been the basis for new discoveries. Note, for example, how many technology companies encourage play within their daily routines.

Exploring the Ways of Animals

A favorite topic for students of all ages, animals both familiar and exotic hold special interest for children. Animals have proved to be favorite topics for poets, too. Here are a few picture books that young children will enjoy:

Mammalabilia by Douglas Florian. Gouache on painted brown paper bags creates charming and unusual illustrations for such poems as "The Mule," a provocative four-line poem that gives the reader a clear picture of this animal. Other collections by the same poet include *In the Swim* and *Insectlopedia*, which features whimsical verse such as "You don't need tickets/To listen to crickets."

Creatures, edited by Lee Bennett Hopkins and illustrated by Stella Ormai. A useful collection of poems about varied animals.

Antarctic Antics: A Book of Penguin Poems, written by Judy Sierra and illustrated by Jose Aruego and Ariane Dewey. Primary level poems about baby penguins and their habitat.

Individual poems about animals that are often included in anthologies of poetry for young people include the following:

"The Woodpecker" by Elizabeth M. Roberts

"Crows" by David McCord

"The Sandhill Crane" by Mary Austin

"The Skunk" by Robert P.T. Coffin

"The Wolf" by Georgia Durston

"Snail" by Langston Hughes

"Snake" by D.H. Lawrence

For more books of poetry about animals, see page 70.

Studying Science Themes

Science suggests many thematic studies that you can design for one or more weeks. Poetry will enhance studies such as those explored here.

THE OCEAN/SEA. The sea is the subject of Alison Shaw's collection *Until I Saw the Sea*. She uses bold, colorful photographs to illustrate such poems as Lilian Moore's "Until I Saw the Sea," John Masefield's "I Must Go Down to the Sea Again," and Robert Louis Stevenson's "At the Seaside," a favorite for young children:

> When I was down beside the sea,
> A wooden spade they gave to me
> To dig the sandy shore.
>
> My holes were hollow like a cup,
> In every hole the sea came up,
> Till it could hold no more.

Other books about the sea include the following:

The Mermaid's Purse, written by Ted Hughes and illustrated by Flora McDonnell. This poet obviously loves the sea and all the animals in it.

The Mermaid and Other Sea Poems, edited by Sophie Windham. Poems about sharks, octopuses, whales, and similar creatures.

OBSERVATION. Talk with students about the importance of careful observation as they learn to work like scientists. "The Blind Men and the Elephant" by John Godfrey Saxe demonstrates how collecting incomplete data can lead one to draw the wrong conclusions:

It was six men of Hindostan,
To learning much inclined,
Who went to see the elephant,
(Though all of them were blind);
That each by observation
Might satisfy his mind.

The first approached the elephant,
And happening to fall
Against his broad and sturdy side,
At once began to bawl,
"Bless me, it seems the elephant
Is very like a wall."

The second, feeling of his tusk,
Cried, "Ho! What have we here
So very round and smooth and sharp?
To me 'tis mighty clear
This wonder of an elephant
Is very like a spear."

The third approached the animal,
And happening to take
The squirming trunk within his hands,
Then boldly up and spake;
"I see," quoth he, "the elephant
Is very like a snake."

The fourth stretched out his eager hand
And felt about the knee,
"What most this mighty beast is like

Is mighty plain," quoth he;
"'Tis clear enough the elephant
Is very like a tree."

The fifth who chanced to touch the ear
Said, "Even the blindest man
Can tell what this resembles most;
Deny the fact who can,
This marvel of an elephant
Is very like a fan."

The sixth no sooner had begun
About the beast to grope
Than, seizing on the swinging tail
That fell within his scope,
"I see," cried he, "the elephant
Is very like a rope."

And so these men of Hindostan
Disputed loud and long,
Each of his own opinion
Exceeding stiff and strong,
Though each was partly in the right,
And all were in the wrong!

Give students an opportunity to base poetry on observation. One good example is the listening walk activity described on page 41, which involves gathering data by using a different sense.

Social Studies

Social studies encompasses a broad variety of subject areas such as geography and history. It leads us to such topics as people and their ways of living around the world, the story of the United States and how it developed over the years, and the study of men and women who have made contributions to the world in various ways. It also clearly deals with multicultural themes.

The social studies topics provide a rich source of subjects for poets, who have created a treasury of material that will add a spark to social studies teaching. Following are suggestions for integrating poetry into social studies lessons. Note that social studies also links with science through such studies as medicine, transportation, and the production of food, and it links with art and music and literature through the humanities, so you'll find additional ideas you can use in your social studies curriculum under those subject areas as well as in this section.

Multicultural Poetry

A gorgeous celebration of poetry by and about African Americans is found in *Words With Wings: A Treasury of African-American Poetry and Art*, selected by Belinda Rochelle. As the editor notes in the introduction,

> If, as Georgia Douglas Johnson says, "Your world is as big as you make it," then the poems and paintings in this book enable us to make our worlds bigger. Poems are words with wings, wings made out of words. But we must help give the poems and art their wings by bringing to them our own experiences and histories, and our willingness to let them take us somewhere new. (p. ii)

Poets represented in this volume include Alice Walker, Langston Hughes, Rita Dove, Lucille Clifton, Ethelbert Miller, Nikki Giovanni, and Maya Angelou. Equally important in this book are the African American artists, including Emilio Cruz, Aaron Douglas, Horace Pippin, Augusta Savage, and Jacob Lawrence.

A second volume that also could be used in a study of African Americans is *Harlem: A Poem by Walter Dean Myers*. Illustrated with bold collage art by the author's son, Christopher Myers, this is a picture of life in Harlem that represents one segment of the history of African Americans living in the United States.

Lessie Jones Little's *Children of Long Ago*, illustrated by Jan S. Gilchrist, is a collection of poetry that depicts the life of African Americans in rural America in the early 1900s. Attractive pastels add to the effectiveness of the poetry.

Look for poetry about other groups in our diverse population as you browse in the library. Be sure to consider poetry as you plan any theme study. Many books of poetry or individual poems about our diverse population will enhance multicultural studies in your classroom, for example, the following books of poetry about African Americans, Latinos, and Native Americans:

African Americans
My Black Me: A Big Book of Poetry, edited by Arnold Adoff

Golden Slippers: An Anthology by Arna Bontemps

Bronzeville Boys and Girls by Gwendolyn Brooks

Greet the Dawn by Paul Dunbar

Spin a Soft Black Song by Nikki Giovanni

Daydreamers by Eloise Greenfield

Something on My Mind by Nikki Grimes

Don't You Turn Back: Poems by Langston Hughes, selected by Lee Bennett Hopkins

Who Look at Me? by June Jordan

DeShawn Days by Toni Medina

In Daddy's Arms I Am Tall: African Americans Celebrating Fathers, edited by Javaka Steptoe

Latinos

Angels Ride Bikes and Other Fall Poems by Francisco X. Alarcón

Still Waters of the Air: Poems by Three Modern Spanish Poets, edited by Richard Lewis

Confetti: Poems for Children by Pat Mora

Love to Mama: A Tribute to Mothers by Pat Mora

The Tree Is Older Than You Are: A Bilingual Gathering of Poems and Stories From Mexico With Paintings by Mexican Artists, edited by Naomi Shihab Nye

Mother Goose in Spanish/Poesías de la Madre Oca by Alastair Reid and Anthony Kerrigan

Neighborhood Odes by Gary Soto

Native Americans

The Earth Is Sore: Native Americans on Nature by Aline Amon

Moonsong Lullaby by Jamake Highwater

Songs of the Dream People by James Houston

The Song of Hiawatha by Henry Wadsworth Longfellow

Reflections on Illusion—Reality by Ramaho Navajo Students

War Cry on a Prayer Feather by Nancy Wood

Introducing Thematic Studies for Older Students

A strong introduction to a thematic study, a highly recommended method of teaching, is a poem that introduces the topic. You don't need to read the whole poem for some of the long classic poems that early poets wrote. Just use the best-known lines, usually the first verse, which sets the tone and serves to introduce older students to these well-known poems that are part of the American heritage. Following are sample ideas.

LEADERSHIP OR SLAVERY. Read this first stanza of a classic poem about Abraham Lincoln's death, "O Captain! My Captain" by Walt Whitman. The first of three verses presents the metaphor of a country as a ship that has lost its captain:

> O Captain! My Captain! Our fearful trip is done,
> The ship has weather'd every rack, the prize we sought is won,
> The port is near, the bells I hear, the people all exulting,
> While follow eyes the steady keel, the vessel grim and daring;
> But O my heart! heart! heart!
> O the bleeding drops of red,
> Where on the deck my Captain lies,
> Fallen cold and dead.

REVOLUTION OR WAR. Henry Wadsworth Longfellow's narrative poem about Paul Revere begins with these well-known lines, which would work well as an introduction to the study:

> Listen, my children, and you shall hear
> Of the midnight ride of Paul Revere,
> On the eighteenth of April, in Seventy-five;
> Hardly a man is now alive
> Who remembers that famous day and year.

This poem is presented in a lovely edition illustrated by Ted Rand. Historical notes are included, as well as a double-page spread featuring a map that locates the happenings described in Longfellow's poem. The book provides a great guide for developing this theme, beginning with an emphasis on the Revolutionary War in the young United States.

DEATH OR FRIENDSHIP. More advanced students might respond to a passage from the work of William Shakespeare, for example, these words spoken by Marc Antony in *Julius Caesar*:

Friends, Romans, countrymen, lend me your ears;
I come to bury Caesar, not to praise him,
The evil that men do lives after them;
The good is oft interred with their bones;
So let it be with Caesar. The noble Brutus
Hath told you Caesar was ambitious:

If it were so, it was a grievous fault.
Here, under leave of Brutus and the rest—
For Brutus is an honorable man;
So are they all, all honorable men—
Come I to speak in Caesar's funeral.

He was my friend, faithful and just to me:
But Brutus says he was ambitious;
And Brutus is an honorable man.

Friendship is a popular theme for young children, too. Salley Mavor's collection of poems, *You and Me: Poems of Friendship*, includes poetry that you could use in the early elementary grades. Or, read Jacqueline Woodson's charming book, *The Other Side*, illustrated beautifully by E.B. Lewis, which tells of children who cross the "racial divide." Talking about this story could lead to the writing of poems about making friends.

IMMIGRATION OR DIVERSITY. A study of "Immigration" or "The Increasing Diversity in the U.S. Population" might well begin with an introduction to the Statue of Liberty and the poem by Emma Lazarus inscribed on the statue. Thinking + Lesson Plan 21 in Appendix A describes a lesson based on Lazarus's poem, which is presented on the next page.

LIVING IN THE CITY. Even younger students will benefit from a thematic study focusing on city life. You might begin with Christopher Myers's *Black Cat*. Here, the city is shown through the eyes of a cat that moves through the subways of New York, slinks down nighttime streets, and climbs brick walls lined with bottles. The poetry is filled with rhythms and powerful images as Myers questions, "Black cat, black cat,/we want to know/where's your home,/where do you go?" Note that the book-length poem about Harlem by Walter Dean Myers,

THE NEW COLOSSUS

Not like the brazen giant of Greek fame,

With conquering limbs astride from land to land;

Here at our sea-washed, sunset gates shall stand

A mighty woman with a torch, whose flame

Is the imprisoned lightning, and her name

Mother of Exiles. From her beacon-hand

Glows world-wide welcome, her mild eyes command

The air-bridged harbor that twin cities frame.

"Keep, ancient lands, your storied pomp!" cries she

With silent lips. "Give me your tired, your poor,

Your huddled masses yearning to breathe free,

The wretched refuse of your teeming shore,

Send these, the homeless, tempest-tost to me,

I lift my lamp beside the golden door."

— EMMA LAZARUS

mentioned in the section on poetry by African Americans, would be an excellent follow-up for this book (both are illustrated by Christopher Myers).

Jane Yolen compiled another collection of varied poems about city living, *Sky Scrape/City Scape: Poems of City Life*, which is illustrated by Ken Condon.

Our second largest city is featured in an attractive picture book, *Angels Ride Bikes and Other Fall Poems*, which features poems by Francisco X. Alarcón and brilliant illustrations by Maya Christina Gonzalez. Poems are in both English and Spanish. These poems celebrate Los Angeles as the promised land, as it is for many Mexican immigrants in California. The poet includes a warm note about his family, which could be inspiring to young readers. These two talented people also collaborated on *Laughing Tomatoes* and *From the Bellybutton of the Moon*.

Many individual poems have been written about the city, for example, "Snow in the City" by Rachel Field and "Rudolph Is Tired of the City" by Gwendolyn Brooks. Have students search for city poems in a variety of poetry anthologies.

Poetry Linked to a Different Culture

Haiku is an interesting form of poetry for students to write. The following books provide models and suggest ways of presenting this Japanese form of poetry:

My Own Rhythm: An Approach to Haiku by Ann Atwood, with photographs by the author. Biographical information about the best known of the Japanese masters of haiku, beginning with Basho, then Issa, his student, and Buson. Includes examples of their haiku, as well as the author's own, illustrated by artful colored photographs.

Stone Bench in an Empty Park, compiled by Paul B. Janeczko with photographs by Henri Silberman. Haiku written by contemporary poets.

Cricket Songs: Japanese Haiku, compiled by Harry Behn

More Cricket Songs: Japanese Haiku, compiled by Harry Behn

In a Spring Garden, edited by Richard Lewis and illustrated by Ezra Jack Keats

Students can write haiku, presenting their original verses artistically, as shown in Figure 12.

FIGURE 12

Folded slightly overlapping...
...tied with ribbon

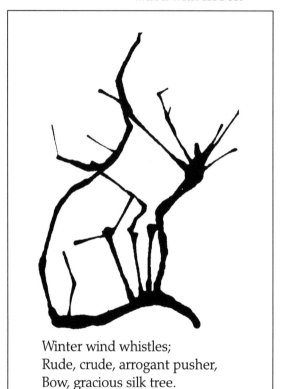

Winter wind whistles;
Rude, crude, arrogant pusher,
Bow, gracious silk tree.

Focus on a Country

One way to begin a study of geography is to read "Maps" by Dorothy B. Thompson. As you prepare to study a specific country in geography, include poetry as a way of introducing some of the literature of the people. With the study of India, for example, you might locate poems by Rudyard Kipling or the writing of the famous Indian poet Tagore. Look for collections like these:

Moon, For What Do You Wait? Poems by Tagore, edited by Richard Lewis and illustrated by Ashley Bryan. Wonderful use of language, as in "The hills are like shouts of children who raise their arms, trying to catch stars."

Poems From India, written by Daisy Aldan and illustrated by Joseph Low. Includes a short history of Indian poetry for advanced students.

Introduce a study of Alaska or Canada with poems from this book:

Poems of the Eskimo, edited by Richard Lewis and illustrated by Jessie Oonark. Includes an interesting introduction "Life as It Was" by anthropologist Edmund Carpenter. Oonark's drawings depict charming images from nature and the Eskimo's relationship with nature.

Translating Poetry

Students may be interested in reading poetry in different languages. They should be aware that we often translate poetry from the original language, as poets did for the haiku in the books listed earlier. I translated "Canción del Pirata (Song of the Pirate)," which tells of a pirate's feeling for his boat and the sea, from the work of Spanish poet José de Espronceda:

Que es mi barco mi tesoro;	My boat is my treasure;
Que es mi Diós la libertad;	Liberty is my god;
Mi ley la fuerza y el viento;	My law, force and the wind;
Mi única patria la mar.	My only homeland, the sea.

This poem can be displayed in both languages as part of a display of pictures and poems about the sea. There are many examples of poetry in translation in books such as Alma Flor Ada's *Gathering the Sun: An Alphabet in Spanish and English,* illustrated by Simón Silva, in which the poetry is presented in both languages.

Conclusion

In this chapter, we have explored various possibilities for incorporating poetry in subjects across the curriculum. Featuring poetry related to art and music reaches out to many students who may not be academically oriented. Sharing poetry related to other subject areas provides a different perspective from the usual textbook approach. In Chapter 8, we will explore different ways of celebrating poetry.

I'M NOBODY! WHO ARE YOU ?

I'm nobody! Who are you?

Are you nobody, too?

Then, there's a pair of us—don't tell!

They'd banish us, you know.

How dreary to be somebody!

How public, like a frog,

To tell your name the livelong day

To an admiring bog!

— EMILY DICKINSON

I'm Nobody! Who Are You?
Celebrating Poetry

Celebrate poetry in your classroom. Your enthusiasm will be contagious, and your students will join in the celebration. With your students, reach out to celebrate poetry in your school and in the larger community as well. You can also join national efforts to celebrate poetry. Together, you can assume a leadership role in making everyone around you aware of poetry and what it has to offer us all.

In this chapter, we'll first cover how you can celebrate poetry in your classroom. From there, we'll move on to consider how you can bring about a school-wide poetry celebration, and we'll look at ways poetry is celebrated in the United States. Finally, we'll discuss how you can begin to write your own poetry.

Celebrating Poetry in Your Classroom

Appreciate your students' original poetry, and encourage them to make it public and to publish it. Facilitate their publishing poems orally as well as in print within the classroom. Also help students explore ways of reaching out to a greater public through magazines and newspapers.

Poetry on Display

Designate a special place for poetry on a large bulletin board. Although sometimes you will display poems by adult poets that students have selected, often this space should be used to display students' original poems. Encourage students to enhance the presentation of their poems through some of the following strategies.

SHAPE POEMS. Display original poems on shapes that reflect the content of the poem—a shoe, an apple, a tree. For a holiday, have each student cut out an appropriate shape on which to display a holiday poem—pumpkins, black cats, Christmas trees, a shamrock.

TISSUE PAPER ART. Bring in tissue paper of varied colors that students can crumple and paint on to achieve interesting effects. Eric Carle has used this kind of colorful art in his collections of poetry such as *Animals Animals*, which students can examine for ideas.

ILLUSTRATIONS. Suggest a variety of supplies for illustrating original poems, for example, colored pencils and pens, crayons, cloth, watercolors, finger paint, and small objects—tiny shells, feathers, gravel, nails—whatever fits the subject.

COLOR POEMS. When students compose poems about colors, have them place their poems on a color wheel like the one on the opposite page.

A Personal Poetry Anthology

Older students who have worked extensively with poetry will be interested in making a selection of poetry that pleases them to create personal or "signature" anthologies. By choosing a few special poems that speak especially to them, they will create a sort of self-portrait, for their choices reveal something of who they are. Students can publish their poems on sheets of paper collected into a book with a cover, or they can create signature anthologies as described subsequently.

Encourage students to take their time as they pore over books of poetry, discovering poems that have something powerful to say to them. It is important to bring in a large selection of poetry books for students to use in their searching so they are exposed to a sufficient variety of poems from which to make meaningful choices. They can write in cursive handwriting, print with calligraphy, or use the computer to copy their poems.

Students can publish the poems they choose as signature anthologies by folding a large sheet of paper into many "pages." This is what publishers do when they publish books; each book is composed of many signatures. In this case, "signature" has a double meaning. These anthologies can be displayed on each student's desk when parents are invited to school.

Class Poetry Collections

Students also enjoy adding their individual poems to a class publication, which can be produced with little difficulty. Try some of the following ideas.

THE COLOR WHEEL...

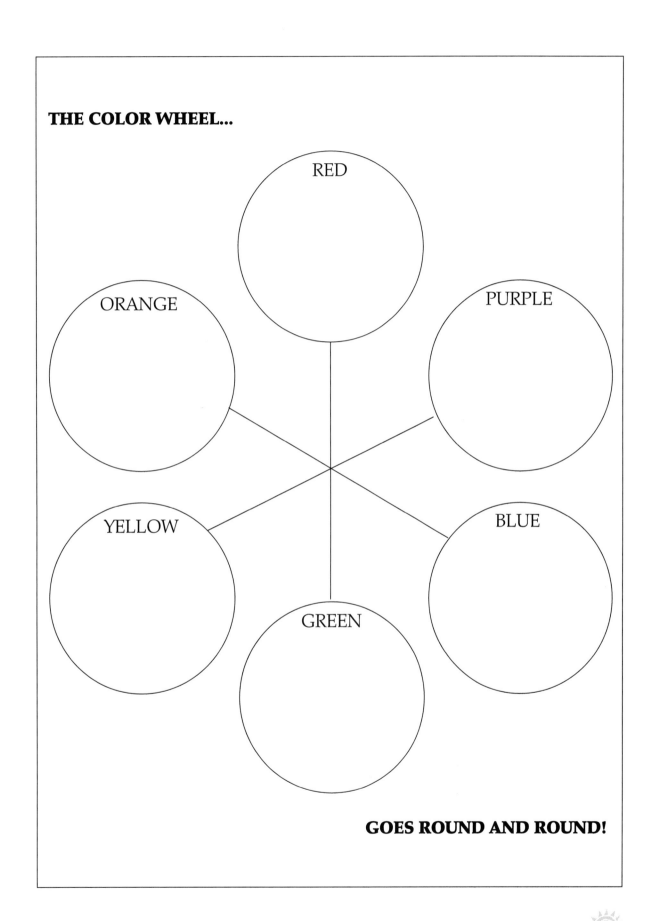

GOES ROUND AND ROUND!

RINGED NOTEBOOK INSTANT PUBLICATION. When students are working with a specific form of poetry as part of a lesson you are presenting, you can provide a colorful three-ringed notebook in which any student can place a sheet on which he or she has copied a poem. Put a label on the front of the notebook bearing a title such as *Lively Limericks, Our Haiku, Spring Has Sprung!*, or *Autumn Days*. Thus, you have an instant publication to which all children can contribute. Leave the notebook on a reading table where children can read it at their leisure. Later, selections can be made from this collection if you decide to create a more formal booklet of poems by your students at the end of the year.

CLASS COLLECTION OF HAIKU. After introducing students to haiku, have each student select the best poem he or she has written to include in a slim booklet of haiku, which is decorated with blown ink art (see Figure 13).

ACCORDION BOOK. Show students how to fold a simple accordion booklet made of any kind of stiff paper. One poem by each member of a cooperative learning group could be displayed in such a booklet. Individual students could also use

FIGURE 13

this type of booklet to display one illustrated line of a favorite poem on each page. Or, it might serve to display several original poems by a single student who then presents the book as a gift for a holiday—Christmas, Hanukkah, Mother's Day, or a birthday, to name only a few.

OUR FAVORITE POEMS. For this activity, each student selects a favorite poem to place in a class collection. The poems can be typed with the computer so that students can vary the spacing and choose interesting fonts to present their poems. After printing their poems, students can use various techniques to decorate or illustrate their favorite poems. The sheets can then be bound with a simple plastic binding to create an attractive book that can be used in the classroom or placed in the school library where other students can enjoy it, too. If students are especially enthusiastic about the project, each one could prepare two copies of his or her favorite poem so that two copies of the full collection can be made. Then, one copy can remain in the classroom while the other is placed in the library.

Recording Favorite Poems

A variation on the printed collection of favorite poems is the recorded set of poems made by members of a class. After selecting a poem to present, each student will need to practice reading the poem aloud a number of times before recording it. Have students work in pairs or small groups to rehearse their readings, checking on one another's pronunciation and the clarity with which the words are spoken. Discuss with students the importance of reading their poems effectively, reading fluently and with appropriate expression. You might share these ideas with students:

- Touch poetry with your voice.

- Poetry is meant to be read or spoken aloud.

- Read, reread as you savor the meaning.

After the recording is made, use it at your listening center. Provide printed copies of each poem, bound together in order of appearance on the tape, to give support to readers who are following the recorded poems. This is an excellent activity for slower readers or students who are learning English as a second language. You might work with another teacher who also has students record their favorite poems. Then, you can exchange the two tapes so students can listen to friends reading their favorite poems aloud.

A Schoolwide Poetry Celebration

Share your enthusiasm for poetry by assuming a leadership role in helping teachers and students in your school celebrate poetry in some of the ways suggested here. See the poem on the opposite page, which is meant for you, but which your students may find inspiring also. Following are some ideas for celebrating poetry schoolwide.

Poetry in the Library

Be sure your school's librarian knows of your interest in poetry. Make a point of suggesting books to order for the library that are available for all teachers and students, but will also support your plans to infuse poetry into your daily lesson plans. Any of the titles suggested throughout this book are appropriate for library purchase, and here are a few additional suggestions:

Picture Books

Old MacDonald Had a Farm by Shari Halpern

There Was an Old Lady Who Swallowed a Fly, written by Simms Taback and illustrated by Pam Adams

Poetry Topics for Older Students

William Shakespeare & the Globe, written and illustrated by Aliki

Animal Acrostics, written by David Hummon and illustrated by Michael Maydak

Suggest that poetry books be on display in the library to attract student and teacher attention as they come and go. You might consider taking one or two new books to your next teacher's meeting to mention what the books have to offer. Pass the books around so that teachers actually open them and look at them.

Presenting a Poetry Program

Work with older students to prepare a poetry program for other classes in your school or a nearby school. First, they need to consider the audience. The poetry they choose will be very different if their audience is a group of first and second graders than if the audience is a group of their peers or parents.

It should be fun for middle school students to plan and present a program for children in the primary grades. First, however, it might require some research

\IF...

If

It

Is

To

  Be,

It

Is

Up

To

  Me!

on their part to find the kind of poetry these children would enjoy. You might begin by brainstorming with your students about what they think the young students might like. Write suggestions on the board as they are made, for example,

- Mother Goose rhymes

- Short poems

- Poems about animals

If it appears that the students don't have enough ideas about the kind of poetry young children like, talk about how they might find out. For example, they could interview the teachers of those grades in their schools. Then, they would need to seek out the kind of poetry required.

Talk with your students about such practical matters as the following:

- Length of the program

- How many different poems could be presented in that time

- Adding variety to their presentation

- How to entertain their audience

- What they want to share with the children; that is, why are they putting on this program?

After listing a number of such items on the board, have the class form cooperative learning groups to talk about these ideas. This permits everyone to have input into the discussion. A recorder in each group should write down suggestions and questions raised. When the large group reconvenes, a person from each group can share one particularly good suggestion or question discussed in their cooperative learning group.

This kind of planning takes time, but students learn a great deal through engaging in such thinking processes. Be sure that they frequently address the following questions:

- How are we doing so far?

- What do we need to do next?

Eventually, they can devise a program something like this, assuming an audience of young children:

Introduction

Several students carrying umbrellas enter reciting

> *Rain, rain, go away!*
>
> *Come again some other day.*
>
> *Rain, rain, go away!*
>
> *Miss Day's sixth grade wants to play!*

Small-group recitations with motions

> I'm a Little Teapot!
>
> Pease Porridge Hot

Group singing

> Sing a Song of Sixpence
>
> Hey, Diddle, Diddle

A series of acting out Mother Goose rhymes

> Little Boy Blue
>
> Jack and Jill
>
> Old Mother Hubbard
>
> Little Miss Muffet

Group singing (audience participation)

> Eentsy, Weentsy Spider
>
> This Old Man

There are many possibilities for such a presentation. Students might like to include other poems, for example, Vachel Lindsay's "The Little Turtle" or "Whisky Frisky." They could also present something by A.A. Milne, perhaps "Furry Bear," or Rose Fyleman's "Mice."

The emphasis should remain on enjoying the poetry as the older students share it with young children. Both groups will benefit.

Sharing Poetry With Parents

Students of all ages will enjoy performing a poetry program for a special parents' night or for a performance in their classroom.

Upper elementary grade children and middle schoolers will enjoy learning a familiar holiday poem like Clement Moore's classic work, 'Twas the Night Before Christmas," which begins with these familiar lines:

'Twas the night before Christmas,

When all through the house

Not a creature was stirring,

Not even a mouse.

The stockings were hung by the chimney with care,

In hopes that Saint Nicholas soon would be there.

Although the work is rather long, children usually have little difficulty following the events spelled out in verse. A lovely illustrated version by Ruth Sanderson might be helpful in supplying pictures to aid memorization. Anita Lobel illustrated another attractive version you might consider.

Poets in the Schools

Arrange to have a poet visit your school to talk with groups and to help individual students work with poetry over a period of time. Local poets are usually available for a relatively small fee. Inquire about a "Poets in the Schools Program" that many school districts make available. Such programs involve hiring a poet to work within one school over a period of time. The intent is to help teachers engage students in writing poetry.

You might also show special videotapes about poets and their work with students such as *The Power of the Word* (PBS) and *The Language of Life* (PBS) by Bill Moyers, which are recommended for older students.

Poetry Performances

Poetry Alive is a professional company based in Asheville, North Carolina, that has been performing at schools, libraries, and various celebratory events across the United States since 1984. Members of this troupe present poetry as drama, planning appropriate scripts and engaging members of the audience as participants in the presentation. Their presentations often combine a range of emotions—sorrow, hilarity, and sincerity—and their repertoire includes both contemporary and classic poems.

Poetry Alive is available for teacher workshops and offers various published materials—books, CD-ROMs, and audiotapes. For scheduling and fee information, contact them by e-mail at poetry@poetryalive.com or online at http://www.poetryalive.com. Their phone number is 800-476-8172.

Poetry Readings

In the adult world, poetry readings have become popular. A microphone is set up in a bookstore, library, club room, or room connected to a professional convention, and amateur poets are invited to read their original poetry. People gather to hear what others have to say and what kind of poetry they are writing. The audience usually applauds appreciatively after each reading, partly because they realize that it takes courage to expose your writing to the public. Some poems that sound especially good may receive a standing ovation.

In an elementary or middle school, you could hold a poetry reading periodically after school. Publicize this event so that students who are enthusiastic writers of poetry can prepare one or two poems to present before an audience. Students should sign up by a given date to be included on a printed program, which can be made easily with computer art. Make sure that a few teachers and the principal, as well as interested parents, attend to help provide a sizable audience and to lead the applause.

Poetry on a National Scale

Let students know that adults are also interested in poetry. It's not just something to be done in school. Make them aware of national activities that promote poetry such as those described in this section. You and your class can become involved in some of these activities. Note that many of these groups make a point of preparing materials for teachers to use in their classrooms.

National Poetry Month

Designated as National Poetry Month, sponsored by the Academy of American Poets, April is one time of the year to place a special emphasis on poetry. See the March issues of journals such as *The Reading Teacher* and *Language Arts* for information about poetry contests and material especially for classroom use. Also, see what is available at websites such as http://www.poets.org. See Thinking + Lesson Plan 22 in Appendix A for a culminating activity.

Make a point of sharing poetry with your students during this month. Bring in interesting collections of poetry such as *It's a Woman's World: A Century of Women's Voices in Poetry*, compiled by Neil Philip. Or, introduce Nikki Grimes's poems about shoes in her book, *Shoe Magic*, illustrated by Terry Widener, to stimulate student writing.

The Children's Book Council is an excellent source of material to help you plan a celebration during Poetry Month, as they recognize one week in April as Young People's Poetry Week. You can find out what they have to offer by visiting their website, http://www.cbcbooks.org. Their mailing address is The Children's Book Council, 12 W. 37th Street, 2nd Floor, New York, NY 10018-7480.

Another source of material is *Poetic Power*, a free newsletter for teachers, which you can obtain from Creative Communication, 90 North 100 East, Logan, UT 84321 or online at http://www.poeticpower.com. The Internet is another excellent source for information on organizations related to poetry. Here are some websites to explore:

Academy of American Poets	http://www.poets.org
The Children's Book Council	http://www.cbcbooks.org
Poets & Writers Magazine	http://www.pw.org
Creative Communication	http://www.poeticpower.com
National Council of Teachers of English	http://www.ncte.org
Poetry Society of America	http://www.poetrysociety.org

Black Poetry Week

The third week in October is designated as Black Poetry Week. Share poetry from Davida Adedjouma's collection, *The Palm of My Heart: Poetry by African American Children*, illustrated by Gregorie Christie. This book was an honor book for the Coretta Scott King award for illustrations in children's literature by an African American artist.

Also introduce students to James Weldon Johnson's song, "Lift Ev'ry Voice and Sing," which is recognized as the African American national anthem. This song is presented in *Lift Ev'ry Voice and Sing*, which is illustrated by Jan Spivey Gilchrist. Johnson was a school principal. He wrote the poem and his brother, J. Rosamond Johnson, composed the music in 1900 to celebrate Abraham Lincoln's birthday. The words to this poem are as follows:

Lift every voice and sing

Till earth and heaven ring.

Ring with the harmonies of Liberty;

Let our rejoicing rise

High as the listening skies,

Let it resound loud as the rolling seas.

Sing a song full of the faith that the dark past has taught us,

Sing a song full of hope that the present has brought us,

Facing the rising sun of our new day begun,

Let us march on 'til victory is won.

Postage Stamps

The United States Postal Service has created a series of stamps that feature noted American poets. Students can write a letter to the Postal Service to nominate a poet to be honored on a future stamp. They will need to know something about the poet in order to provide a convincing rationale for featuring that poet on a new stamp. Poets already honored are T.S. Eliot (22-cent stamp), Emily Dickinson (8-cent stamp), Paul Laurence Dunbar (10-cent stamp), Walt Whitman (5-cent stamp), and Marianne Moore (25-cent stamp).

Poet Laureates

Beginning in 1937, the Library of Congress annually has appointed a U.S. poet to its Library of Congress Poetry Position. The first poet appointed to this position was Joseph Auslander, who wrote the poem "A Blackbird Suddenly," which older students will enjoy. Others who have held the position include Robert Lowell, William Carlos Williams, and Robert Frost. Only a few women have been included, for example, Louise Bogan, Leonie Adams, Elizabeth Bishop, Josephine Jacobsen, Maxine Kumin, and Gwendolyn Brooks. None of these poets write especially for children; however, you'll occasionally find a poem or two by these nationally recognized poets in an anthology of poetry for children. Furthermore, Louis Untermeyer, who was the recognized poet in 1961, has been in the forefront of promoting children's poetry.

In 1986, the Library of Congress decided to designate the selected poet as the official Poet Laureate of the United States. Thus far, there have been 11 Poet Laureates, each of whom has made a distinctive contribution:

Robert Penn Warren	1986–1987
Richard Wilbur	1987–1988
Howard Nemerov	1988–1990
Mark Strand	1990–1991
Joseph Brodsky	1991–1992
Mona Van Duyn	1992–1993
Rita Dove	1993–1995
Robert Hass	1995–1997
Robert Pinsky	1997–2000
Stanley Kunitz	2000–2001
Billy Collins	2001–2002

The assignment of the Poet Laureates is to promote poetry in the United States. They usually make appearances to talk about poetry and to read poetry aloud, their own and that of others. Several advanced students might like to research these poets to discover who they are and what kind of poetry they write. They could share their findings with the rest of the class.

Appointed in June 2001, Billy Collins is Distinguished Professor of English at Lehman College, City University of New York, where he has taught for 30 years. His latest book is *Sailing Alone Around the Room*. The Librarian of Congress, James Billington, announced Collins's appointment as Poet Laureate, saying, "Billy Collins' poetry is widely accessible. He writes in an original way about all manner of ordinary things and situations with both humor and a surprising contemplative twist. We look forward to his energizing presence this year." Students can watch for news of Billy Collins's activities in the local newspaper and on television.

Robert Pinsky, the only Poet Laureate to serve three terms, made an interesting contribution when he went around the country inviting ordinary people to read their favorite poems aloud. Some of these readings have been featured on national television.

Pinsky and his staff developed a packet of materials designed to help anyone conduct a poetry reading in their community. This would be an exciting activity to undertake, perhaps working with local representatives of your English and reading professional groups. If you are interested, you can obtain materials to help you get started by writing Robert Pinsky, Favorite Poem Project, 236 Bay State Road, Boston, MA 02215. You can also get information about the project by e-mail at favpoem@bu.edu or online at http://www.favoritepoem.org.

Continue to watch for news of national poet laureates as new ones are appointed. Many states and cities also have appointed poet laureates. You could initiate an effort to appoint a poet laureate in your community. You might even select a poet laureate for your school.

This kind of involvement of people in the community would certainly be inspiring to our young people, wouldn't it? It's worth thinking about.

Teachers Write Poetry, Too

Teachers like you often write and publish poetry. Original poems are frequently published in such journals as *Language Arts* and *The Reading Teacher*. Reading these poems may help you realize that poetry is not something sacrosanct or complex that you can't handle or even produce. These teachers are speaking directly to you. Teacher and poet Steven L. Layne (2001) wrote a number of poems about teaching that have been published in the book *Life's Literacy Lessons: Poems for Teachers*. He states in the preface, "Discovering the truth of personal experience inside a simple poem engenders a wonderful bond of community" (p. xiii).

The first piece of writing I ever had published was a poem. I remember how thrilled I was to see it in print. This poem is reproduced on the next page so that you can share it with your colleagues (Tiedt, 1962).

Try writing poetry yourself as you express your ideas about what you know best—teaching and children. Perhaps you have other special interests to express or would like to comment on life. The events of September 11, 2001, have moved many to write poems, some expressing grief, fear, or a greater sense of patriotism. Writing poetry offers a catharsis and is a wonderful way to share something of yourself with family and friends.

Conclusion

In this final chapter, we have explored ways of sharing poetry within the classroom as well as celebrating poetry in the larger community. Activities feature

THE CHALLENGE

Are you afraid, teacher,
When his dark eyes probe yours,
And he speaks that questing word—Why?
"Why does four plus six equal ten?
Why do chickens lay eggs?
Why does tomorrow never come?
Why, teacher?"

Are you fearful, teacher,
When her hand grasps yours,
And she earnestly asks, "How?
How do we know green is green?
How does the spider spin a web?
How does it feel to die?
How, teacher?"

Can you go with them, teacher?
Can you free them to explore,
To question, to experiment, to find?
Can you free them from the mesh
Of basal readers, graded texts,
Free them to grow and to learn?
Can you, teacher?

— IRIS M. TIEDT

ways of publishing original student writing, but they also include ways of sharing poetry with other students and with parents. The appendixes of this book present a series of lesson plans designed to help you infuse poetry into your curriculum and additional resources selected to assist you in continuing your growth as a person who cares to celebrate poetry.

Now I have reached a point where I absolutely must stop writing this book! But, there is so much more I would like to share with you. I would love to reproduce all the wonderful poems that you might enjoy sharing with your students, but there are books and books full of them. I would like to tell you about all the lovely picture books that present poetic language especially written for children, but there are more and more of them published every year.

So, I must leave you to explore further on your own. Go to your local library to browse through the poetry books it has to share with you. Thus, the poets and their poetry will speak to you directly, touching your sensibilities with here a little whimsy, there some joy, and perhaps, a bit of beauty, too.

I'd be pleased to hear how poetry works for you and your students. You can e-mail me at irismt@att.net.

My best to all of you,

Iris

Thinking + Lesson Plans

T H I N K I N G + L E S S O N P L A N 1
You Come, Too: An Invitation (Grades 3–8)

Expected Outcomes

The learner will
1. listen to "The Pasture" by Robert Frost.
2. discuss the meaning of the poem and specific vocabulary.
3. write a short paragraph to begin a poetry portfolio.

Resources

Make a copy of "The Pasture" by Robert Frost (see page 14).

Directions

Step I: Read the poem "The Pasture" aloud to students. Ask students to visualize what is happening in this poem: "Can you picture what the poet is talking about in this poem?" Have them listen as you read it aloud again. You also may wish to display a transparency or poster of the poem after you read it aloud.

Step II: Have students take turns telling what they "see" in the poem. Discuss the meaning of specific words, for example, *totter*. Ask students if they know any words that mean something like *totter*. Mention *tot* and *teeter totter*.

Step III: If possible, show students a picture of Robert Frost in his later years. Ask the students how they feel about this poet's saying "You come, too." Have students write several sentences or a paragraph about this poem and the poet who wrote it. This could be the first entry in each student's poetry portfolio.

Assessment

Each student will write a paragraph in his or her poetry portfolio. At a later time, review this paragraph in an individual conference designed to ascertain each student's reaction to the first several poetry experiences.

THINKING + LESSON PLAN 2
Introducing Pat Mora (Grades 3–8, adjusted for ability levels)

Expected Outcomes

The learner will

1. read poetry and stories written by Pat Mora.
2. learn about the life and work of this poet.
3. illustrate one of her poems.

Resources

Collect copies of the many books for young people written by Pat Mora (see page 17). Check her website for updated information: http://www.patmora.com. Have art supplies available.

Directions

Step I: Share information about Pat Mora and read one of her books aloud to the students. Share several of her poems. Emphasize the fact that she writes for young people and that many of her works are presented in both English and Spanish.

Step II: Display as many books as you can collect from local libraries. Provide time for students to read Mora's stories and poems. Direct students to select one poem that they would especially like to illustrate. Older students can read entries about this author in such library references as *Contemporary Authors*.

Step III: Have each student copy a poem using interesting fonts on a computer. After printing their poem on a sheet of paper, have students decorate the presentation of the poem. Students should then punch holes at the left side of the page and put their poem into a class publication titled *Presenting Poetry by Pat Mora*.

Assessment

1. Students will participate in this class activity.
2. Students will receive Pass/Fail evaluations based on their placing a page in the class poetry book.

THINKING + LESSON PLAN 3
Orange Is a Tiger Lily! Writing Poems About Colors (Grades 2–8)

Expected Outcomes
The learner will
1. observe and name colors in our world.
2. listen to poetry about colors.
3. write a poem about a selected color.

Resources
Reproduce on a transparency the lines about orange reproduced in Chapter 1 (these lines make up about one fourth of the full poem). Obtain a copy of *Hailstones and Halibut Bones* by Mary O'Neill, the book from which this poem was taken. Mount a large sheet of butcher paper on the wall to serve as a word wall. Obtain sheets of different colored construction paper, including orange.

Directions
Step I: Ask students to tell you what colors they see around the room. Print the words in a column on the word wall as they are named: black, green, red. (See that orange is listed if no one names it.)

Step II: Ask students to list some things that are red—apples, a bird, lipstick. Then, work with several other colors in turn to stimulate students' thinking about colors that they often see. Share the transparency of the lines about orange with them, saying, "Here are some lines a poet named Mary O'Neill wrote about the color orange." Read the lines aloud. State that this poet enjoyed colors so much that she wrote a number of poems and published them in this book, then say, "Here is what she wrote about red." Share a few lines about several other colors. (Don't try to read all the poems.)

Step III: Say, "I think that we could write poems about color, too. Let's try one together. Suppose we think about blue as an example. Before we make a poem, let's think about things we know that are blue." Make a list on the board: sky, cornflower, part of the U.S. flag, yarn, a rug, sadness. Then, write "Blue is" on the board, asking, "Who has an idea for our poem?" Write the lines as suggested (note that lines do not have to rhyme).

> Blue is a cornflower
> Growing in my garden,
> Blue is a rug
> In the library corner.

Step IV: Say, "Now choose your favorite color. Write it on a clean sheet in your poetry portfolio. Make a list of all the things you know that are that color." Walk around the room to see that all are compiling a list; supply an idea to help a slower student get going. After they have a chance to list a number of items, suggest that they begin a poem just as you did on the board. Read a few lines aloud from their papers as some students get started.

Assessment
1. Mount sheets of varied construction paper irregularly on a large bulletin board. Give students white paper on which to copy their poems as they finish them. They can place their poems near the appropriate color on the display. All students should create a poem to display. Gather together those who do not complete a poem within a reasonable time. Encourage them to help one another by suggesting items for a particular color.
2. Have students read their poems aloud, a few at a time. Use the poems as reading material for less able students or those who are still learning English.

THINKING + LESSON PLAN 4
The Invention of Umbrellas: Dramatizing a Funny Poem (Grades 2–8)

Expected Outcomes

The learner will

1. listen to and read a humorous poem.
2. map the plot of the story told by a poet.
3. participate in acting out a poem.

Resources

Ask a student or two to copy Oliver Herford's poem "The Elf and the Dormouse" on the computer (see page 22). Duplicate the poem for each student.

Directions

Step I: Read "The Elf and the Dormouse" aloud. Ask students to think about what is happening in this poem. Then, read it aloud again as they visualize the action described. Give each student a copy of the poem to read. You may want to read it again as they follow their copy. Have someone check the meaning of *dormouse* and *lamented*.

Step II: Have students work in cooperative learning groups using large sheets of paper to map the trails of the elf, the dormouse, and the location of the toadstool. After they have drawn the trails, the members of each group can illustrate the map, showing perhaps a cluster of toadstools at the edge of a meadow, the dormouse's home, and so on.

Step III: Invite a group of students to act out the story as the rest of the class reads the poem. Discuss how the acting was done with suggestions for improving it. Then, have two or more sets of actors dramatize the poem again while the rest of the students read.

Assessment

1. All students receive Pass/Fail evaluations based on their participation.
2. Students will perform this dramatization for another class, perhaps in a large area outdoors or in the multipurpose room.

THINKING + LESSON PLAN 5
Windy Days: A Topic for All Abilities (Grades K–8)

Expected Outcomes

The learner will

1. read poems about the wind.
2. compare the images of the wind made by different poets.
3. collaborate on a class poem about the wind.

Resources

Make copies of Christina Rossetti's poem "Who Has Seen the Wind?" (see page 26) for younger students plus "Wind" (see page 25) for older students. Present the poem and song orally for first graders.

Directions

Step I: Read "Who Has Seen the Wind?" aloud. After each verse ask, "How do we know the wind is around if we can't see it?" (1—The leaves move or rustle. 2—The trees bend, move back and forth.)

Step II: Explain that we often sing poems. Name a song they know, for example, "Row, Row, Row Your Boat." Say the words to that song aloud to show the class that this song began as a poem. Teach the children how to sing the lyrics of "Who Has Seen the Wind?" If you need help, ask a parent or another teacher (or perhaps a student) to play the tune.

Step III: For older students, compare the images of the wind in poems by different people. Have students supply ideas for a class poem beginning with this pattern:

We know the wind is there

When _____,

_____,

Or _____.

We know the wind is here

When_____,

_____,

Or _____.

Assessment

All students receive Pass by participating.

THINKING + LESSON PLAN 6
Experiencing Metaphor: Clouds (Grades 2–8)

Expected Outcomes

The learner will

1. hear a short poem that presents a creative metaphor.
2. use more advanced thinking skills by interpreting the meaning in a metaphor.

Resources

Prepare copies of the worksheet on page 30 focusing on the poem "White Sheep" so that all students have a copy. You could probably present this activity orally with some first graders.

Directions

Step I: Read the short poem "White Sheep" aloud to the class. Ask, "What do you think the poet is talking about in this poem?" Let several students answer, even if they all say much the same thing. Then say, "Now picture what the poet is seeing as I read the poem again."

Step II: Give each student a copy of the worksheet. Read the poem aloud together. Have students answer the questions orally. Encourage varied answers for Question 2. Ask, "Have you ever looked at the clouds and thought they looked like something interesting?"

Step III: Have each student complete the worksheet. Students should read the poem and answer both questions. Any students who have difficulty should work together in small groups. They can practice reading the poem aloud in unison.

Assessment

Students will take this worksheet home to share with family members. Direct them to read the poem aloud and to tell someone about what the poem means. The person they read to is to sign the bottom of the sheet to indicate that the student did follow these directions.

THINKING + LESSON PLAN 7
Listen! What Do You Hear? Taking a Listening Walk (Grades K–8)

Expected Outcomes

The learner will
1. take a walk to observe sounds.
2. join in creating a word wall of "sound words."
3. create a group poem about sounds.

Resources

Mount a large piece of paper on a side wall. Prepare to take your students for a short listening walk near your school. Each student should have something to write on.

Directions

Step I: Ask students to close their eyes and just listen. Ask if they hear any sounds—feet shuffling, the clock ticking, a paper rustling, breathing, a cough. You may provide a few extra sounds—tapping with a pencil, a bell, scraping of a chair being moved.

Step II: Begin a wall display of sound words as students list the kinds of things they hear: ticking, rustling, coughing. Then brainstorm together other sounds they have heard—singing, sniffling, snoring, clapping, talking. After accumulating a number of sound words, explain that you and they are going on a listening walk to observe all the sounds they can hear. Have each student fold an 8½"×11" piece of paper into fourths, so it will be stiff enough to write on. Walk through the school in "follow the leader" fashion and outside onto the playground, then onto nearby streets, if appropriate. Stop occasionally so students can record sound words.

Step III: Back in the classroom, have students take turns suggesting words for the list on the wall. You might begin categorizing some of the words, for example, soft sounds, loud sounds, scary sounds. Then, begin writing a group poem titled "Listen!" that follows this pattern:

Listen!   Listen!
The wind is blowing,   Planes are zooming,
Children singing.   A bell is ringing!

Assessment

Children will participate in this group activity.

THINKING + LESSON PLAN 8
Whisky Frisky: Imitating a Poetry Model (Grades 4–8)

Expected Outcomes

The learner will
    1. discuss the pattern in a rhymed poem about a squirrel.
    2. follow this pattern to create a similar poem about another animal.

Resources

Make copies of "The Squirrel" (see page 43). Have assorted crayons and colored pencils as well as 8½"×11" drawing paper ready to distribute. Display pictures of a wide variety of animals, including a squirrel.

Directions

Step I: Point out the pictures of animals, asking students to name the various animals. Read the rhythmic poem "The Squirrel" aloud as students listen. Then, give them copies of the poem so they can read it aloud with you.

Step II: Ask students what they notice about the pattern this anonymous poet used to compose the first stanza of this poem, for example, "The poem begins with several words that describe the actions of the squirrel." "There are 4 lines." "Lines 2 and 4 rhyme."

Step III: Tell students to choose one of the animals pictured and begin working on a poem that describes that animal following the same pattern used in the first verse of "The Squirrel." First they need to think about the kinds of movements their animal makes. They will also need to make a rhyme list as described on pages 121–122. Talented students may continue their poems following the patterns of the other stanzas.

Assessment

Use the following rubric for evaluation of this writing activity:
    5   Outstanding—Writing more than 4 lines.
    3   Excellent—Completing a 4-line rhyming poem following the pattern.
    1   Good—A line or two completed.
Permit students to work on their poems further to achieve at least an Excellent rating.

THINKING + LESSON PLAN 9
Bells, Bells, Bells: Musical Language (Grades 6–8)

Expected Outcomes

The learner will
    1. listen to Poe's poem about bells.
    2. read lines of this poem together.

Resources

Obtain a copy of Edgar Allan Poe's "The Bells" (see page 44 for the first verse and discussion of Poe's work).

Directions

Step I: Read the first verse of "The Bells" aloud. Then, display this verse on a transparency so that students can read the poem. Have students tap out the rhythm of the lines as you read it aloud again.

Step II: Ask students to join you in reading the poem aloud together.

Step III: Read the other verses of the poem as students listen to the different kinds of bells the poet describes. Discuss the symbolism of the different bells described.

Assessment

Students receive Pass assessments as they participate in experiencing Poe's poem.

THINKING + LESSON PLAN 10
Busy Buzzing Bees: Musical Sounds (Grades 2–8)

Expected Outcomes

The learner will

1. listen to examples of alliteration.
2. write alliterative lines.

Resources

See pages 44–45 for additional information about alliteration. Locate poems that illustrate alliteration, for example, Rhoda Bacmeister's "Galoshes," Rowena Bennett's "The Witch of Willowby Wood," or Walter de la Mare's "Silver" (see page 45), depending on the ability level of your students.

Directions

Step I: Read a poem aloud to the class. Write examples of alliteration on the board to show students how the poet has repeated sounds. Have students repeat some of the alliterative phrases to get the feel of this musical effect.

Step II: Invite students to create alliterative phrases by presenting a short list of animals, for example, puppy, tiger, monkey, snake, lion. Ask them to suggest "sound alikes" to describe the appearance or actions of an animal, expanding the phrase:
Puppy—playful. Expanded: Pretty playful puppies
Tiger—terrible. Expanded: Ten terrible tigers

Step III: As homework, provide students with a list of perhaps 10 nouns that they can play with at home to see how many phrases they can create. (This is an invitation for parents to enjoy word play with their child.)

Assessment

1. Students receive a Pass if they bring their worksheet back to school with one or two alliterative phrases.
2. This lesson will be judged successful if students later recognize examples of alliteration in poetry or prose and if they use alliterative phrases in their writing occasionally.

THINKING + LESSON PLAN 11
Jingle, Jangle: Experiencing Onomatopoeia (Grades 2–8)

Expected Outcomes

The learner will

1. learn to recognize examples of onomatopoeia.
2. create a word wall that lists examples of onomatopoeia.
3. write free verse that combines sounds and rhythms.

Resources

See page 46 for additional information about onomatopoeia. Obtain a copy of Rhoda Bacmeister's "Galoshes." Some of the same poems used in Thinking + Lesson Plan 10 will be useful in this lesson, too. Prepare a large sheet of paper on which to create a word wall.

Directions

Step I: Read aloud the poem "Galoshes," emphasizing the lines that contain such words as *stamp* or *tramp* and *stuck in the muck and the mud*. Explain that the poet has used words that sound like what they mean. We often use such words in our speech, for example, *jingle* and *jangle*. Invite students to begin listing such examples on a word wall.

Step II: Categorize the words as you see groupings that go together, for example, noises, music, flowing, sharp, loud. Note that this activity increases vocabulary. Some words shared may need explaining so all students understand the meanings.

Step III: Encourage students to read the lists on the word wall and to begin composing lines that combine rhythms and sounds, for example,

> Jingle, jangle, Jumpity Jim.
> Leaping lizards, Liza Jane.

Assessment

1. Using various colored pens, students will write lines they have composed on a large sheet of paper mounted on the wall.
2. Students will use onomatopoeia occasionally as they write poetry and prose after experiencing this lesson.

THINKING + LESSON PLAN 12

Star Light, Star Bright: Developing a Speaking Repertoire (Grades K–8)

Expected Outcomes

The learners will
1. share poems they know.
2. perform poems they all know with others.

Resources

Locate various books of poetry. Have several students copy the poems you select (see Step II) on the computer for reproduction.

Directions

This oral language activity focuses on building a class repertoire of poems they can say together much as they might sing songs (see pages 54–59 for additional information).

Step I: Invite students to recite poems they know, for example, "Star Light," verses from Mother Goose, or a jump-rope song like "Teddy Bear, Teddy Bear." If several people know the same poem, they can join in teaching the poem to the whole class. Select a new poem periodically to teach to the class, for example, "I Know an Old Lady Who Swallowed a Fly" or "'Fire! Fire!' Cried Mrs. McGuire!" (see page 36).

Step II: At least once a week, invite the class to recite several poems in their growing repertoire together. Ask, "Which of our poems would you like to start with?" Remind students of the first line before they begin, giving them a little time to adjust their thinking before you begin the recitation with them. Print some of these poems for reading practice for students in the English as a Second Language program or for slower readers. This will help them memorize the words so they can participate. Gradually, develop a ringed notebook collection of class favorites.

Step III: Offer to have your class present some of the poems to another class. As part of the presentation, have students teach the other class one of the poems so they can join in, too.

Assessment

1. Students will participate in oral language activities with increasing enjoyment.
2. Students will request an opportunity to recite poems in chorus and call for favorites.

THINKING + LESSON PLAN 13
Like a Thunderbolt! Making Comparisons (Grades 6–8)

Expected Outcomes

The learner will
1. recognize similes in poetry.
2. read a poem that requires more sophisticated thinking.
3. create similes.

Resources

Make a copy of "The Eagle" by Alfred Lord Tennyson (see page 60) for each student. Also, make a transparency of the printed poem. Do *not* include the title on the transparency.

Directions

Step I: First, show the poem on a transparency. Read it aloud to the class. Ask, "What is happening in this poem?"

Step II: Say, "Think about what the poet is describing as I read the poem again." Then, ask students to write on a slip of paper what they think the poet is describing. After all have recorded their answers, let students share their answers. (If, by chance, no one realizes that the author is talking about an eagle, you may have to give the class some hints or ask leading questions.)

Step III: Ask, "What is a *thunderbolt*?" Say, "'Like a thunderbolt' is a comparison of two things. We call this kind of image a simile." Give students some things they might compare: "What is a book like or what is a dog like?" For example, a sports fan might say, "My dog is like a wary fullback defending his goal." For homework, ask students to look around their home and find five things about which to create similes to enter in their poetry portfolios.

Assessment

Students will share similes in cooperative learning groups. Students will choose the three best in each group to display on a bulletin board.

THINKING + LESSON PLAN 14
Fallen Leaves Are Cornflakes: Introducing the Metaphor (Grades 3–8)

Expected Outcomes

The learner will

1. listen to and read a poem containing a metaphor.
2. brainstorm examples of metaphors.
3. create a poem based on a metaphor.

Resources

This lesson builds on Thinking + Lesson Plan 13 by introducing the metaphor. Make a copy of "December Leaves" (see page vi). A follow-up lesson could be designed around the metaphor in "I Like to See It Lap the Miles" (see page 88) for more advanced students.

Directions

Step I: Ask students to imagine the picture the poet paints in the poem you are going to read. Read "December Leaves" aloud. Have a number of students share the pictures that came to their minds as they listened. Show students a transparency of this poem and have them read it aloud with you. Ask them to identify the comparisons the poet is making for the leaves, lawn, wind, sky, and snow.

Step II: Explain the difference between a simile and a metaphor. This poet says, "leaves are cornflakes." She could have said, "The leaves are *like* cornflakes," which would be a simile. Have students turn to the similes in their poetry portfolios. Ask students to review their similes and then try turning them into metaphors.

Step III: Have each student select his or her favorite metaphor and write a short poem about it.

The students' poems may rhyme or not and may be any length, just so they extend the idea of the metaphor. As students progress, have some ideas read aloud as a way of stimulating thinking. If a student needs help in developing his or her metaphor, ask the class to make suggestions.

Assessment

Students will produce poems that develop a metaphor in some way. Have students include their poems in a class publication titled *Leaves Are Cornflakes*.

THINKING + LESSON PLAN 15
Planning a Mother Goose Presentation (Grades 4–8)

Expected Outcomes

The learner will

1. read Mother Goose rhymes.
2. collaborate with a group on presenting at least one rhyme.
3. participate in a class presentation for a primary grade class.

Resources

Bring in a number of collections of Mother Goose rhymes from the library. Arrange with a primary grade teacher to have your students present a program to his or her class sometime in the future. Refer to Chapter 5 for suggestions about developing this project.

Directions

Step I: Explain how important it is for all primary grade children to know the Mother Goose rhymes that are part of our heritage from Europe. Tell the students that you have volunteered them to present a selection of these verses to _____'s class. Say, "I hope you won't mind helping me with this project. First of all, we need to decide which verses we will present and just how each verse will be presented."

Step II: Number off by fives or sixes to create cooperative learning groups of four to six students each. Direct them to select two or three verses that they would be interested in presenting. (Allow plenty of time for poring over the collections of rhymes.) Bring the groups together to find out the first choice for each group. If there is a duplication, you may have to draw straws and go to second or third choices. List the verses selected on the board. Discuss possible ways of presenting a verse and have the groups decide on what method each will use. Note these choices on the board also. In addition to verses presented by each group, add a few more that the whole group will chant or sing.

Step III: Allow time for practicing and then a full rehearsal. Have several students create an attractive printed program, and schedule the performance.

Assessment

The program will be presented at least once. The response of the primary grade children should be ample proof of how successful the students' efforts were.

THINKING + LESSON PLAN 16
Listing Poems (Grades K–8)

Expected Outcomes

The learner will
1. brainstorm ideas about a topic.
2. collaborate on writing a group listing poem.
3. write an original listing poem (for older students).

Resources

Refer to page 112 for additional information about writing listing poems. Use the excerpt from "Swift Things Are Beautiful" by Elizabeth Coatsworth (see page 106) for students in grades 3–8. Adjust the activity and expectations to fit the maturity and ability level of your students.

Directions

Step I: Brainstorm ideas about any appropriate topic—a holiday, the season, a field trip, an event. List all the words and phrases suggested by students on the board, continuing until you have a fairly long list.

Step II: Invite students to suggest lines to go with one that you provide, depending on the subject, for example, "The circus is coming to town," "Halloween will soon be here," or "It's springtime; it's springtime!" Complete a short, unrhymed poem together to show students how a listing poem is created. Students should review the list on the board to get ideas.

Step III: As homework for older students, each student will write an original listing poem on a topic of his or her choice. Review just how you went about creating a poem in class. Have students list the steps in their poetry portfolios. You may have students choose their topics and begin brainstorming ideas in class so they have a good start before tackling this homework independently.

Assessment

1. All students will participate in brainstorming ideas and creating a group poem.
2. Older students will produce listing poems, fully edited, to include in a class publication titled *These Are Our Favorite Things!*

"If I Were King!" Listing Poems 2 (Grades 2–8)

Expected Outcomes

The learner will

1. listen to a picture book read-aloud.
2. brainstorm ideas around the theme suggested by the book.
3. write a listing poem about the theme.

Resources

Obtain a copy of Fred Hiatt's book *If I Were Queen of the World* and/or Judith Viorst's poem "If I Were King."

Directions

Step I: Read the selected work aloud. Discuss what students would do if they were king (or queen). List ideas on the board.

Step II: Have students write individual poems "If I Were King" or "If I Were Queen" listing all the things they would do.

Step III: Display the poems on a bulletin board decorated with golden crowns that students cut from construction paper.

Assessment

1. Students will participate in listing ideas after reading the book or poem.
2. Students will produce a short listing poem to display.

THINKING + LESSON PLAN 18
Questioning: Writing Free Verse (Grades 3–8)

Expected Outcomes

The learner will

1. listen to and read poems by Hilda Conkling.
2. observe the pattern used in her free verse.
3. imitate one of Conkling's poems to create a new one.

Resources

Obtain copies of several of Hilda Conkling's poems. Copy one example on a transparency (see page 114 for additional information). Displaying pictures of different animals, including a mouse, on the bulletin board would be helpful.

Directions

Step I: Read several of Hilda Conkling's poems aloud, including "Little Mouse" (see page 114).

Step II: Show "Little Mouse" on a transparency. Ask students to identify the questions that the poet asks.

Step III: Have students imitate Conkling's questioning technique to create an original poem that addresses a different animal. Students may work on their poems at home to complete them.

Assessment

1. Students will participate in the class discussion about Conkling's poems.
2. Students will produce short free verse poems like Conkling's to contribute to a class publication.

THINKING + LESSON PLAN 19
Writing Limericks (Grades 3–8)

Expected Outcomes

The learner will

1. listen to a number of limericks.
2. identify the form and rhyme scheme of a limerick.
3. compose original limericks.

Resources

See pages 126–128 for information about limericks. Place "A Young Farmer of Leeds" on a transparency for use in introducing this lesson. Do *not* use an example by Edward Lear, as he uses a varied rhyming pattern.

Directions

Step I: Read several limericks aloud.

Step II: Display a sample limerick on a transparency so that students can identify the pattern followed by the poet. Invite students to read the poem aloud with you. Then, have them tell you which lines rhyme (1, 2, and 5; 3 and 4).

Step III: Have students work in pairs to create an original limerick. Suggest that most limericks begin with these traditional words: *There was* or *There once was*.

Assessment

1. Students will participate in the class discussion of limericks.
2. Most students will produce limericks to place in a class book titled *Lively Limericks!*

T H I N K I N G + L E S S O N P L A N 2 0
Illustrating a Poem (Grades 3–8)

Expected Outcomes

The learner will

1. select a favorite poem to copy using the computer.
2. illustrate the poem.
3. place the poem in a class collection of favorites to place in the school library.

Resources

Bring in a large collection of poetry books from the library. Also, have various art supplies available.

Directions

Step I: Students will spend time browsing through poetry books to select a favorite poem. They should be prepared to tell why they chose a particular poem.

Step II: Take the class to the computer lab (or schedule time in the classroom) so students can copy the poem they select. Show them how to select an interesting font to use. Encourage them to try more than one font so they compare to choose one they like best.

Step III: Have students illustrate their poems. Then, collect the poems in a volume titled *Our Favorite Poems*.

Assessment

1. Students will select poems to present using the computer. Each will then copy and illustrate one poem.
2. Each student will share the poem he or she selected with the class either by reading it aloud or recording it for the listening center.
3. Students will produce a class publication that can be placed in the school library.

THINKING + LESSON PLAN 21
Focusing on Diversity: Immigrants (Grades 4–8)

Expected Outcomes

The learner will

1. read Emma Lazarus's poem "The New Colossus," which appears on the Statue of Liberty.
2. discuss the meaning of the poem.
3. learn more about the immigration process and becoming a U.S. citizen.

Resources

Have a large collection of poetry books, especially those that relate to multiculturalism. See pages 154–155 for suggestions.

Directions

This is a multicultural lesson that focuses on the diversity in our population. This is a good culminating activity for Poetry Month (April).

Step I: Read "The New Colossus" aloud (see page 158). Discuss what this poem means and why it appears on the Statue of Liberty.

Step II: Have students investigate the topic of immigration on the Internet. Follow up with a discussion of how immigrants become new citizens of the United States.

Step III: Have students create a bulletin board display in the school hallway featuring this poem and the information about immigration that students have learned. This activity could be featured on Columbus Day or another suitable date. Use Thinking + Lesson Plan 16 to guide students to compose listing poems about the topic of immigration or immigrants. Their poems could be part of the display.

Assessment

1. Students will share in gathering information and preparing the bulletin board display.
2. Students will write listing poems about immigrants or immigration.
3. Students will share their findings with other classes, including poetry recitations, for example, choric speaking.

T H I N K I N G + L E S S O N P L A N 2 2
Planning a Culminating Celebration: Poetry Month (Grades 3–8)

Expected Outcomes

The learner will
  1. brainstorm in small groups.
  2. participate in planning a program.
  3. participate in presenting a poetry program to parents.

Resources

Bring in an assortment of poetry anthologies from the library. Have paper available for planning groups.

Directions

Step I: Talk with students about all the poetry activities they have engaged in during the past months. Make a list on the board as a way of reviewing the year's work.

Step II: Suggest planning a presentation for parents as a way of sharing what students have learned. You might plan the program for the end of April, which is National Poetry Month. Have students work in cooperative learning groups as they brainstorm how they might share some of the poems they especially like and activities they enjoyed that are listed on the board. They also can refer to their Poetry Portfolios to remind them of all they did. After groups have had time to think together, suggest that each group choose one activity that it would like to contribute to the program.

Step III: Students will consider the activities suggested to be sure there is variety and no repetition. They will rehearse the program.

Step IV: Students will invite their parents to an afternoon event at which they will present a brief program titled perhaps *Poetry Is For You, Too!* Students can make a printed program and serve a simple snack of cookies and punch for their guests.

Assessment

  1. Students will participate in the planning activities.
  2. Students will participate in presenting the poetry program.

Further Resources for the Teacher

The ideas presented in this book and the poems and books suggested are enough to get you started teaching with poetry in your K–8 classroom. In this appendix, you'll find resources that will help you locate more information. Included, too, is a list of poetry books that have won the Caldecott Award.

Professional Journals

Following are addresses for journals to which you or your school's library might wish to subscribe. Those marked with an asterisk are included with membership in a professional organization that presents conferences and provides support for educators. All include information related to the use of poetry in K–8 classrooms at various times during the year.

Book Links: Connecting Books, Libraries, and Classrooms. American Library Association, 50 Huron St., Chicago, IL 60611; http://www.ala.org; published bimonthly.

* *English Journal.* National Council of Teachers of English, 1111 W. Kenyon Rd., Urbana, IL 61801; http://www.ncte.org. Available with membership in NCTE; directed to middle school and secondary school teachers.

* *Journal of Adolescent & Adult Literacy.* International Reading Association, 800 Barksdale Rd., Newark, DE 19714; http://www.reading.org. Available with membership in IRA; directed to middle school and secondary school teachers.

Journal of Children's Literature. Children's Literature Assembly, National Council of Teachers of English, 1111 W. Kenyon Rd., Urbana, IL 61801; http://www.ncte.org. Available with membership in NCTE plus membership in the Assembly.

* *Language Arts.* National Council of Teachers of English, 1111 W. Kenyon Rd., Urbana, IL 61801; http://www.ncte.org. Available with membership in NCTE; directed to elementary and middle school teachers.

The New Advocate. Christopher-Gordon Publishers, 480 Washington St., Norwood, MA 02062. Directed to elementary and middle school teachers.

* *The Reading Teacher*. International Reading Association, 800 Barksdale Rd., Newark, DE 19714; http://www.reading.org. Available with membership in IRA; directed to elementary and middle school teachers.

Teachers & Writers. 5 Union Square West, New York, NY 10003-3306. Suitable for upper elementary, middle school, and secondary teachers.

Selected Articles

Brown, T.W., & Laminack, L.L. (1999). Let's talk a poem. *Young Children, 44,* 49–52.

Dakin, M.E. (2001). The Poet, the CEO, and the first-grade teacher. *Harvard Educational Review, 71,* 269–284.

Ford, M.P. (1989). *Reaching the heart: Quality poetry instruction for young children.* Paper presented at Annual Convention, Association for Childhood Education International, Indianapolis, IN.

Galda, L. (1989). Children's poetry. *The Reading Teacher, 43,* 1.

Lukasevich, A. (1984). Making poetry a natural experience for young children. *Childhood Education, 61,* 36–42.

Pinsky, R. (2001, September). The physicality of poetry. *Teachers & Writers, 31,* 1–4.

Schneider, D. (2001, April/May). Something beautiful: Reading picture books, writing poetry. *Book Links, 10*(5), 31–34.

Statman, M. (2000). Listener in the snow: The practice and teaching of poetry. *Teachers & Writers, 31,* 12–13.

Walders, D. (1999, April 28). Rhyme and reason: How a good poem can change the rhythm of a class. *Education Week, 33,* 4: 3,12.

Professional Books

This list presents books that provide additional information about using poetry in the classroom. The books listed here are meant to supplement those discussed specifically within the text.

Barton, B., & Booth, D. (1995). *Mother Goose goes to school.* Portland, ME: Stenhouse.

Booth, D., & Moore, B. (1988). *Poems, please! Sharing poetry with children.* Portland, ME: Stenhouse.

Chatton, B. (1993). *Using poetry across the curriculum: A whole language approach.* Phoenix, AZ: Oryx.

Collom, J. (1998). *Moving windows: Evaluating the poetry children write.* New York: Teachers & Writers' Collaborative.

Collom, J., & Noethe, S. (1999). *Poetry everywhere: Teaching poetry writing in school and in the community.* New York: Teachers & Writers' Collaborative.

Cullinan, B. (Ed.). (1996). *A jar of tiny stars: Poems by NCTE award-winning poets.* Urbana, IL: National Council of Teachers of English; Honesdale, PA: Boyds Mills Press.

Cullinan, B., & Harrison, D. (1999). *Easy poetry lessons that dazzle and delight (grades 3–6).* New York: Scholastic.

Cullinan, B., Scala, M., & Schroder, V. (1995). *Three voices: An invitation to poetry across the curriculum.* Portland, ME: Stenhouse.

Deutsch, B. (1987). *Poetry handbook: A dictionary of terms.* Totowa, NJ: Barnes & Noble.

Dunning, S., & Stafford, W. (1992). *Getting the knack: 20 poetry writing exercises.* Urbana, IL: National Council of Teachers of English.

Fagin, L. (1997). *The list poem: A guide to teaching & writing catalog verse.* New York: Teachers & Writers' Collaborative.

Flynn, N., & McPhillips, S. (2000). *A note slipped under the door: Teaching from poems we love.* Portland, ME: Stenhouse.

Glover, M.K. (1999). *A garden of poets: Poetry writing in the elementary classroom.* Urbana, IL: National Council of Teachers of English.

Hansen, M.P., & Bilch, L. (Eds.). (1999). *Instant activities for poetry (grades 3–6).* New York: Scholastic.

Hewitt, G. (1998). *Today you are my favorite poet: Writing poetry with teenagers.* Boston: Boynton/Cook.

Higginson, W., & Harter, P. (1996). *The haiku handbook: How to write, share, and teach haiku.* Hong Kong: Kodansha.

Jago, C. (1999). *Nikki Giovanni in the classroom: "The same ol' danger but a brand new pleasure."* Urbana, IL: National Council of Teachers of English.

Jago, C. (2000). *Alice Walker in the classroom: "Living by the word."* Urbana, IL: National Council of Teachers of English.

Janeczko, P.B. (Ed.). (1994). *Favorite poetry lessons (grades 4–8).* New York: Atheneum.

Janeczko, P.B. (Ed.). (1994). *Poetry from A to Z: A guide for young writers.* New York: Atheneum.

Janeczko, P.B. (Ed.). (1999). *How to write poetry.* New York: Scholastic.

Janeczko, P.B. (Ed.). (2001). *A poke in the I: A collection of concrete poems.* Cambridge, MA: Candlewick.

Koch, K. (1990). *Rose, where did you get that red? Teaching great poetry to children.* New York: Vintage.

Koch, K. (1998). *I never told anybody: Teaching poetry writing to old people.* New York: Teachers & Writers' Collaborative.

Koch, K. (1999). *Making your own days: The pleasures of reading and writing poetry.* New York: Scribners.

Koch, K. (2000). *Wishes, lies, and dreams: Teaching children to write poetry* (2nd ed.). New York: Harper.

Livingstone, M.C. (1991). *Poem-making: Ways to begin writing poetry.* New York: HarperCollins.

Michaels, J. (1999). *Risking intensity: Reading and writing poetry with high school students.* Urbana, IL: National Council of Teachers of English.

Moon, B. (2001). *Studying poetry: Activities, resources, and texts.* Urbana, IL: National Council of Teachers of English.

Morice, D. (1999). *How to make poetry comics.* New York: Teachers & Writers' Collaborative.

Morice, D. (2000). *The adventures of Dr. Alphabet: 104 unusual ways to write poetry in the classroom and in the community.* New York: Teachers & Writers' Collaborative.

Opitz, M. (2000). *Rhymes and reasons: Literature and language play for phonological awareness.* Portsmouth, NH: Heineman.

Padgett, R. (2000). *Poetic forms: 10 audio programs hosted by Ron Padgett.* New York: Teachers & Writers' Collaborative.

Padgett, R. (Ed.). (2000). *The T & W handbook of poetic forms* (2nd ed.). New York: Teachers & Writers' Collaborative.

Polonsky, M. (1996). *The poetry reader's toolkit.* New York: NTC Publishing.

Routman, R. (2000). *Kids' poems.* New York: Scholastic.

Somers, A.B. (1999). *Teaching poetry in high school.* Urbana, IL: National Council of Teachers of English.

Sunsenez, J. (1999). *Teaching poetry: Yes you can (grades 4–8).* New York: Scholastic.

Tannenbaum, J. (2000). *Teeth, wiggly as earthquakes: Writing poetry in the primary grades.* Portland, ME: Stenhouse.

Tiedt, I.M. (1983). *The language arts handbook.* Englewood Cliffs, NJ: Prentice-Hall.

Tiedt, I.M. (1989). *Exploring books with children.* Boston: Houghton Mifflin.

Tiedt, I.M. (2000). *Teaching with picture books in the middle school.* Newark, DE: International Reading Association.

Tiedt, P., & Tiedt, I.M. (2002). *Multicultural teaching: A handbook of activities, information, and resources* (6th ed.). Boston: Allyn & Bacon.

Tiedt, P., Tiedt, I.M., & Tiedt, S.W. (2001). *Language arts activities in the classroom* (3rd ed.). Boston: Allyn & Bacon.

Weisbart, J. (2001). *Joyful ways to teach young children to write poetry*. New York: Scholastic.

Selected Websites

The following websites supplement those included within the list of professional journals.

Academy of American Poets
http://www.poets.org

The ALAN Review
http://Scholar.lib.vt.edu/ejournals/ALAN/alan-review.html

Bookwire
http://www.bookwire.com

The Children's Book Council
http://www.cbcbooks.org

The Horn Book
http://www.hbook.com

The Lion and the Unicorn
http://Muse.jhu.edu/journals/uni

Pen American Center
http://www.pen.org

Poetry Society of America
http://www.poetrysociety.org

Poets & Writers
http://www.pw.org

Teachers & Writers Collaborative
http://www.twc.org

Caldecott Award-Winning Children's Poetry Books

The following poetry books have won the Randolph J. Caldecott Award given annually by the American Library Association.

1945

Prayer for a Child, illustrated by Elizabeth Orton Jones; text by Rachel Field. (Macmillan)

Honor Book: *Mother Goose,* illustrated by Tasha Tudor. (Oxford University Press)

1946

Honor Book: *Sing Mother Goose,* illustrated by Marjorie Torrey; music by Opal Wheeler. (Dutton)

1947

Honor Book: *Sing in Praise: A Collection of the Best Loved Hymns,* illustrated by Marjorie Torrey; text selected by Opal Wheeler. (Dutton)

1955

Honor Book: *Book of Nursery and Mother Goose Rhymes,* illustrated by Marguerite de Angeli. (Doubleday)

1956

Frog Went A-Courtin', illustrated by Feodor Rojankovsky; text retold by John Langstaff. (Harcourt)

1959

Honor Book: *The House That Jack Built: La Maison Que Jacques A Batie* by Antonio Frasconi. (Harcourt)

1962

Honor Book: *Fox Went Out on a Chilly Night: An Old Song* by Peter Spier. (Doubleday)

1963

Honor Book: *The Sun Is a Golden Earring,* illustrated by Bernarda Bryson; text by Natalia M. Belting. (Holt)

1964

Honor Book: *Mother Goose and Nursery Rhymes,* illustrated by Philip Reed. (Atheneum)

1972

Honor Book: *If All the Seas Were One Sea* by Janina Domanska. (Macmillan)

1982

Honor Book: *A Visit to William Blake's Inn: Poems for Innocent and Experienced Travelers,* illustrated by Alice & Martin Provensen; text by Nancy Willard. (Harcourt)

1997

Honor Book: *Hush! A Thai Lullaby,* illustrated by Holly Meade; text by Minfong Ho. (Melanie Kroupa/Orchard Books)

1998

Honor Book: *There Was an Old Lady Who Swallowed a Fly* by Simms Taback. (Viking)

Bloom, H. (2001). *The joys of reading*. Boston: Houghton Mifflin.

The Children's Book Council. (1976). *Poetry, children and children's books*. New York: Author.

Demerdjian, T. (2001, February). Poetry consultant helps English learners 'speak out loud.' *The Council Chronicle, 16*, 4.

Ford, M. (1987). *Quality poetry instruction for young children*. Unpublished doctoral dissertation, University of Indiana, Bloomington.

Gardner, H. (1999). *The well-disciplined mind: What all students should understand*. Paper presented at annual meeting of the American Educational Research Association, Montreal, Canada.

Koch, K. (2000). *Wishes, lies, and dreams: Teaching children to write poetry*. New York: HarperPerennial.

Kuskin, K. (1979). Acceptance speech for National Council of Teachers of English Award for Excellence in Poetry for Children. Presented at the 1979 National Council of Teachers of English annual convention in Atlanta, GA.

Mackintosh, M. (1924). *Poetry teaching*. Urbana, IL: National Council of Teachers of English.

Schneider, D. (2001, April/May). Something beautiful: Reading picture books, writing poetry. *Book Links, 10*(5), 31–34.

Sepura, B.J. (1994). Integrating poetry into the daily curriculum. *The Reading Teacher, 47*, 54–57.

Terry, A. (1974). *Poetry preferences* (Research Report). Urbana, IL: National Council of Teachers of English.

Tiedt, I.M. (1962, November). The challenge. *The Educational Forum, XXVII*, p. 78.

Tiedt, I.M. (1970). Exploring poetry patterns. *Elementary English, 47*(8), 1082–1085.

Tiedt, I.M. (2000). *Teaching with picture books in the middle school*. Newark, DE: International Reading Association.

Tiedt, P., & Tiedt, I.M. (2002). *Multicultural teaching: A handbook of activities, information and resources* (6th ed). Boston: Allyn & Bacon.

Tiedt, P., Tiedt, I.M., & Tiedt, S. (2001). *Language arts activities in the classroom*. Boston: Allyn & Bacon.

Tom, T. (1969). *Poetry instruction in grades 4–6*. Unpublished doctoral dissertation. Harvard University, Cambridge, MA.

Poetry Collections and Children's Literature Cited

Ackerman, K. (Ed.). (1990). *A brighter garden: Poetry by Emily Dickinson*. New York: Philomel.

Ada, A.F. (1997). *Gathering the sun: An alphabet in Spanish and English*. New York: Lothrop, Lee & Shepard.

Adedjouma, D. (1998). *The palm of my heart*. New York: Lee & Low.

Adoff, A. (1974). *My black me: A big book of poetry*. New York: Dutton.

Adoff, A. (1979). *Eats*. New York: Lothrop.

Adoff, A. (1986). *Sports pages*. New York: Lippincott.

Adoff, A. (Ed.). (1997). *I am the darker brother: An anthology of modern poems by African Americans*. New York: Simon & Schuster.

Adoff, A. (2000). *The basket counts*. New York: Simon & Schuster.

Alarcón, F.X. (1997). *Laughing tomatoes and other spring poems*. San Francisco: Children's Book Press.

Alarcon, F.X. (1998). *From the bellybutton of the moon and other summer poems*. San Francisco: Children's Book Press.

Alarcón, F.X. (1999). *Angels ride bikes and other fall poems*. San Francisco: Children's Book Press.

Aldan, D. (1969). *Poems from India*. New York: Thomas Crowell.

Aliki. (2000). *William Shakespeare & the Globe*. New York: HarperCollins.

Amon, A. (1981). *The earth is sore*. New York: Atheneum.

Anglund, J.W. (1989). *A little book of poems & prayers*. New York: Simon & Schuster.

Anglund, J.W. (Illus.). (1960). *A Mother Goose ABC: In a pumpkin shell*. San Diego: Harcourt.

Atwood, A. (1973). *My own rhythm: An approach to haiku*. New York: Scribner.

Bagert, B. (Ed.). (1995). *Poetry for young people: Edgar Allan Poe*. New York: Sterling.

Bailey, A.C. (1996). *To remember Robert Louis Stevenson*. New York: McKay.

Baring-Gould, W.S., & Baring-Gould, C. (1962). *The annotated Mother Goose: Nursery rhymes old and new, arranged and explained*. New York: Potter.

Baron, V.O. (1969). *Here I am!* New York: Dutton.

Barrett, J. (1998). *Things that are most in the world*. New York: Simon & Schuster.

Barton, J.S. (1998). *Little feelings*. Amherst, NY: Prometheus.

Baxter, N. (Ed.). (1996). *The children's classic poetry collection*. New York: Smithmark.

Behn, H. (Ed.). (1964). *Cricket songs: Japanese Haiku*. San Diego: Harcourt.

Behn, H. (Ed.). (1971). *More cricket songs: Japanese Haiku*. San Diego: Harcourt.

Belting, N. (1962). *The sun is a golden earring*. New York: Holt.

Belting, N. (1964). *Calendar moon*. New York: Holt.

Belting, N. (1965). *The earth is on a fish's back*. New York: Holt.

Belting, N. (1974). *Whirlwind is a ghost dancing*. New York: Dutton.

Bender, M. (1999). *All the world's a stage: A pop-up biography of William Shakespeare*. San Francisco: Chronicle Books.

Bontemps, A. (1941). *Golden slippers: An anthology*. New York: Harper.

Brenner, B. (2000). *Voices: Poetry and art from around the world*. Washington, DC: National Geographic Society.

Brooke, L. (1922). *Ring o'roses: A nursery rhyme picture book*. New York: Warne.

Brooks, G. (1956). *Bronzeville boys and girls*. New York: Harper.

Brown, C. (1999). *Polkabats and octopus slacks: 14 stories*. Boston: Houghton Mifflin.

Brown, C. (2000). *Dutch sneakers and flea keepers: 14 more stories*. Boston: Houghton Mifflin.

Brown, M. (1991). *Good night, moon*. New York: Harper.

Brown, M. (1991). *The runaway bunny*. New York: Harper.

Brown, M.T. (1994). *Scared silly: A book for the brave*. Boston: Little, Brown.

Bunting, E. (1999). *Butterfly house*. New York: Scholastic.

Caldecott, R. (n.d.). *Hey diddle diddle picture book*. New York: Warne.

Carle, E. (1999). *The very lonely firefly*. New York: Philomel.

Carlson, L.M. (Ed.). (1994). *Cool salsa: Bilingual poems on growing up Latino in the United States.* New York: Holt.

Carroll, J.A., & Wilson, E.E. (Eds.). (1997). *Poetry after lunch: Poems to read aloud.* Spring, TX: Absey.

Carroll, L. (2001). *Alice's adventures in wonderland.* New York: HarperCollins.

Catalano, D. (1998). *Frog went a-courting: A musical play in six acts.* Honesdale, PA: Boyds Mills.

Chall, M.W. (1992). *Up north at the cabin.* New York: Lothrop.

Chaucer, G. (1988). *Canterbury tales.* (B. Cohen, Trans.). New York: Lothrop, Lee & Shepard.

Ciardi, J. (1962). *You read to me, I'll read to you.* New York: Lippincott.

Cleary, B. (1965). *The Mouse and the motorcycle.* New York: Morrow.

Clifton, L. (1969). *Good times.* New York: Random.

Clifton, L. (1987). *Some of the days of Everett Anderson.* New York: Holt.

Clifton, L. (1989). *Good woman: Poems and a memoir 1969–1980.* Rochester, NY: BOA Editions.

Clifton, L. (2000). *Blessing the boats: New and selected poems 1988–2000.* Rochester, NY: BOA Editions.

Clinton, C. (Ed.). (2000). *I, too, sing America: Three centuries of African American poetry.* New York: Audio Bookshelf.

Cole, J., & Calmenson, S. (1999). *Give the dog a bone: Stories, poems, jokes, and riddles about dogs.* New York: Scholastic.

Collay, R., & Dubrow, J. (1998). *Stuartship.* Eugene, OR: Flower Press.

Collins, B. (2001). *Sailing alone around the room.* New York: Random House.

Copeland, J.S. (1993). *Speaking of poets: Interviews with poets who write for children and young adults.* Urbana, IL: National Council of Teachers of English.

Copeland, J.S., & Copeland, V.L. (1995). *Speaking of poets 2: More interviews with poets who write for children and young adults.* Urbana, IL: National Council of Teachers of English.

Cousins, L. (1996). *Jack and Jill and other nursery rhymes.* New York: Dutton.

Davis, K. (1999). *I hate to go to bed!* San Diego: Harcourt Brace.

de Angeli, M. (Illus.). (1954). *Marguerite de Angeli's book of nursery and Mother Goose rhymes.* Garden City, NY: Doubleday.

de Paola, T. (1985). *Tomie de Paola's Mother Goose.* New York: Putnam.

de Regniers, B.S., Moore, E., & White, M.M. (1988). *Sing a song of popcorn.* New York: Scholastic.

Denton, K.M. (1998). *A child's treasury of nursery rhymes.* New York: Kingfisher.

Doris, M. (1997). *Morning girl.* Garden City, NY: Doubleday.

Dotlich, R.K. (1998). *Lemonade sun and other summer poems.* Honesdale, PA: Boyds Mills.

Dunbar, P.L. (1978). *Greet the dawn.* New York: Atheneum.

Dyer, J. (1996). *Animal crackers: A delectable collection of pictures, poems, and lullabies for the very young.* Boston: Little, Brown.

Eagle, K. (1999). *Humpty dumpty.* Dallas, TX: Whispering Coyote Press.

Edens, C. (1998). *The glorious Mother Goose.* New York: Atheneum.

Faber, D. (1964). *Robert Frost: America's poet.* Englewood Cliffs, NJ: Prentice Hall.

Feeling, T., & Greenfield, E. (1993). *Daydreamers.* New York: Dutton.

Florian, D. (1997). *In the swim.* San Diego: Harcourt.

Florian, D. (1998). *Insectlopedia.* San Diego: Harcourt.

Florian, D. (1999). *Winter eyes.* New York: Greenwillow.

Florian, D. (2000). *Mammalabilia.* San Diego: Harcourt.

Galdone, P. (1960). *The house that Jack built*. New York: McGraw-Hill.

Galdone, P. (1960). *Old Mother Hubbard and her dog*. New York: McGraw-Hill.

Galdone, P. (1960). *The old woman and her pig*. New York: McGraw-Hill.

Galdone, P. (1964). *Tom, Tom, the piper's son*. New York: McGraw-Hill.

Galdone, P. (1966). *The history of Simple Simon*. New York: McGraw-Hill.

Gilchrist, J.S. (Illus.). (1995). *Lift ev'ry voice and sing*. New York: Scholastic.

Giovanni, N. (1971). *Spin a soft black song*. New York: Hill and Wang.

Giovanni, N. (1996). *The sun is so quiet*. New York: Holt.

Goldstein, B. (1992). *What's on the menu?* New York: Viking.

Goldstone, B. (1998). *The beastly feast*. New York: Holt.

Graham, J.B. (1999). *Flicker flash*. Boston: Houghton Mifflin.

Graham, J.B. (2000). *Touch the poem*. New York: Blue Sky/Scholastic.

Greenfield, E. (1993). *Daydreamers*. New York: Dutton.

Grimes, N. (1978). *Something on my mind*. New York: Dial.

Grimes, N. (1997). *It's raining laughter*. New York: Dial.

Grimes, N. (2000). *Shoe magic*. New York: Orchard.

Grover, E. (Ed.). (1915). *Mother Goose: The original Volland edition*. New York: Checkerboard Press.

Guthrie, W. (1998). *This land is your land*. Boston: Little, Brown.

Hacker, J.H. (1984). *Carl Sandburg*. New York: Watts.

Halpern, S. (1997). *Old MacDonald had a farm*. New York: North-South.

Hamanaka, S. (1999). *I look like a girl*. New York: Morrow.

Harrison, M., & Stuart-Clark, C. (1995). *The new Oxford treasury of children's poems*. Oxford, UK: Oxford University Press.

Hartmann, W. (1994). *One sun rises: An African wildlife counting book*. New York: Dutton.

Heide, F.P. (2000). *Some things are scary*. Cambridge, MA: Candlewick.

Hiatt, F. (1997). *If I were queen of the world*. New York: Simon & Schuster.

Highwater, J. (1981). *Moonsong lullaby*. New York: Lothrop.

Hines, A.G. (2001). *Pieces: A year in poems & quilts*. New York: Greenwillow.

Hoberman, M.A. (1998). *The llama who had no pajama*. San Diego: Harcourt Brace.

Hopkins, L.B. (Ed.). (1969). *Don't you turn back: Poems by Langston Hughes*. New York: Knopf.

Hopkins, L.B. (1985). *Creatures*. San Diego: Harcourt.

Hopkins, L.B. (1985). *Munching: Poems about eating*. Boston: Little, Brown.

Hopkins, L.B. (Ed.). (1988). *Side by side: Poems to read together*. New York: Simon & Schuster.

Hopkins, L.B. (Ed.). (1998). *Climb into my lap: First poems to read together*. New York: Holt.

Hopkins, L.B. (2000). *Yummy: Eating through a day*. New York: Simon & Schuster.

Hornby, G. (1975). *Poems for children and other people*. New York: Crown.

Houston, J. (1972). *Songs of the dream people*. New York: Atheneum.

Hubbell, P. (1998). *Boo! Halloween poems and limericks*. Rochester, NY: Marshall Cavendish.

Hudson, W. (Ed.). (1993). *Pass it on: African-American poetry for children*. New York: Scholastic.

Hughes, L.A. (Ed.). (1975). *America's favorite poems*. Waukesha, WI: Country Beautiful Corporation.

Hughes, T. (2000). *The mermaid's purse*. New York: Knopf.

Hummon, D. (1999). *Animal acrostics*. Philadelphia: Dawn.

Isaacs, A. (1998). *Cat up a tree: A story in poems*. New York: Dutton.

Jacobs, J. (1984). *The fables of Aesop*. New York: Macmillan.

Jacobs, W.J. (1975). *Edgar Allan Poe: Genius in torment*. New York: McGraw Hill.

James, S. (Ed.). (2000). *Days like this: A collection of small poems*. Cambridge, MA: Candlewick.

Janeczko, P.B. (Ed.). (2000). *Stone bench in an empty park*. New York: Orchard.

Johnston, T. (Ed.). (2000). *It's about dogs*. San Diego: Harcourt.

Jordan, J. (1969). *Who look at me?* New York: Thomas Crowell.

Jordan, J., & Bush, T. (Eds.). (1979). *The voices of the children*. New York: Holt.

Kamen, G. (1985). *Kipling: Storyteller of east and west*. New York: Atheneum.

Keats, E.J. (1996). *The snowy day*. New York: Viking.

Keller, R. (Illus.). (1979). *Edna St. Vincent Millay's poems selected for young people*. New York: Harper.

Kellogg, S. (2000). *Give the dog a bone*. Minneapolis, MN: Sea Star Books.

Koch, K. (1973). *Rose, where did you get that red?* New York: Random House.

Koch, K., & Farrell, K. (Eds.). (1985). *Talking to the sun: An illustrated anthology of poems for young people*. New York: Holt.

Kohl, H., & Cruz, V.H. (1970). *Stuff*. New York: World.

Krull, K. (Ed.). (1994). *Comedies, tragedies (and what the neighbors thought)*. New York: Harcourt.

LaFontaine. (1806). *A hundred fables*. London: Bodley Head.

Lansky, B. (1991). *Kids pick the funniest poems*. New York: Meadowbrook Press.

Lansky, B. (1999). *The new adventures of Mother Goose: Gentle rhymes for happy times*. New York: Atheneum.

Layne, S.L. (2001). *Life's literacy lessons: Poems for teachers*. Newark, DE: International Reading Association.

Larrick, N. (Ed.). (1988) *Cats are cats*. New York: Philomel.

Larrick, N. (Ed.). (1990). *Mice are nice*. New York: Philomel.

Lewis, J.P. (1999). *The bookworm's feast: A potluck of poems*. New York: Dial.

Lewis, R. (1965). *In a spring garden*. New York: Dial.

Lewis, R. (1967). *Moon, for what do you wait? Poems by Tagore*. New York: Atheneum.

Lewis, R. (Ed.). (1970). *Still waters of the air: Poems by three modern Spanish poets*. New York: Dial.

Lewis, R. (1971). *Poems of the Eskimo*. New York: Simon & Schuster.

Lillegard, D. (2000). *Wake up house: Rooms full of poems*. New York: Knopf.

Little, L.J. (1988). *Children of long ago*. New York: Philomel.

Livingstone, M.C. (Ed.). (1989). *Halloween poems*. New York: Holiday.

Livingstone, M.C. (1989). *Poems for fathers*. New York: Holiday.

Lobel, A. (Illus.). (1984). *'Twas the night before Christmas*. New York: Knopf.

Lobel, A. (1986). *The Random House book of Mother Goose: A treasury of 306 timeless nursery rhymes*. New York: Random House.

Logue, M. (1998). *Love: The story of Elizabeth Barrett Browning*. Chicago: The Child's World.

Longfellow, H.W. (1960). *The song of Hiawatha*. New York: Dutton.

Longfellow, H.W. (1990). *Paul Revere's ride*. Ill. T. Rand. New York: Dutton.

Lottridge, C.B. (1996). *Mother Goose: A sampler*. Toronto, Ontario, Canada: Groundwood.

MacLachlan, P. (1994). *All the places to love*. New York: HarperCollins.

Mavor, S. (1997). *You and me: Poems of friendship*. New York: Orchard.

McCaughrean, G. (1985). *The Canterbury tales.* Chicago: Rand-McNally.

McFarlane, S. (1992). *Jessie's island.* Boston: Orca.

McLerran, A. (1991). *Roxaboxen.* New York: Lothrop.

Medina, T. (2001). *DeShawn days.* New York: Lee & Low.

Melmed, L.K. (1999). *Jumbo's lullaby.* New York: Lothrop.

Merriam, E. (1969). *The inner city mother goose.* New York: Simon & Schuster.

Merriam, E., & Larrick, N. (1973). *Male and female under 18.* New York: Avon.

Mora, P. (1992). *A birthday basket for Tia.* New York: Simon & Schuster.

Mora, P. (1994). *The desert is my mother: El desierto es mi madre.* Houston: Arte Publico.

Mora, P. (1995). *The gift of the poinsettia: El regalo de la flor de nochebuena.* Houston: Arte Publico.

Mora, P. (1996). *Confetti: Poems for children.* New York: Lee & Low.

Mora, P. (1998). *Delicious hullabaloo: Pachanga deliciosa.* Houston, TX: Arte Publico.

Mora, P. (1998). *This big sky.* New York: Scholastic.

Mora, P. (2000). *My own true name: New and selected poems for young adults.* Houston, TX: Arte Publico.

Mora, P. (2001). *The bakery lady: La senora de la panaderia.* Houston, TX: Piñata Books.

Mora, P. (2001). *Listen to the desert: Oye al desierto.* Phoenix, AZ: Clarion.

Mora, P. (2001). *Love to mama: A tribute to mothers.* New York: Lee & Low.

Morrison, L. (1995). *Slam dunk: Poems about basketball.* New York: Hyperion.

Moss, J. (1997). *Bone Poems.* New York: Workman.

Myers, C. (Illus.). (1997). *Harlem: A poem by Walter Dean Myers.* New York: Scholastic.

Myers, C. (1999). *Black cat.* New York: Scholastic.

Myers, W.D.(1993). *Brown angels.* New York: HarperCollins.

Nye, N.S. (Ed.). (1995). *The tree is older than you are: A bilingual gathering of poems and stories from Mexico with paintings by Mexican artists.* New York: Simon & Schuster.

Nye, N.S. (2000). *Come with me: Poems for a journey.* New York: Greenwillow.

O'Neill, M. (1989). *Hailstones and halibut bones: Adventures in color* (2nd ed.). Garden City, NY: Doubleday.

Opie, I. (Ed.). (1996). *My very first Mother Goose.* Cambridge, MA: Candlewick.

Opie, I. (Ed.). (1999). *Here comes Mother Goose.* Cambridge, MA: Candlewick.

Orie, S.D. (1995). *Did you hear wind sing your name? An Oneida song of spring.* New York: Walker.

Pellowski A., et al. (1971). *Have you seen a comet? Children's art and writing from around the world.* New York: Day.

Pettit, J. (1996). *Maya Angelou: Journey of the heart.* New York: Dutton.

Philip, N. (2000). *It's a woman's world: A century of women's voices in poetry.* New York: Dutton.

Prelutsky, J. (1995) *The gargoyles on the roof.* New York: Greenwillow.

Prelutsky, J. (1977). *It's Halloween.* New York: Greenwillow.

Prelutsky, J. (Ed.). (1983). *The Random House book of poetry for children: A treasury of 572 poems for today's child.* New York: Random House.

Prelutsky, J. (1984). *The new kid on the block.* New York: Greenwillow.

Prelutsky, J. (1986). *Read-aloud rhymes for the very young.* New York: Knopf.

Prelutsky, J. (1990). *Something big has been here.* New York: William Morrow.

Prelutsky, J. (1996). *A pizza the size of the sun: Poems.* New York: Greenwillow.

Prelutsky, J. (1996). *Tyrannosaurus was a beast.* New York: Greenwillow.

Prelutsky, J. (Ed.). (1997). *The beauty of the beast: Poems from the animal kingdom*. New York: Knopf.

Prelutsky, J. (Ed.). (1998). *Imagine that! Poems of never-was*. New York: Knopf.

Prelutsky, J. (Ed.). (1999). *The 20th century children's poetry treasury*. New York: Knopf.

Prelutsky, J. (2000). *It's raining pigs and noodles: Poems*. New York: Greenwillow.

Rackham, A. (Illus.). (1969). *Mother Goose: The old nursery rhymes*. New York: Watts.

Ramaho Navajo students. (1983). *Reflections on illusion—reality*. Santa Fe, NM: Pine Hills Media Center.

Reef, C. (2000). *Paul Laurence Dunbar: Portrait of a poet*. Salt Lake City, : Enslow.

Reid, A., & Kerrigan, A. (1968). *Mother Goose in Spanish/Poesias de la Madre Oca*. New York: Thomas Crowell.

Rochelle, B. (Ed.). (2001). *Words with wings: A treasury of African-American poetry and art*. New York: HarperCollins.

Rosen, M. (1993). *Poems for the very young*. New York: Kingfisher.

Rounds, G. (Illus.). (1988). *Old MacDonald had a farm*. New York: Holiday.

Rounds, G. (Illus.). (1990). *I know an old lady who swallowed a fly*. New York: Holiday.

Rummel, J. (1998). *Langston Hughes*. Broomall, PA: Chelsea House.

Rylant, C. (1982). *When I was young in the mountains*. New York: Dutton.

Rylant, C. (1992). *Best wishes*. Los Angeles: Owen.

Rylant, C. (2000). *In November*. San Diego: Harcourt.

Sanderson, R. (Illus.). (1997). *'Twas the night before Christmas*. Boston: Little, Brown.

Schneider, R. (Illus.). (1978). *I'm nobody! Who are you?: Poems of Emily Dickinson for children*. Owings Mill, MD: Stemmer House.

Schnur, S. (1997). *Autumn: An alphabet acrostic*. Phoenix, AZ: Clarion.

Schwartz, A. (1999). *And the green grass grew all around*. New York: Harper.

Seuss, Dr. (1937). *And to think that I saw it on Mulberry Street*. New York: Vanguard.

Shaw, A. (1998). *Until I saw the sea*. New York: Holt.

Sierra, J. (1996). *Good night, dinosaurs*. Phoenix, AZ: Clarion.

Sierra, J. (1998). *Antarctic antics: A book of penguin poems*. San Diego: Harcourt.

Sierra, J. (2000). *There's a zoo in room 22*. Philadelphia: Gulliver Books.

Silverstein, S. (1974). *Where the sidewalk ends*. New York: Harper.

Silverstein, S. (1996). *Falling up*. New York: HarperCollins.

Smith, C.R. (1999). *Rimshots: Basketball pix, rolls, and rhythms*. New York: Dutton.

Smith, C.R. (2001). *Short takes: Fast-break basketball poetry*. New York: Dutton.

Soto, G. (1992). *Neighborhood odes*. San Diego: Harcourt.

Stanley, D., & Vennema, P. (1998). *Bard of Avon: The story of William Shakespeare*. New York: Morrow.

Steptoe, J. (2001). *In Daddy's arms I am tall: African Americans celebrating fathers*. New York: Lee and Low.

Stevenson, J. (1998). *Popcorn*. New York: William Morrow.

Stevenson, J. (1999). *Candy Corn*. New York: Greenwillow.

Stevenson, J. (1999). *Sweet Corn*. New York: Beech Tree.

Stevenson, J. (Ed.). (2000). *Cornflakes: Poems*. New York: Greenwillow.

Taback, S. (1997). *There was an old lady who swallowed a fly*. New York: Viking.

Tenggren, G. (Illus.). (1956). *The Tenggren Mother Goose*. Boston: Little, Brown.

Thayer, E.L. (2000). *Casey at the bat: A ballad of the Republic sung in the year 1888*. Ill. C. Bing. New York: Handprint Books.

Thorpe, Q. (2000). *Take it to the hoops, Magic Johnson*. New York: Hyperion.

Tudor, T. (Illus.). (1944). *Mother Goose*. New York: Walck.

Untermeyer, L. (1998). *The Golden Books family treasury of poetry*. New York: Golden Books.

Updike, J. (1999). *A child's calendar*. New York: Holiday House.

Watts, I. (1999). *Divine and moral songs for children*. Morgan, PA: Soli Deo Gloria.

Whipple, L. (1989). *Eric Carle's animals animals*. New York: Puffin.

Whipple, L. (1991). *Eric Carle's dragons dragons & other creatures that never were*. New York: Philomel.

Wilbur, R. (2000). *The pig in the spigot: Poems*. San Diego: Harcourt.

Wildsmith, B. (Illus.). (1965). *Brian Wildsmith's Mother Goose*. New York: Watts.

Windham, S. (Ed.). (1994). *The mermaid and other sea poems*. New York: Scholastic.

Wood, N. (1991). *War cry on a prayer feather*. Denver, CO: Colorado Centennial Commission.

Woodson, J. (2001). *The other side*. New York: Putnam.

Wong, J. (1996). *A suitcase of seaweed and other poems*. New York: McElderry.

Wright, B.F. (Illus.). (1992). *The real Mother Goose*. Totowa, NJ: Barnes & Noble.

Yolen, J. (1995). *Alphabestiary: Animal poems from A to Z*. Honesdale, PA: Boyds Mills.

Yolen, J. (1996). *Sky scrape/City scape: Poems of city life*. Honesdale, PA: Boyds Mills.

Younger, B. (1998). *Purple mountain majesties: The story of Katharine Lee Bates and "America the Beautiful."* New York: Dutton.

— COPYRIGHT ACKNOWLEDGMENTS —

We thank the following poets, publishers, and agents for the use of copyrighted material, as listed. Sincere efforts have been made to trace copyrights and to obtain appropriate permission to use all previously published poetry, as required. Unless otherwise indicated, the poet holds the copyright. In the event of any question arising as to the use of material, the author and publisher, while expressing regret for inadvertent error, will be pleased to make the necessary corrections to future printings.

Bennett, R. Five lines from "The Witch of Willowby Wood." In *Story-Teller Poems.*

Bennett, R. "Modern Dragon."

Burgess, G. "I Wish That My Room Had a Floor."

Carman, B. Lines from "A Vagabond Song."

Carroll, L. "How Doth the Little Crocodile."

Coatsworth, E. "Swift Things Are Beautiful." Copyright © Macmillan Publishing Company.

Conkling, H. "Dandelion." In *Poems by a Little Girl.*

Conkling, H. "Little Mouse in Gray Velvet." In *Poems by a Little Girl.*

de la Mare, W. "Silver." In *The Complete Poems of Walter de la Mare.* Copyright ©1969 by Literary Trustees of Walter de la Mare.

Dickinson, E. "I'm Nobody! Who Are You?" In *Poems by Emily Dickinson.* Copyright © Roberts Brothers.

Dickinson, E. "I Like to See It Lap the Miles." In *Poems by Emily Dickinson.* Copyright © Roberts Brothers.

Dickinson, E. "Autumn." In *Poems by Emily Dickinson.* Copyright © Roberts Brothers.

Farjeon, E. "What Is Poetry?" In *Eleanor Farjeon's Poems for Children.* New York: Harper & Row.

Frost, R. "The Pasture." In *The Complete Works of Robert Frost.* New York: Holt, Rinehart and Winston.

Fyleman, R. "I Think Mice Are Nice." In *Fifty-One New Nursery Rhymes* by Rose Fyleman. New York: Doubleday. Reprinted by permission.

Herford, O. "The Elf and the Dormouse."

Housman, A.E. "Loveliest of Trees."

Hughes, L. "Hold Fast Your Dreams." In *The Dream Keeper and Other Poems*. New York: Knopf.

Hughes, L. "Mother to Son." In *The Dream Keeper and Other Poems*. New York: Knopf.

Hugo, V. "Be Like the Bird."

Jacobs, L. "City Pigeons." In *Alphabet of Girls*. New York: Holt.

Lazarus, E. "The New Colossus."

Lear, E. "The Jumblies."

Lear, E. "There Once Was a Man With a Beard."

Lindsay, V. "The Little Turtle." In *Johnny Appleseed and Other Poems*. New York: Macmillan. Copyright © Elizabeth Lindsay.

Longfellow, H.W. "Paul Revere's Ride."

Merriam, E. "There Was a Crooked Man." In *The Inner City Mother Goose*. New York: Simon & Schuster.

Milne, A. "The End." In *When We Were Very Young*. New York: Dutton.

Moore, C. "'Twas The Night Before Christmas."

Morley, C. Eight lines from "Smells (Junior)." In *The Rocking Horse*. New York: Harper & Row.

Nash, O. "The Panther." In *Verses From 1929 On*. Boston: Little, Brown.

O'Neill, M. "What Is Orange?" In *Hailstones and Halibut Bones*. New York: Doubleday. Reproduced with permission.

Rossetti, C. "Who Has Seen the Wind?"

Service, R.W. "The Cremation of Sam McGee." Copyright © The Service Estate.

Stevenson, R.L. "At the Seaside." In *Garden of Verses*.

Stevenson, R.L. "Requiem." In *Garden of Verses*.

Stevenson, R.L. "The Wind." In *Garden of Verses*.

Tennyson, A.L. "The Eagle."

Thayer, E. "Casey at the Bat." San Francisco *Examiner*, June 3, 1888.

Tiedt, I.M. "The Challenge."

Whitman, W. "I Hear America Singing."

Whitman, W. "This Moment Yearning and Thoughtful."

Whitman, W. Lines from "O Captain, My Captain."

Whitman, W. Lines from "Song of the Open Road."

Widdemer, M. "The Secret Cavern."

Wolfe, H. "The Blackbird." In *Kensington Gardens*.

— INDEX —

References followed by *f* indicate figures.

A

ABBE, GEORGE: "The Passer," 149

ACADEMY OF AMERICAN POETS, 208

ACCORDION BOOK, 166–167

ACKERMAN, KAREN: *A Brighter Garden: Poetry by Emily Dickinson,* 17–18

ACROSTICS, 131–132

ACTION POEMS, 49–50

ADA, ALMA FLOR: *Gathering the Sun,* 161

"ADAM AND EVE AND PINCHME," 49

ADAMS, LEONIE, 175

ADEDJOUMA, DAVIDA: *The Palm of My Heart,* 174

ADOFF, ARNOLD: *The Basket Counts,* 149; *Eats,* 63; *I Am the Darker Brother,* 29; *My Black Me: A Big Book of Poetry,* 154; *Sports Pages,* 149

AESOP, 76

"A FLEA AND A FLY IN A FLUE," 127

AFRICAN AMERICANS: poetry by, 32, 39, 154–156, 174

"AFRICAN LULLABY," 64

"AFTERNOON ON A HILL" (MILLAY), 10

THE ALAN REVIEW, 208

ALARCÓN, FRANCISCO X.: *Angels Ride Bikes and Other Fall Poems,* 155, 159

ALDAN, DAISY: *Poems from India,* 161

ALDIS, DOROTHY: "Brooms," 140

ALIKI: *William Shakespeare & the Globe,* 168

ALLITERATION, 44–46, 191

"AMERICA THE BEAUTIFUL" (BATES), 144

AMON, ALINE: *The Earth Is Sore: Native Americans on Nature,* 155

AND TO THINK THAT I SAW IT ON MULBERRY STREET (SEUSS), 27

ANGELOU, MAYA, 69

ANGLUND, JOAN WALSH: *A Little Book of Poems & Prayers,* 64; *A Mother Goose ABC: In a Pumpkin Shell,* 101

ANIMALS: poetry on, 70–71, 150–151

"ANNABEL LEE" (POE), 17

ANONYMOUS: "Adam and Eve and Pinchme," 49; "A flea and a fly in a flue," 127; "African Lullaby," 64; "Betty Botter," 20, 65; "The Eentsy, Weentsy Spider," 51; "'Fire! Fire!' Cried Mrs. McGuire," 20, 36, 55, 83; "How much wood could a wood chuck chuck," 53; "Hush, little baby, don't say a word," 146–147; "I am a gold key," 49; "If all the seas were one sea," 150; "I'm a Little Teapot," 49–50; "I saw Esau," 54; "A Kite," 62; "Molly, my sister, and I fell out," 120; "Mr. Nobody," 58–59; "Not last night, but the night before," 55; "On top of spaghetti," 50–52; "Out and In," 53; "Pease porridge hot," 50; "Peter Piper picked a peck of pickled peppers," 53; "Rain, rain, go away," 62; "Relativity," 142; "The Secret," 56; "Sleep, baby, sleep," 64; "A sleeper from the Amazon," 54; "The Squirrel," 42–44, 189; "Teddy bear, teddy bear," 48; "There's one wide river to cross," 66–67; "There was an old man of Blackheath," 20; "White coral bells," 145; "White sheep, white sheep," 29–31, 187; "A Young Farmer of Leeds," 127, 200

"THE ANT AND THE GRASSHOPPER" (JACOBS), 77

"ANTONIO, ANTONIO" (RICHARDS), 42

"ARITHMETIC" (SANDBURG), 142

ART, 135–141

ASSESSMENT: in lesson plans, 182–203; poetry portfolios, 32–34; of student knowledge of Mother Goose rhymes, 97–98; of students' poetry exposure, 21

ATHLETICS, 148

"AT THE SEASIDE" (STEVENSON), 151

ATWOOD, ANN: *My Own Rhythm: An Approach to Haiku,* 159

AUSLANDER, JOSEPH: "A Blackbird Suddenly," 125, 175

AUSTIN, MARY: "The Sandhill Crane," 151

"AUTUMN" (DICKINSON), 139

B

"BAA, BAA, BLACK SHEEP," 96

BACMEISTER, RHODA: "Galoshes," 46, 191–192

BAGERT, BROD: *Poetry for Young People: Edgar Allan Poe,* 17, 80

BAILEY, ALICE COOPER: *To Remember Robert Louis Stevenson,* 68

"THE BALLOON MAN" (FYLEMAN), 140

BARING-GOULD, WILLIAM S. AND CEIL: *The Annotated Mother Goose,* 101

BARON, VIRGINIA A.: *Here I Am!,* 107

BARRETT, JUDI: *Things That Are Most in the World,* 113

BARTON, JUDY SPAIN: *Little Feelings,* 41

"THE BASE STEALER" (FRANCIS), 149

Bates, Katharine Lee: "America the Beautiful," 144

Baxter, Nicola: *The Children's Classic Poetry Collection,* 18

Beautiful images, 76

Behn, Harry: *Cricket Songs: Japanese Haiku,* 159; *More Cricket Songs: Japanese Haiku,* 159

"Be like the bird" (Hugo), 12

"The Bells" (Poe), 44, 190

Belting, Natalie, 76

Bender, Michael: *All the World's a Stage,* 68

Bennett, Rowena: "A Modern Dragon," 72, 140; "The Witch of Willowby Wood," 44–45, 191

"Betty Botter," 20, 65

Biade, Folami, 38

Billington, James, 176

Bishop, Elizabeth, 175–176

"A Blackbird Suddenly" (Auslander), 125, 175

Black Poetry Week, 174–175

Blake, William, 136

Blessing the Boats (Clifton), 16

"The Blind Men and the Elephant" (Saxe), 152–153

Bloom, H., 13

Bogan, Louise, 175

Bontemps, Arna: *Golden Slippers: An Anthology,* 155

Books: accordion, 166–167; covers for, 139; of haiku, 166f

Bookwire, 208

Brenner, Barbara: *Voices: Poetry and Art from Around the World,* 138

Brodsky, Joseph, 176

Brooke, Leslie: *Ring O'Rosies: A Nursery Rhyme Picture Book,* 101

Brooks, Gwendolyn, 39, 176; *Bronzeville Boys and Girls,* 155; "Rudolph Is Tired of the City," 159

"Brooms" (Aldis), 140

Brown, Marc T.: *Scared Silly,* 74

Brown, Margaret Wise: *Good Night, Moon,* 64; *The Runaway Bunny,* 64

Brown Angels (Myers), 32

Browning, Elizabeth Barrett, 69

Bunting, Eve: *Butterfly House,* 71

Burgess, Gelette: "I wish that my room had a floor," 127; "The Purple Cow," 139–140

C

CALDECOTT, RANDOLPH: *Hey Diddle Diddle Picture Book,* 101

CALDECOTT AWARD: winners of, 209–210

CARLE, ERIC: *Eric Carle's Animals Animals,* 70; *Eric Carle's Dragons Dragons and Other Creatures That Never Were,* 72; *The Very Lonely Firefly,* 70–71

CARLSON, LORI M.: *Cool Salsa,* 29

CARMAN, BLISS: "A Vagabond Song," 10

CARROLL, JOYCE A., AND EDWARD E. WILSON: *Poetry After Lunch,* 29

CARROLL, LEWIS, 40; "How doth the little crocodile," 85; "The Walrus and the Carpenter," 7; "You are old, Father William," 57

CARRYL, CHARLES EDWARD: "The Plaint of the Camel," 7

CARRYL, GUY WETMORE: "Little Miss Muffett," 83

"CASEY AT THE BAT" (THAYER), 148

CATALANO, DOMINIC: *Frog Went A-Courting: A Musical Play in Six Acts,* 148

CELEBRATION OF POETRY, 163–179; in classroom, 163–167; national, 173–177, 203; schoolwide, 168–173

CHALL, MARSHA W.: *Up North at the Cabin,* 113

CHAUCER, GEOFFREY: *Canterbury Tales,* 78–79

"CHICAGO" (SANDBURG), 114

CHILDREN'S BOOK COUNCIL, 175

THE CHILDREN'S BOOK COUNCIL, 208

CIARDI, JOHN: "Mummy Slept Late and Daddy Fixed Breakfast," 20; "The Reason for the Pelican," 7

CINQUAIN, 116–117

"CITY" (HUGHES), 87

CITY LIFE: poems on, 157–158

"CITY PIGEONS" (JACOBS), 5–6

CLASS POETRY COLLECTIONS, 164–167

CLASSROOM: celebrating poetry in, 163–167

CLEARY, BEVERLY, 21

CLICHES, 86

CLIFTON, LUCILLE, 16–17, 32

CLINTON, CATHERINE: *I, Too, Sing America,* 29

COATSWORTH, ELIZABETH: "Down the rain falls," 7; "Swift things are beautiful," 106, 112–113, 197

COFFIN, ROBERT P. T.: "The Skunk," 151

COLE, JOANNA, AND STEPHANIE CALMENSON: *Give the Dog a Bone,* 147

COLLAY, RYAN: *Stuartship,* 79

COLLINS, BILLY, 176

COLOR POEMS, 164, 165*f*, 185

"COMMISSARIAT CAMELS" (KIPLING), 70

COMMUNICATION: poetry and, 5–9; poet-student, facilitating, 18–19

CONCRETE POETRY, 140–141

CONKLING, HILDA: "Little mouse in gray velvet," 114, 199

CONTEMPORARY AUTHORS, 15

COPELAND, JEFFREY S.: *Speaking of Poets*, 69; *Speaking of Poets 2* (with Vicky L. Copeland), 69

COUNTED SYLLABLES, 116–117

COUNTED WORDS, 116

COUNTING RHYMES, 141–142

COUPLETS, 123–125

COUSINS, LUCY: *Jack and Jill and Other Nursery Rhymes*, 92

COX, KENYON: "The Octopussycat," 84

"CRADLE SONG OF THE ELEPHANTS" (DELVALLE), 64

CRAPSEY, ADELAIDE, 116

CREATIVE LEVEL: of approach to poetry, 31

CRICKET, 107

"CROWS" (MCCORD), 151

CULTURAL EXPLORATION: poetry for, 159–161

CURRICULUM: poetry across, 135–161

D

DAVIES, WILLIAM H.: "Leisure," 9

DAVIS, KATIE: *I Hate to Go to Bed!*, 41

DE ANGELI, MARGUERITE: *Marguerite de Angeli's Book of Nursery and Mother Goose Rhymes*, 101

DEATH: poems on, 156–157

"DECEMBER LEAVES" (STARBIRD), vi, 195

DE ESPRONCEDA, JOSÉ: "Canción del Pirata (Song of the Pirate)," 161

DEHN, PAUL: "Little Miss Muffett," 20

DEKKER, THOMAS: "Golden Slumbers," 64

DE LA MARE, WALTER: "Silver," 44–45, 83, 191

DELVALLE, ADRIANO: "Cradle Song of the Elephants," 64

DEMERDJIAN, T., 115

DENTON, KADY MACDONALD: *A Child's Treasury of Nursery Rhymes*, 92

DE PAOLA, TOMIE: *Tomie de Paola's Mother Goose*, 92

DE REGNIERS, B.S., 8; *Sing a Song of Popcorn*, 64

DIAMANTE, 117–118; form for, 119*f*

DICKINSON, EMILY, 17–18, 175; "Autumn," 139; "I like to see it lap the miles,"
    72, 88–89, 195; "I'm nobody! Who are you?," 162; "Morning," 138

DINOSAURS, 71–72

DISCUSSION, 27; of writing poetry, 115

"THE DIVER" (ROSS), 149

DIVERSITY: poems on, 157, 202; teaching for, 31–32

DORRIS, MICHAEL, 21

DOTLICH, REBECCA KAI: *Lemonade Sun and Other Summer Poems*, 38

"THE DOUBLE-PLAY" (WALLACE), 149

DOVE, RITA, 176

"DOWN THE RAIN FALLS" (COATSWORTH), 7

DRAGONS, 72

DUETS: for voice choir, 57–58

DUNBAR, PAUL L., 69, 175; *Greet the Dawn*, 155

DURSTON, GEORGIA: "The Wolf," 151

DYER, JANE: *Animal Crackers*, 64

E

EAGLE, KIN: *Humpty Dumpty*, 102

"THE EAGLE" (TENNYSON), 60, 87, 194

EDENS, COOPER: *The Glorious Mother Goose*, 92

EDUCATION INDEX, 15–16

"THE EENTSY, WEENTSY SPIDER," 51

ELEMENTARY ENGLISH, 15, 136

"ELETELEPHONY" (RICHARDS), 20, 83

"THE ELF AND THE DORMOUSE" (HERFORD), 22–24, 185

ELIOT, T.S., 175

"THE END" (MILNE), 64

ENGLISH AS A SECOND LANGUAGE PROGRAM: poetry for, 47

ENSEMBLE POEMS: for voice choir, 56–57

EPITAPHS, 132–133

F

FABER, DORIS: *Robert Frost: America's Poet*, 68

FARJEON, ELEANOR: "What Is Poetry?," 2–3

FARRAR, JOHN: "Watching Clouds," 140

FAVORITE POEM PROJECT, 177

FEELINGS: poems on, 40–41

FERLINGHETTI, LAWRENCE, 16

FIELD, RACHEL: "I'd like to be a lighthouse," 140; "Snow in the City," 159

"'FIRE! FIRE!' CRIED MRS. McGUIRE," 20, 36, 55, 83

FISHER, AILEEN: "Skins," 87; "Wind," 25

FLORIAN, DOUGLAS: *Mammabilia,* 138, 150; *Winter Eyes,* 38

"FOG" (SANDBURG), 20, 114

FOLK SONGS, 147–148

FORD, M., 20

FOUND POETRY, 79–80

"FOUR LITTLE FOXES" (SARETT), 125

FRANCIS, ROBERT: "The Base Stealer," 149; "Pitches," 149

FREE VERSE, 109–115, 199

FRIENDSHIP: poems on, 156–157

FROST, ROBERT, 1, 4–5, 68, 175; "The Pasture," 1, 13–14, 182; "Stopping by Woods on a Snowy Evening," 143–144

FUNNY RHYMES, 49

"FURRY BEAR" (MILNE), 171

FYLEMAN, ROSE: "The Balloon Man," 140; "I think mice are nice," 21, 136–137, 171

G

GALDONE, PAUL, 92

"GALOSHES" (BACMEISTER), 46, 191–192

GAME SONGS, 48–49

GARDNER, H., 22

THE GARGOYLES ON THE ROOF (PRELUTSKY), 7

GEOGRAPHY, 160–161

GIOVANNI, NIKKI, 39; *Spin a Soft Black Song,* 155; *The Sun Is So Quiet,* 28, 64

"GOD'S WORLD" (MILLAY), 9

"GOLDEN SLUMBERS" (DEKKER), 64

GOLDSTEIN, BOBBYE: *What's On the Menu?,* 63

GOLDSTONE, BRUCE: *The Beastly Feast,* 40

GOOD NIGHT, MOON (BROWN), 64

GOOD TIMES (CLIFTON), 16

GOOD WOMAN: POEMS AND A MEMOIR (CLIFTON), 16

GRAHAM, JOAN B.: *Flicker Flash,* 141; *Touch the Poem,* 141

"THE GRASSHOPPER AND THE ANT" (LA FONTAINE), 77–78

GREENFIELD, ELOISE, 39; *Daydreamers,* 155

GRIMES, NIKKI: *It's Raining Laughter,* 38; *Shoe Magic,* 174; *Something on My Mind,* 155

GROVER, EULALIE: *Mother Goose: The Original Volland Edition,* 18

GUITERMAN, ARTHUR: "Habits of the Hippopotamus," 83; "Under the Goal Posts," 149

GUTHRIE, WOODY: *This Land Is Your Land,* 53, 147

H

"HABITS OF THE HIPPOPOTAMUS" (GUITERMAN), 83

HACKER, JEFFREY H.: *Carl Sandburg,* 68

HAIKU, 159; presentation of, 166*f*

HAILSTONES AND HALIBUT BONES (O'NEILL), 22, 24, 113, 185

HALLOWEEN, 72–74; couplets on, 124–125

HALPERN, SHARI: *Old MacDonald Had a Farm,* 168

HAMANAKA, SHEILA: *I Look Like a Girl,* 67

HARRISON, MICHAEL, AND CHRISTOPHER STUART-CLARK: *The New Oxford Treasury of Children's Poems,* 18, 62

HARTMAN, WENDY: *One Sun Rises,* 71

HASS, ROBERT, 176

HEALTH, 148–149

HEIDE, FLORENCE, 40; *Some Things Are Scary,* 41, 74

HERFORD, OLIVER: "The Elf and the Dormouse," 22–24, 185

HIATT, FRED: *If I Were Queen of the World,* 113, 198

HIGHWATER, JAMAKE: *Moonsong Lullaby,* 155

"THE HIGHWAYMAN" (NOYES), 83

HINES, ANNA GROSSNICKLE: *Pieces: A Year in Poems & Quilts,* 136

HOBERMAN, MARY ANN: *The Llama Who Had No Pajama,* 40

HOPKINS, LEE B.: *Climb Into My Lap,* 38; *Side by Side,* 38

HOPKINS, LEE BENNETT: *Creatures,* 150; *Munching: Poems About Eating,* 63; *Yummy: Eating Through a Day,* 63

THE HORN BOOK, 208

HORNBY, GEORGE: *Poems for Children and Other People,* 136

HOUSMAN, A.E.: "Loveliest of Trees," 84

HOUSTON, JAMES: *Songs of the Dream People,* 155

"HOW DOTH THE LITTLE BUSY BEE" (WATTS), 85–86

"HOW DOTH THE LITTLE CROCODILE" (CARROLL), 85

"How much wood could a wood chuck chuck," 53

"How pleasant to know Mr. Lear" (Lear), 127

Hubbell, Patricia: *Boo! Halloween Poems and Limericks,* 74; "Shadows," 20

Hudson, Wade: *Pass It On,* 39

"Hughbert and the Glue" (Kuskin), 20

Hughes, Langston, 32, 39, 69; "City," 87; *Don't You Turn Back,* 155; "Snail," 151

Hughes, Linda Ann: *America's Favorite Poems,* 18

Hughes, Ted: *The Mermaid's Purse,* 151

Hugo, Victor: "Be like the bird," 12

Hummon, David: *Animal Acrostics,* 168

humor, 6–7, 39–40, 49; in poems for Readers Theatre, 82–83

"Hush, little baby, don't say a word," 146–147

I

"I am a gold key," 49

"I'd like to be a lighthouse" (Field), 140

"If all the seas were one sea," 150

"I hear America singing" (Whitman), 115, 134

I Know an Old Lady Who Swallowed a Fly (Rounds), 52

"I like to see it lap the miles" (Dickinson), 72, 88–89, 195

illustration: displaying, 164; of poetry, 135–138, 201

I Look Like a Girl (Hamanak), 67

"I love little pussy" (Taylor), 85

images: beautiful, 76; exploring, 86–89; visualizing, 139–140

"I'm a little teapot," 49–50

immigration, 202; poems on, 157

"I'm nobody! Who are you?" (Dickinson), 162

independent readers: reading poetry to, 38

independent reading: poetry for, 67–68

India: poetry of, 160–161

inferential level: of approach to poetry, 29

In November (Rylant), 67

Isaacs, Anne: *Cat Up a Tree,* 40

"I saw Esau," 54

"'I,' Says the Poem" (Merriam), 18

"I Talk, I Say, I Speak" (Shapiro), 113

"I think mice are nice" (Fyleman), 21, 136–137, 171

"I WENT TO THE ANIMAL FAIR," 39–40

"I WISH THAT MY ROOM HAD A FLOOR" (BURGESS), 127

J

"JACK AND JILL," 95

JACOBS, JOSEPH: "The Ant and the Grasshopper," 77

JACOBS, LELAND: "City Pigeons," 5–6

JACOBS, WILLIAM JAY: *Edgar Allan Poe: Genius in Torment,* 68

JACOBSEN, JOSEPHINE, 176

JAMES, SIMON: *Days Like This,* 38

JANECZKO, PAUL B.: *Stone Bench in an Empty Park,* 159

JAPAN: poetry of, 159

JOHNSON, ANGELA, 38

JOHNSON, JAMES WELDON: "Lift Ev'ry Voice and Sing," 174

JOHNSTON, TONY: *It's About Dogs,* 70

JORDAN, JUNE: *The Voices of the Children* (with Torri Bush), 107; *Who Look at Me?,* 155

JOURNALS: professional, 207–208

"THE JUMBLIES" (LEAR), 82–83

JUMBO'S LULLABY (MELMED), 67

JUMP-ROPE SONGS, 48, 54–55

K

KAMEN, GLORIA: *Kipling: Storyteller of East and West,* 69

KEATS, EZRA JACK, 139

KEATS, JOHN, 136

KELLOGG, STEVEN: *Give the Dog a Bone,* 142

KEY, FRANCIS SCOTT: "The Star-Spangled Banner," 144

KIPLING, RUDYARD, 69, 160; "Commissariat Camels," 70; "On the road to Mandalay," 148

"A KITE," 62

KOCH, KENNETH, 1; *Rose, Where Did You Get That Red?,* 107; *Talking to the Sun* (with Kate Farrell), 18

KOHL, HERBERT, AND VICTOR H. CRUZ: *Stuff,* 107

KRULL, KATHLEEN: *Lives of the Writers: Comedies, Tragedies (and What the Neighbors Thought),* 15

KUMIN, MAXINE, 176

KUNITZ, STANLEY, 176

KUSKIN, KARLA, 2, 13; "Hughbert and the Glue," 20

L

LA FONTAINE, JEAN DE, 77; "The Grasshopper and the Ant," 77–78

LANGUAGE: love of, poetry and, 5–6

LANGUAGE ARTS, 15–16, 136, 173, 177

LANSKY, BRUCE: *Kids Pick the Funniest Poems,* 63; *The New Adventures of Mother Goose,* 101–102

LARRICK, NANCY: *Cats Are Cats,* 70

LATINOS: poetry by, 32, 39, 155

LAWRENCE, D.H.: "Snake," 151

LAYNE, S.L., 177

LAZARUS, EMMA: "The New Colossus," 158, 202

LEADERSHIP: poems on, 156

LEAR, EDWARD, 7, 40; "How pleasant to know Mr. Lear," 127; "The Jumblies," 82–83; "The Table and the Chair," 57–58

LEHRER, TOM: "Pollution," 83

"LEISURE" (DAVIES), 9

LENSKI, LOIS: "People," 140

LESSON PLANS WITH POETRY, 181–203; adapting for different levels, 24–25; designing, 19–25; form for, 22–24, 23*f*

LEWIS, J. PATRICK: *The Bookworm's Feast: A Potluck of Poems,* 74

LEWIS, RICHARD: *Moon, For What Do You Wait? Poems by Tagore,* 161; *Poems of the Eskimo,* 161; *In a Spring Garden,* 159; *Still Waters of the Air,* 155

LIBRARY: poetry in, 168

A LIBRARY FOR JUANA (MORA), 17

LIBRARY OF CONGRESS, 175

"LIFT EV'RY VOICE AND SING" (JOHNSON), 174

LILLEGARD, DEE: *Wake Up House: Rooms Full of Poems,* 74

LIMERICKS, 20, 126–128; writing, 200

LINDSAY, VACHEL: "The Little Turtle," 75*f*, 171; "Whisky Frisky," 171

THE LION AND THE UNICORN, 208

LISTENING TO POETRY, 41–46

LISTENING WALK, 41–42, 188

LISTING POEMS, 112–113, 197–198

LITERACY INSTRUCTION: Mother Goose and, 93–94; with poetry, 61–63

LITERAL LEVEL: of approach to poetry, 29

LITTLE, LESSIE JONES: *Children of Long Ago,* 154

"LITTLE MISS MUFFETT" (CARRYL), 83

"LITTLE MISS MUFFETT" (DEHN), 20

"LITTLE MOUSE IN GRAY VELVET" (CONKLING), 114, 199

"THE LITTLE TURTLE" (LINDSAY), 75*f*, 171

LIVES OF THE WRITERS: COMEDIES, TRAGEDIES (AND WHAT THE NEIGHBORS THOUGHT) (HEWITT), 15

LIVINGSTONE, MYRA COHN: *Halloween Poems*, 74; *Poems for Fathers*, 64

LOBEL, ARNOLD: *The Random House Book of Mother Goose*, 92

LOGUE, MARY: *Love: The Story of Elizabeth Barrett Browning*, 69

"LONE DOG" (MCLEOD), 20

LONGFELLOW, HENRY WADSWORTH: "Paul Revere's Ride," 156; *The Song of Hiawatha*, 155

"LOVELIEST OF TREES" (HOUSMAN), 84

LOWELL, ROBERT, 175

LULLABIES, 146

M

MACKINTOSH, M., 19

MACLACHLAN, PATRICIA: *All the Places to Love*, 113

"MAPS" (THOMPSON), 160

MARBLEIZED PAPER, 139

MASEFIELD, JOHN, 136; "Sea Fever," 83, 151

MATHEMATICS, 141–143

MAVOR, SALLEY: *You and Me: Poems of Friendship*, 157

MCCORD, DAVID: "Crows," 151; "Song of the Train," 8, 42, 64, 72; "This Is My Rock," 125

MCFARLANE, SHERYL: *Jessie's Island*, 113

MCLEOD, IRENE R.: "Lone Dog," 20

MCLERRAN, ALICE: *Roxaboxen*, 113

MEDINA, TONI: *DeShawn Days*, 155

MELMED, LAURA KRAUSS: *Jumbo's Lullaby*, 67

MERRIAM, EVE, 40; *Inner City Mother Goose*, 102; "'I,' Says the Poem," 18; *Male and Female Under 18:* (with Nancy Larrick), 107

MERRYMAN, MILDRED P.: "The Pirate Don Durk of Dowdee," 44

METAPHOR, 86–89, 187, 195

MILLAY, EDNA ST. VINCENT: "Afternoon on a Hill," 10; *Edna St. Vincent Millay's Poems Selected for Young People*, 136; "God's World," 9; "Travel," 72–73

MILLER, JOAQUIN, 136

MILNE, A. A.: "The End," 64; "Furry Bear," 171

"A MODERN DRAGON" (BENNETT), 72, 140

"Molly, my sister, and I fell out," 120

Monkhouse, Cosmos: "There once was a lady from Niger," 20, 127

"Moonlight" (Uschold), 87

Moore, Clement: "Twas the night before Christmas," 172

Moore, Lilian: "Until I saw the sea," 151

Moore, Marianne, 175

Mora, Pat, 17, 32, 183; *Confetti,* 28, 64, 155; *Love to Mama: A Tribute to Mothers,*
     155; *My Own True Name,* 39

Morley, Christopher: "Smells (Junior)," 7

"Morning" (Dickinson), 138

Morrison, Lillian: *Slam Dunk: Poems About Basketball,* 149

Moss, Jeff: *Bone Poems,* 71

Mother Goose, 91–104; "Baa, baa, black sheep," 96; continuing stories of, 102;
     history of, 100–101; in the primary grades, 91–96; introducing to older stu-
     dents, 97–105; "Jack and Jill," 95; "Little Boy Blue," 104; presentation of,
     98–99, 196; *The Real Mother Goose,* 92; "Simple Simon," 90; "Sing a song
     of sixpence," 103; teachings of, 99–100; "The noble Duke of York," 44; writ-
     ing parodies of, 101–102

Moyers, Bill, 172

"Mr. Nobody," 58–59

Mullin, Edward: "There once was an old kangaroo," 20

multicultural teaching with poetry, 31–32, 202; poems for, 39, 154–155

"Mummy Slept Late and Daddy Fixed Breakfast" (Ciardi), 20

music: creating, 146–147; poems set to, 25–26, 31, 96, 130, 144–148; poetry and,
     8, 143–148

Myers, Christopher: *Black Cat,* 157

Myers, Walter Dean: *Brown Angels,* 32; *Harlem,* 154, 157–159

My Own True Name (Mora), 17

N

Nash, Ogden, 7, 40

National Council of Teachers of English, 19; Award for Excellence in Poetry
     for Children, 13

National Poetry Month, 173–174; lesson plan for, 203

Native Americans: poetry by, 155

Nemerov, Howard, 176

"The New Colossus" (Lazarus), 158, 202

The New Oxford Treasury of Children's Poems, 18, 62

"Night" (Sandburg), 87

"The noble Duke of York," 44

"Not last night, but the night before," 55

Noyes, Alfred: "The Highwayman," 83

Nye, Naomi Shihab: *Come With Me,* 29; *The Tree Is Older Than You Are,* 155

O

Observation: poetry on, 152–153

Ocean: poetry on, 151

"The Octopussycat" (Cox), 84

Older students: Mother Goose rhymes for, 97–104; poetry books for, 29; reading development in, 64–69; reading poetry to, 38–39; and rhyme lists, 122

Old MacDonald Had a Farm (Rounds), 52

O'Neill, Mary: *Hailstones and Halibut Bones,* 22, 24, 113, 184; "What Is Orange?," 4

Onomatopoeia, 46, 192

"On the road to Mandalay" (Kipling), 148

"On top of spaghetti," 50–52

Opie, Iona: *Here Comes Mother Goose,* 92; *My Very First Mother Goose,* 92

Oral language skills. *See* reading aloud; saying poems aloud

Orie, Sandra DeCoteau: *Did You Hear Wind Sing Your Name?,* 28

"Out and In," 53

P

Paper: marbleized, 139

Parents: poetry collections for, 63–64; poetry program for, 171–172; and Readers Theatre, 83–84; and voice choir, 58–59

Parker, Dorothy, 40

Parodies: for Readers Theatre, 84–86; writing, 101–102

"The Passer" (Abbe), 149

"The Pasture" (Frost), 1, 13–14, 182

"Paul Revere's Ride" (Longfellow), 156

"Pease porridge hot," 50

Pellowski, A., et al.: *Have You Seen a Comet?,* 107

Pen American Center, 208

"People" (Lenski), 140

Perrault, Charles: *Contes de Ma Mere l'Oye,* 101

"Peter Piper picked a peck of pickled peppers," 53

Pettit, Jane: *Maya Angelou: Journey of the Heart,* 69

PHILIP, NEIL: *It's a Woman's World: A Century of Women's Voices in Poetry,* 174

PHONEMIC AWARENESS, 61, 94

PHOTOGRAPHS: of poets, 15–16

PHYSICAL EDUCATION, 148–149

PINSKY, ROBERT, 176–177

"THE PIRATE DON DURK OF DOWDEE" (MERRYMAN), 44

"THE PIT AND THE PENDULUM" (POE), 80

"PITCHES" (FRANCIS), 149

"THE PLAINT OF THE CAMEL" (CARRYL), 7

PLEASING WORDS DISPLAY, 108

POE, EDGAR ALLAN, 17, 68; "The Bells," 44, 190; "The Pit and the Pendulum," 80; "The Raven," 17

POEMS: action, 49–50; color, 164, 165*f*, 184; content of, 39–41; familiar, 46–48; listing, 112–113, 197–198; shape, 163

POETIC POWER, 175

POET LAUREATES, 175–177

POETRY: across curriculum, 135–161; celebrating, 163–179; characteristics of, 2–4; concrete, 140–141; definition of, 1–3; discovering, 1–11; found, 79–80; getting acquainted with, 13–19; for independent reading, 67–68; levels of approach to, 29–31; listening to, 41–46; literacy instruction with, 61–63; patterns in, 116–120; performances of, 172–173; and Readers Theatre, 81–86; reading aloud, 25–29, 37–59; in reading program, 61–89; recording, 167; rhymed: forms of, 120–129; saying aloud, 46–59, 193; selecting, 17–18, 81; special effects in, 42–46; by teachers, 177, 178*f*; teaching with, 13–35; on themes, 70–74; translating, 161; unrhymed, 109–115, 199; writing, 107–133, 197–200

POETRY ALIVE, 172–173

POETRY COLLECTIONS: class, 164–167; personal, 74–75, 164

POETRY DAILY, 17

POETRY DISPLAYS, 65–67, 163–164

POETRY PORTFOLIOS, 32–34, 203

POETRY POSTERS, 102–104, 138*f*

POETRY READINGS, 173

POETRY SOCIETY OF AMERICA, 208

POETS: books on, 68–69; getting acquainted with, 13–19; school visits by, 172

POETS & WRITERS, 208

"POLLUTION" (LEHRER), 83

PORTFOLIOS: poetry, 32–34, 203

POSTAGE STAMPS: poets on, 175

POSTERS: creating, 102–104

PRELUTSKY, JACK, 40; *The Beauty of the Beast*, 28; *The Gargoyles on the Roof*, 7; *Imagine That! Poems of Never-Was*, 40; *It's Halloween*, 74; *It's Raining Pigs and Noodles*, 28, 38; *The New Kid on the Block*, 28; *A Pizza the Size of the Sun*, 28; *The Random House Book of Poetry for Children*, 18; *Read-Aloud Rhymes for the Very Young*, 38; *Something Big Has Been Here*, 28; *The 20th Century Children's Poetry Treasury*, 18; *Tyrannosaurus Was a Beast*, 71

PREREADERS: reading poetry to, 37–38

PRESENTATION: of haiku, 160*f*, 166*f*; of Mother Goose rhymes, 98–99, 196; of poem, 185; of poetry program, 168–171

PREWRITING ACTIVITIES, 107–109

PRIMARY GRADE STUDENTS: Mother Goose rhymes for, 91–94; poetry books for, 63

PROFESSIONAL JOURNALS, 204–205

PROSE: versus poetry, 76–80

"THE PURPLE COW" (BURGESS), 139–140

Q

QUATRAIN, 128–129

"QUESTIONS" (RIDLOW), 20

QUINTAIN, 120

QUINZAINE, 118

R

RACKHAM, ARTHUR: *Mother Goose: The Old Nursery Rhymes*, 101

"RAIN, RAIN, GO AWAY," 62

RAMAHO NAVAJO STUDENTS: *Reflections on Illusion—Reality*, 155

"THE RAVEN" (POE), 17

READERS THEATRE: poetry and, 81–86

READING ALOUD, 25–29, 37–59; Mother Goose, 93; in reading instruction, 62–63

READING PROGRAM: poetry in, 61–89

THE READING TEACHER, 15, 173, 177

"THE REASON FOR THE PELICAN" (CIARDI), 7

RECORDING POETRY, 167

RECREATION, 148–149

REEF, CATHERINE: *Paul Laurence Dunbar: Portrait of a Poet*, 69

REID, ALASTAIR, AND ANTHONY KERRIGAN: *Mother Goose in Spanish/Poesias de la Madra Oca*, 155

"RELATIVITY," 142

"REQUIEM" (STEVENSON), 132

RESEARCH: on teaching with poetry, 19–21

REVOLUTION: poems on, 156

RHYMED POETRY: forms of, 120–129

RHYMING: as poetic skill, 120–123

RHYMING DICTIONARY: creating, 121–123

RHYTHM, 42–44

RICHARDS, LAURA E.: "Antonio, Antonio," 42; "Eletelephony," 20, 83

RIDDLES, 49, 100

RIDLOW, MARCI: "Questions," 20

RIMES, 61

ROBERTS, ELIZABETH M.: "The Woodpecker," 151

ROCHELLE, BELINDA: *Words With Wings,* 154

"ROCK-A-BYE, BABY," 146

ROSEN, MICHAEL: *Poems for the Very Young,* 64

ROSS, W.W.E.: "The Diver," 149

ROSSETTI, CHRISTINA: "Who Has Seen the Wind?," 26, 186

ROUNDS, 145

ROUNDS, GLEN: *I Know an Old Lady Who Swallowed a Fly,* 52; *Old MacDonald Had a Farm,* 52

"RUDOLPH IS TIRED OF THE CITY" (BROOKS), 159

RUMMEL, JACK: *Langston Hughes,* 69

THE RUNAWAY BUNNY (BROWN), 64

RYLANT, CYNTHIA: *In November,* 67; *When I Was Young in the Mountains,* 79

S

SANDBURG, CARL, 68; "Arithmetic," 142; "Chicago," 114; "Fog," 20, 114; "Night," 87

"THE SANDHILL CRANE" (AUSTIN), 151

SARETT, LEW: "Four Little Foxes," 125

SAXE, JOHN GODFREY: "The Blind Men and the Elephant," 152–153

SAYING POEMS ALOUD, 46–59, 193

SCHNEIDER, D., 135

SCHNUR, S.: *Autumn: An Alphabet Acrostic,* 131

SCHOOL: celebration of poetry in, 168

SCHWARTZ, ALVIN: *And the Green Grass Grew All Around,* 147

SCIENCE, 149–153

SCRATCH DESIGNS, 139

SCRIPT: for Readers Theatre: preparing, 82

SEA: poetry on, 151

"Sea Fever" (Masefield), 83, 151

"The Secret," 56

"The Secret Cavern" (Weddemer), 9

Self-worth: poetry and, 8–9

Sensory awareness: poetry and, 7–8

Septolet, 118

Sepura, B., 20–21

Service, Robert W.: "The Cremation of Sam McGee," 38–39

Seuss, Dr.: *And to Think That I Saw It on Mulberry Street,* 27

"Shadows" (Hubbell), 20

Shakespeare, William, 68–69, 136; *Julius Caesar,* 156–157

Shape poems, 163

Shapiro, Arnold: "I Talk, I Say, I Speak," 113

Shaw, Alison: *Until I Saw the Sea,* 151

Sierra, Judy: *Antarctic Antics: A Book of Penguin Poems,* 150; *Good Night, Dinosaurs,* 71; *There's a Zoo in Room 22,* 72

"Silver" (de la Mare), 44–45, 83, 191

Silverstein, Shel: *Falling Up,* 67; *Where the Sidewalk Ends,* 7, 38

Simile, 86–87, 194

"Simple Simon," 90

"Sing a song of sixpence," 103

"Skins" (Fisher), 87

"The Skunk" (Coffin), 151

Slavery: poems on, 156

"Sleep, baby, sleep," 64

"A sleeper from the Amazon," 54

"Smells (Junior)" (Morley), 7

Smith, Charles R.: *Rimshots: Basketball Pix, Rolls, and Rhythms,* 149; *Short Takes: Fast-Break Basketball Poetry,* 149

"Snail" (Hughes), 151

"Snake" (Lawrence), 151

"Snow in the City" (Field), 159

Social studies, 153–161

Solos: for Readers Theatre, 84; for voice choir, 58–59

Some of the Days of Everett Anderson (Clifton), 16

"A Song of Greatness," 21

"Song of Myself" (Whitman), 110–111

"Song of the Open Road" (Whitman), 115

"Song of the Train" (McCord), 8, 42, 64, 72

SONGS, 144–148; books of, 52–53; Mother Goose, 94

SOTO, GARY: *Neighborhood Odes*, 155

SOUNDS: musical, 191; word wall of, 188

SOUND-SYMBOL RELATIONSHIPOS: reinforcement of, 65

SPECIAL EFFECTS IN POETRY, 42–46

SPORTS COLLAGE, 148–149

"THE SQUIRREL," 42–44, 189

STANLEY, DIANE, AND PETER VENNEMA: *Bard of Avon*, 69

STARBIRD, KAYE: "December Leaves," vi, 195

"STAR LIGHT, STAR BRIGHT" (TAYLOR), 47

"THE STAR-SPANGLED BANNER" (KEY), 144

STEPTOE, JAVAKA: *In Daddy's Arms I Am Tall*, 38, 155

STEVENSON, JAMES: *Cornflakes: Poems*, 38

STEVENSON, ROBERT LOUIS, 1, 68; "At the Seaside," 151; "Requiem," 132; "The Swing," 129–130; "Wind," 25; "Windy Nights," 25

STONE SOUP, 107

"STOPPING BY WOODS ON A SNOWY EVENING" (FROST), 143–144

STRAND, MARK, 176

STUDENTS AT DIFFERENT LEARNING LEVELS: adapting lesson plans for, 24–25; reading poems to, 37–39

"SWEET AND LOW" (TENNYSON), 83

"SWIFT THINGS ARE BEAUTIFUL" (COATSWORTH), 106, 112–113, 197

"THE SWING" (STEVENSON), 129–130

T

TABACK, SIMMS: *There Was an Old Lady Who Swallowed a Fly*, 168

"THE TABLE AND THE CHAIR" (LEAR), 57–58

TAGORE, 160

TAYLOR, JANE: "I love little pussy," 85; "Star light, star bright," 47

TEACHERS: Mother Goose collections for, 92; poetry by, 177, 178f; poetry collections for, 63–64; resources for, 207–210

TEACHERS & WRITERS COLLABORATIVE, 208

TEACHING MATERIALS: books, 205–208; for National Poetry Month, 175

TEACHING STRATEGIES, 25–35

"TEDDY BEAR, TEDDY BEAR," 48

TENNYSON, ALFRED, LORD: "The Eagle," 60, 87, 194; "Sweet and low," 83

TERRY, A., 19–20

THACKERAY, WILLIAM MAKEPEACE: "A Tragic Story," 56–57

THAYER, ERNEST: "Casey at the Bat," 148

THEMES: poetry on, 70–74; for science, 151–153; in social studies, 155–159

"THERE ONCE WAS A LADY FROM NIGER" (MONKHOUSE), 20, 127

"THERE ONCE WAS AN OLD KANGAROO" (MULLIN), 20

"THERE'S ONE WIDE RIVER TO CROSS," 66–67

"THERE WAS AN OLD MAN OF BLACKHEATH," 20

"THIS IS MY ROCK" (McCORD), 125

THIS LAND IS YOUR LAND (GUTHRIE), 53, 147

"THIS MOMENT YEARNING AND THOUGHTFUL" (WHITMAN), 8–9

THOMPSON, DOROTHY B.: "Maps," 160

THORPE, QUINCY: *Take It to the Hoop, Magic Johnson,* 149

TIEDT, IRIS M., 2, 26, 32, 104, 117, 130, 177–178

TIEDT, P., 2, 32, 117

TIEDT, S., 2, 117

TISSUE PAPER ART, 164

"TO HELEN" (POE), 17

TOM, T., 19

TONGUE TWISTERS, 53

"A TRAGIC STORY" (THACKERAY), 56–57

TRAINS, 72–73

TRANSLATION: of poetry, 161

"TRAVEL" (MILLAY), 72–73

TRIANGULAR TRIPLETS, 126

TRIPLETS, 125–126

TUDOR, TASHA, 18; *Mother Goose,* 101

"A TUTOR WHO TOOTED THE FLUTE," 54

"TWAS THE NIGHT BEFORE CHRISTMAS" (MOORE), 172

U

"UNDER THE GOAL POSTS" (GUITERMAN), 149

UNRHYMED POETRY, 109–115, 199

UNTERMEYER, LOUIS, 176; *The Golden Books Family Treasury of Poetry,* 18, 63

"UNTIL I SAW THE SEA" (MOORE), 151

UPDIKE, JOHN: *A Child's Calendar,* 138

USCHOLD, MAUDE E.: "Moonlight," 87

V

"A VAGABOND SONG" (CARMAN), 10

Van Duyn, Mona, 176
The Very Lonely Firefly (Carle), 70–71
videotapes: on poetry, 172
Viorst, Judith: "If I Were King," 198
vocabulary: explicit instruction in, 94; love of, poetry and, 5–6
voice choir, 54–59

W

Wallace, Robert: "The Double-Play," 149
"The Walrus and the Carpenter" (Carroll), 7
war: poems on, 156
Warren, Robert Penn, 176
"Watching Clouds" (Farrar), 140
Watts, Isaac: "How doth the little busy bee," 85–86
websites, 175, 208; Pat Mora, 17; of poetry, 173; Poetry Daily, 17
Weddemer, Margaret: "The Secret Cavern," 9
"What Is Orange?" (O'Neill), 4
"What Is Poetry?" (Farjeon), 2–3
Whipple, Laura, and Eric Carle: *Eric Carle's Animals Animals*, 70; *Eric Carle's Dragons Dragons & Other Creatures That Never Were*, 72
"Whisky Frisky" (Lindsay), 171
"White coral bells," 145
"White sheep, white sheep," 29–31, 187
Whitman, Walt, 175; "I hear America singing," 115, 134; *Leaves of Grass,* 115; "O captain! My captain," 156; "Song of Myself," 110–111; "Song of the Open Road," 115; "This moment yearning and thoughtful," 8–9
"Who Has Seen the Wind?" (Rossetti), 26, 186
Wilbur, Richard, 176; *The Pig in the Spigot,* 29
Wildsmith, Brian: *Brian Wildsmith's Mother Goose,* 101
Williams, William Carlos, 175
"Wind" (Fisher), 25
"Wind" (Stevenson), 25
Windham, Sophie: *The Mermaid and Other Sea Poems,* 151
"Windy Nights" (Stevenson), 25
"The Witch of Willowby Wood" (Bennett), 44–45, 191
"The Wolf" (Durston), 151
Wood, Nancy: *War Cry on a Prayer Feather,* 155
"The Woodpecker" (Roberts), 151

WOODSON, JACQUELINE: *The Other Side,* 157

WORDSWORTH, WILLIAM, 16, 136

WORD WALL: for poetry instruction, 34–35; of rhymes, 122–123; of sound words, 188

WRITING POETRY, 107–133, 197–200

Y

YOLEN, JANE: *Alphabestiary,* 68; *Sky Scrape/City Scape: Poems of City Life,* 159

"YOU ARE OLD, FATHER WILLIAM" (CARROLL), 57

YOUNGER, BARBARA: *Purple Mountain Majesties,* 144

YOUNGER CHILDREN: poetry books for, 28–29

"A YOUNG FARMER OF LEEDS," 127, 200

YOUNG PEOPLE'S POETRY WEEK, 175

Franklin Pierce College Library

00138864

DATE DUE

OCT 2 7 2003	
APR 1 9 2004	
NOV 1 8 2009	

GAYLORD   PRINTED IN U.S.A.